To DAD McFAUL
FROM: DAVID & JOANNE — DEC 4/9

A DECADE OF HOCKEY'S GREATEST RIVALRY

COLD WAR

Toronto's Bob Pulford (#20) is about to put the puck past goaltender Gump Worsley (#30) during a scramble in front of the Canadiens net.

A DECADE OF HOCKEY'S GREATEST RIVALRY

COLD WAR

1959–1969

Mike Leonetti *with the photography of Harold Barkley*

HarperCollins*Publishers*Ltd

Montreal's Henri Richard (#16) staged many battles with Toronto's Tim Horton (#7) whenever the Leafs and Canadiens played each other.

*This book is dedicated to my cousin, Gino Granieri,
who taught me all about the Leafs–Canadiens rivalry
and to all hockey fans across Canada.*

First hardcover edition

Canadian Cataloguing in Publication Data

Leonetti, Mike, 1958–
Cold war : a decade of hockey's greatest rivalry, 1959–1969

ISBN 0-00-200081-4

1. Montreal Canadiens (Hockey team)—History. 2. Toronto Maple Leafs
(Hockey team)—History. 3. National Hockey League—History. I. Title.

GV848.M6L46 2001   796.962'64'0971   C2001-900871-6

01 02 03 04 HC 6 5 4 3 2 1

Printed and bound in Canada

The following photos are courtesy The Hockey Hall of Fame:
37, 51, 81, 100 (both), 101, 108, 121, 123, 142 (bottom), 143,
151, 160, 163, 177, 197 (both), 198, 199, 209, 210, 211 (both)

Design: Kimberley Young

Acknowledgements

The writer would like to thank Harold Barkley for his wonderful photography, which made this book possible. Thanks to Nick Pitt and Jim Williamson at Warwick Publishing for finally letting the writer complete this book. A thank-you to the friendly staff at the Hockey Hall of Fame, Phil Pritchard and Craig Campbell for their assistance in finding needed photos to supplement the Barkleys. A very special thanks to Paul Patzkou for his time in compiling invaluable research materials and for his editorial review of the text. Without Paul's efforts this book would not have been possible. The biggest thank-you of all goes to my wife Maria and my son David for their love, support, understanding and most of all their kind patience while this book was being written.

Table of Contents

Foreword

The Montreal Canadiens and the Toronto Maple Leafs have had a wonderful rivalry going back to the late 1920s. I grew up in northwestern Quebec in the town of Rouyn-Noranda, the twin cities. Rouyn was predominately French and Noranda was multilingual. It was here that I learned what rivalries were all about.

Rouyn and Noranda each had their own hockey team. They played in separate leagues, but each year they would play a "best four out of seven" series to see who had bragging rights. This competition carried over to minor hockey at the midget and juvenile level, each side trying to show who had the superior team. Passions ran very high.

Because of radio, English and French, the Maple Leafs (with Foster Hewitt) and the Canadiens (with René Lecavalier) were brought to life in our community. Choosing a team to cheer for was not done lightly. In most cases, the choice was made along language lines. Other teams had some support but the majority was divided between the Canadiens and the Maple Leafs. A great deal of pride was taken in the success of your team. When things did not go well for your team, you were subject to a great amount of razzing. It became a test to remain loyal.

I began playing for the Maple Leafs in the fall of 1960. It was good timing on my part. Toronto had been to the Stanley Cup finals in 1959 and 1960, so prospects looked very good. Farm systems played a large part in the makeup of all National Hockey League teams in that era. Toronto was no different. I was among several players who had joined the Leafs from the Toronto Marlboros or the St. Michael's Majors.

In 1962, the Maple Leafs defeated the Chicago Blackhawks in six games, giving Toronto its first Stanley Cup victory since Bill Barilko's famous overtime goal 11 years earlier. We would win again in 1963 and 1964. Montreal was busy rebuilding with young players from their farm system, and a renewed Canadiens team would win Stanley Cups in 1965 and 1966. In 1967, the last year of the "Original Six" and Canada's Centennial, the Leafs and the Canadiens would meet in the finals once more, with the Leafs winning the Stanley Cup.

The Montreal–Toronto rivalry created great competition and great debate, not only between the players but also between the fans of each team. I was proud to represent the Toronto Maple Leafs. I hope that this book brings back memories and gives readers as much pleasure as it gave me to play in those games.

Best Wishes,
David Keon

*Jean Beliveau gets crunched into the boards by Toronto's Tim
Horton (#7) with Red Kelly (#4) looking to take the puck away.*

The Leafs–Canadiens Rivalry
Prologue

The Toronto Maple Leafs and the Montreal Canadiens had never played a seventh game in a playoff series until the night of April 9, 1964. The two most storied franchises in hockey had staged some memorable post-season series already (in 1947 and 1951 when the Leafs won the Stanley Cup and in 1959 and 1960 when Montreal won the championship) and would do so again (in 1967). However, none of these meetings had the drama of a game seven when a one-contest showdown means the end of the year for one side. The 1964 semi-final series between Canada's teams had drawn great interest from all over Canada and on this crisp early spring evening, the eyes of a nation were focused on the Montreal Forum. Just as the game began, a floral arrangement of 1,500 roses in the shape of a horseshoe appeared just outside the Leafs dressing room. It had been sent by Toronto fans, while thousands of Montreal supporters signed a telegram that was presented to the Canadiens.

Legendary broadcaster Danny Gallivan was doing the play-by-play for *Hockey Night in Canada* that evening with Keith Dancy providing occasional colour commentary. Gallivan's description was all that television viewers needed to enjoy the ending of what had been an exciting series. The series lead had gone back and forth, with each team winning on the road. Great goaltending marked each contest. Goaltenders Johnny Bower of the Leafs and Charlie Hodge of the Canadiens had

Dave Keon was one of the greatest players ever to wear the Maple Leaf uniform.

each recorded shutouts and had played superbly in every game won by their respective teams. Bower's shutout happened in the sixth game of of the series and was redemption for the Leaf netminder, who was criticized as being too old whenever Toronto lost. For Hodge, the entire 1963–64 season finally proved that he was a full-time NHL goalie. On this night only one would emerge as a winner.

Frank Mahovlich, who had enjoyed two great games in the series for the Leafs, took a penalty after just 80 seconds of play, but the Leafs killed it off easily. Bower then had to make a good stop on speedy Canadiens winger Bill Hicke, who broke down the wing. He followed that up with stops on Claude Provost and Henri Richard. Hodge had to make a fine stop on Bob Pulford of the Leafs by using his catching hand. But the Maple Leafs hit the scoreboard first when some good work by Bob Baun, George Armstrong and Don McKenney kept the puck in the Montreal end. Finally, Leafs centre Dave Keon rapped in a loose puck and Gallivan said, "The little man from Noranda [Keon's birthplace] made no mistake." Keon had not scored a goal in the series to date, but this night belonged to the swift Leaf who usually saved his best performances for the games that mattered most.

At 9:40 of the first period, Toronto's Andy

Bathgate was penalized for hooking, but before the penalty was over, Leaf defenceman Tim Horton broke up a Montreal attack at his own blueline. Armstrong picked up the loose puck along the boards and hit a streaking Keon with a breakaway pass. Nobody was going to catch Keon, a gifted skater, although Jean Guy Talbot gave it a valiant effort. Keon went in on Hodge and fired a low shot to the far side of the net and gave the Leafs a 2-0 lead. The two teams exchanged good scoring chances before the first period ended, but there were no more tallies, even though Montreal had to kill off two penalties.

To start the second period, the organist in the Forum played "The Maple Leaf Forever" as the Toronto club took to the ice. The Montreal line of Bill Hicke, Ralph Backstrom and Bobby Rousseau was giving the Leafs all kinds of trouble with their speed, but Bower turned back all 13 Canadien shots on goal in that period. Hodge also faced 13 Toronto shots and had to make a good save on Mahovlich to keep the spread at two goals. The middle period was highlighted by Montreal defenceman Terry Harper dishing out

terrific bodychecks to Bobby Baun and Carl Brewer (who was injured on the play).

The Canadiens were a desperate group in the third period and threw everything they had at the Leafs, firing 18 shots at Bower. The veteran Leaf goalie stopped all but one. After a wild scramble in front of the Leafs net, Backstrom put in a rebound off a Talbot drive. Bower had no chance and Gallivan added, "The place is in an uproar." Hodge had to make good stops to keep the Habs in the game, but the clock was winding down as the action went end to end. Toronto coach Punch Imlach hated this type of game, especially in such an important contest. He would have preferred a close-checking effort by his team but he was helpless to change anything at this point.

Provost broke down the wing when Leaf defenceman Allan Stanley stumbled, but Horton managed to get back and prevented a good shot on goal. Bower then robbed Rousseau from about

Tim Horton was a six-time all-star selection (three times on the first team) during his long career with the Maple Leafs.

Toronto's Frank Mahovlich (#27) was often closely checked by Montreal's Claude Provost (#14) when the two teams played each other.

12 feet out and followed that save with stops on Backstrom and Dave Balon.

Montreal kept the pressure on and the Leafs were given the seemingly obligatory penalty all visiting teams got late in the third period of a game at the Forum when the Habs were trailing. Toronto's Gerry Ehman was called on a borderline trip against Balon at 17:27 and as the Leaf winger fidgeted nervously in the penalty box, his teammates bailed him out with a great penalty-killing effort. Montreal coach Toe Blake played his last card when he pulled Hodge with just 27 seconds to play and a face-off in the Toronto end. Horton won the draw against

Rousseau and the Leafs were able to get the puck down the ice. In the Montreal end, Red Kelly dug the puck out of a corner and fed a pass to a waiting Keon, who slammed the puck into the empty net for a 3-1 lead and a series win. The Leafs poured over the boards to congratulate Keon on his hat trick and Gallivan called it, "a big night for a truly great player."

The 1964 playoffs saw the Leaf dynasty of the 1960s reach its height (although they would have a resurgence in 1967). After defeating Montreal, the Leafs went on to meet Detroit in the finals and beat the Red Wings in another exciting seven-game series that featured more heroics.

Many of the players who helped the Leafs knock off the first-place Canadiens were also instrumental in beating Detroit and giving Toronto its third consecutive Cup. Dave Keon was a big reason why the Leafs were champions three straight times, leading with his tireless checking and timely goals. Small in stature but big in heart, the Toronto centreman always gave it his best, an honest effort night after night. Assigned to check the best centre of the other team (like Montreal's Jean Beliveau), Keon never hooked, held, slashed or mauled his opponent. His superior skating skills and outstanding positional play were all Keon needed to do the job. To beat Keon, the opposition had to make a good play and he never gave anything away without a battle. Clean, honest and durable, Keon was a hero to many who idolized the Leafs in this era.

No team can win without a star, and in the case of the Maple Leafs their most gifted athlete was the "Big M," Frank Mahovlich. Large, fleet-footed and born with a natural flair for scoring picture goals, Mahovlich could take the entire Leaf team upon his broad shoulders and lead them to victory single-handedly. In full flight, he was virtually unstoppable, and when sufficiently roused, he could be dominating. In the 1964 playoffs he had 15 points in 14 games.

As good as the Leafs were up front with players like Keon and Mahovlich, their real anchors were on the blueline and in goal. Tim Horton was a piece of granite as he patrolled the Toronto end of the ice. Intimidating with his legendary strength, Horton's steadiness made him an all-star performer. He also had a knack of saving his best for the post season; in the 1962 playoffs he set a record for defencemen with 13 assists.

If the opposing team got by Horton, they had Johnny Bower to contend with in the Leafs net. A very competitive netminder who even took getting beaten in practice seriously, Bower was great at not giving up the killer goal to the opposition. In 1964, the Leafs twice faced elimination in the sixth game of a series, but Bower would not yield and gave the Leafs the time they needed to win the Cup. The 1964 final game for the Stanley Cup against Detroit was a 4-0 victory. Bower's great reflexes kept the Leafs in many a game for over a decade.

While these four players were the most important for Toronto during this era, other players worthy of considerable mention were

Allan Stanley, Red Kelly, Bob Pulford, Bob Baun and Leafs captain George Armstrong.

While the Leafs were winning Cups in the early 1960s, the Montreal club was quietly rebuilding after a 1960 championship had marked the end of an unprecedented run of five straight titles (a record yet to be tied or beaten). Between 1956 and 1960, the Habs had won five consecutive Stanley Cups with some of the greatest players in the history of the game. But Jacques Plante, Doug Harvey, Bernie Geoffrion, Dickie Moore and the great Maurice "Rocket" Richard had all left the team by the 1964–65 season. The only holdovers from the great teams still with the club were Jean Beliveau, Ralph Backstrom, Jean Guy Talbot, Claude Provost and Henri Richard. In the five years since their last Cup, the Habs had added future stars like Jacques Laperriere, Yvan Cournoyer, J.C. Tremblay and Bobby Rousseau, to name but a few. They also had resurrected the careers of veteran goalies Hodge and Lorne "Gump" Worsley.

By 1965, the city of Montreal was practically demanding the Habs reclaim the Cup. They first

Montreal's Jean Beliveau (#4) won the first-ever Conn Smythe Trophy in 1965, while Leafs goaltender Johnny Bower won four Stanley Cups and two Vezina Trophies in his career with Toronto.

(Hodge had played most of the season) and the Habs hoped home ice would be the difference.

Gallivan opened this broadcast with the simple statement, "The winner gets the Stanley Cup." But any anticipated drama was over quickly as the Canadiens blitzed the Blackhawks early and often. Montreal forced a turnover in the Chicago end as soon as the puck was dropped. Beliveau put a shot past Glenn Hall to give the Canadiens a 1-0 lead after just 14 seconds of play. Beliveau then set up Dick Duff (a former Leaf) for another goal and the Canadiens never looked back.

Worsley made a couple of good stops on Chicago's Bobby Hull (who was booed every time he touched the puck and was checked to a virtual standstill by Claude Provost) on a Blackhawk power-play. He also robbed Camille Henry in close. Cournoyer then grabbed the puck and sped around defenceman Elmer Vasko before beating Hall with a shot for another Canadiens goal.

Phil Esposito took a hooking penalty for Chicago and Montreal defenceman Ted Harris made a good play with a nice pass to Richard, who made it 4-0. For good measure, Harris rocked Eric Nesterenko with an elbow, as the Habs completely dominated the first period.

The second period was rather dull and Chicago showed no signs of making a comeback. There was no further scoring in the second or third periods and only the great work of Hall kept the score at 4-0. As the clock brought the game to an end, the Canadiens leapt over the boards to mob Worsley. The players hoisted Blake on their shoulders and the organist played "For He's a Jolly Good Fellow" when Beliveau was given the first ever Conn Smythe Trophy for his great playoff performance (16 points in 13 games).

Naturally, the crowd booed NHL president Clarence Campbell when he stepped onto the ice to present the Stanley Cup to the Canadiens. The classy Beliveau accepted the Cup and spoke to the crowd in both French and English. He then took the Cup for a skate by himself and the rest of the Canadiens went off to the dressing room. Blake was interviewed on television and with a smile of great relief said of all his Cup wins to

Henri Richard (#16) made a habit of scoring important goals in the playoffs when he excelled the most.

had to get by the Maple Leafs which they did after a tough six-game series, in dethroning the defending champs. The finals saw the Canadiens go up against the Chicago Blackhawks. Each team won their home games to even the series at three wins apiece, with the seventh game scheduled for the Forum on May 1, 1965 (the first time a meaningful hockey game was played in the month of May). In a somewhat surprising move, Blake decided to start Worsley in goal date, "none has given me the satisfaction like this one." The Montreal Cup famine was over.

Blake had every reason to be happy, especially with the performance of his best players, starting with the team captain. Beliveau represented the class of the Canadiens organization like no other player in the great history of Les Glorieux. He had all the statistics that Hall of Fame players produce, but Beliveau's real value was the way he carried himself on and off the ice. One of the bigger players in this era, Beliveau had a grace and style to his play that made him the new idol for the hockey-mad Quebecois who needed a new leader when Maurice Richard retired. But he had such charisma and charm that he was idolized all over Canada (and still is today). Never shy about playing a physical game when he had to, Beliveau still found a way to play the game as a great sportsman and as a leader of a special team.

If Beliveau was the class of the Habs, then Henri Richard was their heart and soul. Perhaps more than any other player, Richard understood what it meant to wear the Canadiens sweater. He must have learned this lesson from his older brother, who showed that if you were from Quebec and played for the Habs, you were more than just a hockey player. The Canadiens represented a nation and a tradition that was unmatched in professional sports. It was a history that the "Pocket Rocket" took very seriously, and when his team needed an important goal, it was often Richard who scored it (see the 1966 and 1971 Stanley Cup finals summaries for further details). When the Canadiens were in the playoffs they seemed to have a special if not mystical spirit that drove them to succeed. That special something was embodied in the person of Henri Richard.

Just as the Leafs were strong on defence, the Habs had their own stars on the blueline and in goal. Jacques Laperriere was a lanky rearguard who used his long reach on defence and his booming shot on offence to become one of the best all-round defencemen in the NHL. Blake relied on the steady Laperriere to anchor his defence and he was rarely disappointed by the stellar work of the future Hall of Fame player. Worsley was brought

to Montreal to get the Canadiens over the top and replace a legend in Plante.

At first, it looked like they had made a mistake. Hodge was getting most of the work and Worsley was often injured. But the 1965 play-

Montreal defenceman Jacques Laperriere (#2) won the Calder Trophy as the NHL's best rookie in 1964.

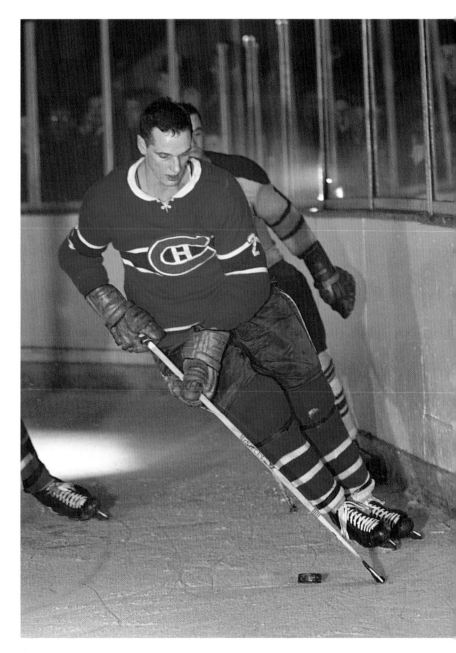

The Montreal Canadiens rescued Lorne "Gump" Worsley from the New York Rangers and won four Stanley Cups with him in net.

offs turned Worsley's career around and he finally won the big game. The pudgy netminder never looked the part, but Worsley was surprisingly quick and he could make the big save at the right moment, which is all the Habs needed with their good goal scoring.

Montreal then went on to win the Cup in 1966, 1968 and 1969. They might have won five in a row again were it not for the '67 Maple Leafs but the Montreal dynasty of the 1960s still had many great players on the team. Other notable performers included J.C. Tremblay (a great playoff performer), Gilles Tremblay, Rousseau, Duff, Provost, Backstrom, Cournoyer, Harris, Harper and goaltender Rogie Vachon.

In the 10-year period from 1959 to 1969, Canada's teams won all the Stanley Cups except for one—a 1961 win by third-place Chicago, even though the Canadiens and Leafs had finished first and second that year. Montreal was transformed radically from the team that won in 1960 to the squad that took the Cup back in 1965. But there was one constant behind the bench in the person of Toe Blake. A crusty curmudgeon when the Canadiens lost, Blake also had a "father knows best" air about him that endeared the coach to his players. The Canadiens knew they were accountable to Blake but he never choked their creativity and allowed them to play the fire-wagon style the team was known for.

Blake had the benefit of great management behind him, first in the person of Frank Selke and then Sam Pollock, both hockey geniuses and innovators in their own right. However, it was the demanding Blake who made the machine run smoothly, and he must have done it right because he is still revered today by anyone who played for him.

In Toronto, George "Punch" Imlach was a one-man act who began his stay in 1958 when the Maple Leafs were floundering. A balding 40-year-old who was a virtual unknown, Imlach took over the entire operation and coached and managed the team to four Cups and six appearances in the finals between 1959 and 1967. Cocky and at times downright arrogant, Imlach made many good personnel moves and reinstalled the defence-first strategy the Leafs had often used to great success in the past. Using a drill sergeant approach to coaching, Imlach gave Leaf players little room to be creative (including the very talented Mahovlich), but the style did prove to be efficient and obviously effective. Imlach had many quirks in his coaching methods; he was also extremely superstitious. He rubbed many of his players the wrong way and many insist they won in spite of their coach because they had the talent to do so.

Not only were the coaches different, so too were the cities the two teams represented during this decade. The Leafs style was much like that of the city of Toronto—staid, conservative and English. The Canadiens were like Montreal—colourful, flashier and French. The Habs played with flair and the moniker "Flying Frenchmen" seemed to fit perfectly, much like "clutch and grab" suited the checking Maple Leafs.

For all their differences, the two teams realized they had a rich history to live up to. In Montreal the exploits of Aurel Joliet, Georges Vezina, Howie Morenz and Maurice Richard were passed down from one generation to the next. Toronto had the names of Charlie Conacher, Syl Apps, Turk Broda and Ted Kennedy firmly engrained in their minds and on the walls of Maple Leaf Gardens. In an era when only six teams competed for the Stanley Cup, it was easier to remember the heroes of an earlier time, but it was also much harder to live up to their accomplishments.

However, this decade of hockey did see a new group of hockey legends grow and take their rightful place in the history of the game. Hockey fans in Canada cheered for either the Maple Leafs or Canadiens, and the Toronto-Montreal rivalry was exciting for anyone who followed the NHL. Each side alternatively respected and hated the other and it made for some great hockey. Every Leafs–Canadiens game was special (14 of them during the season when there were six teams in the league) and each time they met in the playoffs it was a stirring contest. Ask anyone, especially the players who witnessed the rivalry first hand, and they'll tell you there was nothing like it. The two teams exemplified teamwork, dedication, courage and a willingness to battle through tough odds. When they clashed at high speed it was a sight to behold. Hockey has never seen such a rivalry since and may never see one like it again.

Capturing the fierce battles between Montreal and Toronto was award-winning photographer Harold Barkley. An all-star performer in his own right, Barkley travelled to both cities (and all NHL locations) to take his memorable photos. His images give the reader a rinkside seat at the Montreal Forum and Maple Leaf Gardens during many of the classic games between the Leafs and Canadiens. Since Barkley did most of his work for the *Toronto Star*, his photo collection tends to cover that city's team more thoroughly, so his work has been supplemented here with photos from the archives of the Hockey Hall of Fame.

This book recounts in a season-by-season and game-by-game format the intensity of the rivalry and the ultimate triumphs of both teams. It uses the accounts of the time as the primary source of research and places emphasis on the words of the coaches and players. Turn the pages and relive a time when Canada's teams ruled the NHL!

Montreal coach Toe Blake shares his wit and wisdom with star players Jean Beliveau (#4) and Maurice Richard (#9). The Canadiens were looking for their fourth straight Stanley Cup as the 1958–59 season began.

The Leafs–Canadiens Rivalry

1958–59

season summary

Expectations for the Montreal Canadiens and the Toronto Maple Leafs could not have been more different for the start of the 1958–59 season. The Canadiens were going for a record fourth straight Stanley Cup while the Leafs were hoping just to get back into the playoffs. Montreal had just completed a championship season in 1957–58 with what many people said was the greatest team ever assembled. A 43-win, 96-point first-place finish would be hard to repeat, but if a team could do so, the Canadiens were certainly capable. Coach Toe Blake would not let this group of great players become complacent, however. Just to keep the Canadiens on their toes, a few changes were made. Ab McDonald was brought in to replace the veteran Bert Olmstead and defenceman Dollard St. Laurent was picked up by Chicago. Ralph Backstrom would be a fine addition as a rookie, while Bill Hicke was a newcomer on the horizon.

In Toronto, coach Billy Reay was hoping the addition of seasoned pros like Johnny Bower, Allan Stanley and Olmstead (claimed in the intra-league draft from Montreal) would help youngsters like Frank Mahovlich, Dick Duff and Carl Brewer to mature. The Leafs also added an assistant general manager to their organization (via Boston) before the season started in the person of George

"Punch" Imlach. At 40 years of age, the balding and unknown Imlach would prove to be bold, brash and boastful in turning the Leafs' fortunes around once he was named general manager and replaced Reay as coach in November. Imlach almost hired Alf Pike to coach the team but when the two could not agree to terms, Imlach felt he was the best man for the job.

It took the down and nearly out Leafs the entire season to escape the basement of the NHL, but on the final night of the schedule they edged out the New York Rangers for the last playoff berth. The Leafs got great mileage out of their old and young players and were led by Duff (most goals and points), Olmstead (most assists), Brewer (most penalty minutes) and Mahovlich (22 goals and 49 points) to post a 27-32-11 regular season. A player picked up during the season, Gerry Ehman, helped lead the team in the playoffs as the Cinderella Maple Leafs made it all the way to the finals before they ran into the powerful Canadiens.

As expected, the Canadiens romped through the regular season with a 39-18-13 mark, good for 91 points and another first-place finish. The team was loaded with all-stars (Jacques Plante, Tom Johnson, Jean Beliveau and Dickie Moore, who played with a broken wrist on the first team; Henri Richard and Doug Harvey on the second), and award winners (Moore won the Art Ross, Johnson took the Norris Trophy, Plante earned the Vezina Trophy, while Backstrom was named as the best rookie and walked away with the Calder). Beliveau and Moore waged a friendly war during the season to see who would take the scoring title just to keep things interesting for the defending champions. The Habs won eight of the fourteen regular-season games with the Leafs (Toronto won five) and their depth and overall superiority were quite evident in the playoffs.

The upstart Leafs were no match for the Montrealers on paper but they did not go down without a fight. All the games were close and the final contest at the Forum had the Leafs trying to come back from three goals down with the goalie on the bench. Despite injuries to key performers, the Habs still had enough to make Toronto wait longer for a championship.

OCTOBER 16, 1958
Montreal 4 Toronto 3 @ The Forum

In a hard-fought contest, the Maple Leafs came back from a 2-0 deficit, took the lead 3-2 on a goal by Dave Creighton only to lose the game on a late tally by Dickie Moore of the Canadiens. The Habs were led by Moore with two goals and singles by Bernie Geoffrion and Maurice Richard. Toronto got two from Bob Pulford who scored his goals 47 seconds apart in the first period to tie the game at 2-2. On Pulford's second marker, he split the defence of Jean Guy Talbot and Tom Johnson before putting a low shot past goalie Jacques Plante.

The two quick tallies by Pulford inspired the Leafs. Backed by some great goaltending by Johnny Bower, they were even with the Canadiens until 17:09 of the third period when Moore rifled a pass from Henri Richard past Bower for the game winner.

It was the Leafs' third straight loss but they proved to be feisty in this contest, as Frank Mahovlich scuffled with Montreal's Andre Pronovost while Dick Duff and George Armstrong argued with Canadien fans at rink side near the end of the second period. In addition, Bert Olmstead got a 10-minute misconduct for raising his stick at linesman Art Skov. For Montreal, Johnson ran over Bower and earned himself a charging call. The Habs outshot the Leafs 40-39 in the game.

OCTOBER 29, 1958
Montreal 5 Toronto 0 @ Maple Leaf Gardens

Before 13,756 fans, the Canadiens behind the stellar goaltending of Jacques Plante—who made 27 saves to earn his second shutout of the season—

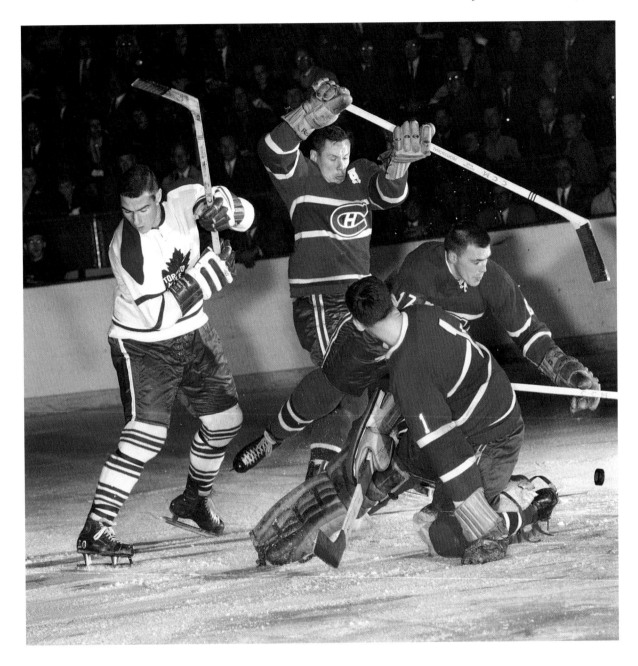

Toronto's Bob Pulford puts one past goalie Jacques Plante (#1) for one of his two goals on October 16, 1958. Defencemen Jean Guy Talbot (#17) and Tom Johnson were unable to stop the hard charging Leaf forward.

showed that the Leafs were not in their class as yet. Montreal rookie Ab McDonald, a smooth-skating, speedy winger, scored his first NHL goal in this game, beating Leaf goalie Ed Chadwick, while Jean Beliveau, Bernie Geoffrion, Dickie Moore and Tom Johnson picked up the other markers. The hapless Leafs had nothing going in this contest (and had only two wins in eight starts) which saw the last Hab goal go into the net after Toronto's Ron Stewart banked a shot into his own goal (it was credited to Moore). A couple of Leafs showed some life when winger Dick Duff got under the skin of Rocket Richard (the Canadiens star roughed up the Leaf player and when Duff tried to retaliate, the Pocket Rocket intervened) and Frank Mahovlich challenged Plante to make a few tough saves. It was the Habs' seventh win in eleven starts.

NOVEMBER 12, 1958
Montreal 4 Toronto 1 @ Maple Leaf Gardens

The Canadiens used two power-play goals and goalie Jacques Plante had a relatively easy game as the Habs romped over the Leafs. Montreal got off to a good start when defenceman Tom Johnson scored a goal after a face-off win by centre Henri Richard just four seconds after a penalty to Toronto's Tim Horton. Jean Beliveau scored with a hard shot on the short side of Leaf goaltender Ed Chadwick to make it 2-0, while Phil Goyette deflected a shot into the Toronto goal to make it 3-0. Billy Harris got one back for the home side (a disputed goal that referee Red Storey let stand) by poking the puck past Plante. But Bernie Geoffrion put in another power-play tally off his own rebound to make it 4-1 for the Habs. Horton was once again in the penalty box. The only effective Leafs in this game were Billy Harris and Frank Mahovlich.

was replacing the injured Jean Beliveau between Bernie Geoffrion and Ab McDonald. The Habs pressed on the attack and fired 37 shots at Bower, but he held them off until Tim Horton and Frank Mahovlich scored for Toronto (both goals coming in the second period). Leaf defenceman Carl Brewer scuffled with Montreal's Don Marshall, taking a punch at the Canadien, who fought back. Bob Pulford and Henri Richard also fought in the game, while Mahovlich brushed referee Red Storey after the Leaf had been high sticked and no penalty call was made. Montreal recalled Marcel Bonin from Rochester for this game to replace the injured Andre Pronovost. This was the first Leafs–Canadiens game for new Toronto coach George "Punch" Imlach.

DECEMBER 18, 1958
Montreal 4 Toronto 1 @ The Forum

Montreal extended their unbeaten streak to nine games with a 4-1 win over the Maple Leafs. The Canadiens went up 3-0 before letting up a little. The Habs got goals from Henri Richard, Bob Turner and Claude Provost to give them a commanding lead. Richard deked around Toronto defenceman Marc Reaume before

"Goaltending had nothing to do with it. It wouldn't have mattered if we used both Chadwick and Bower. We were out skated and out roughed."

Leaf coach Billy Reay (*The Globe and Mail*, October 30, 1958)

DECEMBER 4, 1958
Montreal 2 Toronto 2 @ The Forum

The cellar-dwelling Maple Leafs got a brilliant performance from goalie Johnny Bower and left the Forum with a 2-2 tie. Montreal actually led the game 2-0 on two markers from rookie Ralph Backstrom, both in the first period. Backstrom

depositing a shot past Leaf goalie Johnny Bower. Turner, who played a strong game, fired a 10-foot shot past Bower after taking a pass from Richard. The Montreal defenceman also had one assist in the contest that saw a Canadiens shutout bid get spoiled by a 35-foot blast from the stick of former Hab Bert Olmstead. Dickie Moore rounded out the scoring for Montreal.

DECEMBER 31, 1958
Toronto 2 Montreal 0 @ Maple Leaf Gardens

For the first time in the 1958–59 season, the Maple Leafs beat the Montreal Canadiens 2-0 in a New Year's Eve clash. In front of 13,169 fans

Tom Johnson (centre) poses with fellow Montreal defencemen Jean Guy Talbot and Bob Turner (#11). Johnson scored in consecutive games versus the Leafs on October 29, 1958, and again on November 12, both easy Canadien victories. Turner also played well.

Ralph Backstrom

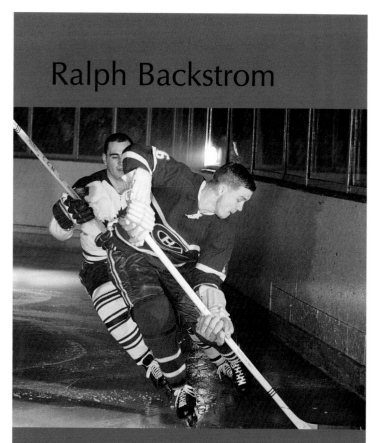

Ralph Backstrom (#6) began his NHL career with Montreal in 1958–59 and he scored 18 goals as a rookie, including two against the Leafs on December 4, 1958. Backstrom nearly signed with the Boston Bruins but at the last minute he decided to go with the Canadiens. He scored his first two NHL goals against Glenn Hall of Chicago on October 23, 1958. He stayed in Montreal until 1971 when he was dealt to the Los Angeles Kings, but not before he scored 215 goals and 287 assists with the Habs.

THE NUMBERS

When Ralph Backstrom won the Calder Trophy as the rookie of the year in 1959, he polled 141 points out of a possible 180, more than twice the number earned by the runner-up, Carl Brewer of the Maple Leafs.

the Leafs got goals from Billy Harris and Gerry Ehman as goaltender Ed Chadwick earned his third shutout of the season (and second in four games). The Leafs played a strong checking game and did very well at killing penalties against the vaunted Habs power-play. The Leafs opened the scoring when Frank Mahovlich whipped a pass to Harris, who made no mistake in beating Jacques Plante in the Montreal goal. Mahovlich also helped set up Ehman (who had been just recently called up from the Hershey Bears) for the Leafs' second goal in the third period. Toronto's Bobby Baun was cross-checked into the boards by Montreal's Al Langlois, but did not miss a shift. Going into January 1959, the NHL standings had Montreal in first with 47 points, followed by Detroit with 35, New York with 35, Chicago and Boston with 34 each and Toronto in last with 26.

JANUARY 8, 1959
Montreal 3 Toronto 0 @ The Forum

Maurice Richard scored his 525th career goal in leading the Canadiens to a 3-0 win over Toronto. As a result of a promotion run by a local French newspaper, a Montreal fan got a car and an autographed puck from the Rocket in honour of the goal. Defenceman Bob Turner played another excellent game with a short-handed goal. Turner blocked a Larry Regan shot and sped away to beat Johnny Bower with a 20-foot shot. The Forum crowd of 13,825 gave him a great ovation. Claude Provost scored the other Montreal goal and Jacques Plante made 25 saves to earn the shutout. The win by Montreal, which featured line matching by coaches Toe Blake and Punch Imlach, kept the Habs up by 10 points on second-place Chicago.

JANUARY 21, 1959
Toronto 3 Montreal 1 @ Maple Leaf Gardens

The Maple Leafs played one of their best games of

> *"The Canadiens have a lot of good hockey players in guys like Beliveau, Geoffrion, Moore, little Rocket, Provost, Johnson and the guy in the nets. There isn't a guy on the team who can't skate."*

Maple Leafs assistant general manager King Clancy (*The Montreal Gazette*, February 6, 1959)

the year as they inched ever closer to a playoff spot. Goalie Ed Chadwick was superb in goal, making 33 of 34 saves in front of the largest crowd of the season (14,107 fans). He got help from Bert Olmstead, Billy Harris and Dick Duff who scored the Leaf goals. Ron Stewart set up Olmstead for his goal, a 25-foot slapper past Jacques Plante, while Harris knocked in a pass from Duff for his marker. Duff knocked in his own rebound for his goal. Tom Johnson got the lone Canadiens tally, while the Leafs had two players in the penalty box, but then Duff got his score to make it 3-1. The Canadiens' Phil Goyette, normally a mild-mannered type, took a serious run at the Leafs' Carl Brewer but the Toronto defender saw him coming and managed to deliver the first blow. As a result, Goyette suffered a rib cartilage injury. The Leafs generally out-bumped the Canadiens and handed the Montreal squad just their third loss in 24 starts.

FEBRUARY 5, 1959
Toronto 6 Montreal 3 @ The Forum

Dick Duff and Frank Mahovlich each scored twice for the visiting Maple Leafs, who downed the Habs 6-3 before 13,896 fans. Jacques Plante started in net for the Habs but was replaced after two periods (suffering a groin injury) by Claude Pronovost, a goalie called up from the Montreal Royals of the Quebec Hockey League. The Leaf power-play was working well and Duff also scored a shorthanded goal (his 19th of the year) for Toronto, who was backstopped by goalie Ed Chadwick. Montreal got their goals from Ian Cushenan, Ralph Backstrom and Dickie Moore (his 27th of the season). The win gave the Leafs 43 points and moved them within two of fourth-place Boston.

FEBRUARY 11, 1959
Montreal 5 Toronto 2 @ Maple Leaf Gardens

Led by Jean Beliveau's three goals and one assist, the visiting Canadiens ran over the Maple Leafs 5-2 before 13,858 spectators. The big Montreal centre's hat trick brought his goal total on the season to 26. Then Beliveau took a run at the Leafs' Dick Duff. The Leaf winger was pinned against the boards and never saw Beliveau coming. Duff was cut for five stitches to the forehead. Marc Reaume and George Armstrong came to the aid of their fallen teammate. Bob Turner came into the fray to assist Beliveau and exchanged high sticks with Reaume. At the end of the fracas, Beliveau was given a five-minute major for cross-check-ing, and in the penalty box Reaume and Turner tried to continue the battle. Frank Mahovlich, already in the sin bin for high sticking, scuffled with the Montreal players, try-ing to get at Beliveau while Turner and Ab

Toronto goalie Ed Chadwick shut out the highflying Habs 2-0 on December 31, 1958. In his career as a Leaf, Chadwick played in 180 games and posted a 57-89-34 record with 14 shutouts and 2.96 goals-against average. He was dealt to Boston in 1961.

McDonald tried to protect their teammate. Police were called in to separate the combatants (in a single penalty box) and 10-minute misconducts were handed out. Marcel Bonin and Don Marshall also scored for the Habs while Bert Olmstead and Barry Cullen responded for Toronto. Defenceman Carl Brewer assisted on both Toronto goals and was the best Leaf player of the night.

FEBRUARY 25, 1959
Toronto 3 Montreal 2 @ Maple Leaf Gardens

The next two meetings between Toronto and Montreal saw the clubs split a pair of games. The Leafs staged a rally to pull out the first game after being down 2-0. Phil Goyette and Jean Beliveau had given the Habs a two-goal lead but the Leafs, desperate to get out of the cellar, got goals from Frank Mahovlich, Bert Olmstead and Gerry Ehman (who also recorded two assists) to win the game. The victory moved the Leafs to within seven points of the fourth-place New York Rangers.

MARCH 5, 1959
Montreal 2 Toronto 1 @ The Forum

The Canadiens won the game 2-1 at the Forum despite some great goaltending by the Leafs' Johnny Bower. Bower stopped 34 of 36 shots but was beaten by

Dick Duff enjoyed his best NHL season in 1958–59 when he scored 29 times and had 53 points (both career high totals). He had some good games against the Canadiens, including a two-goal effort on February 5, 1959, in a 6-3 Leaf win at the Forum.

Dickie Moore (his 34th of the year) and Claude Provost. Marcel Bonin set up Moore for the winners, who were missing both Henri Richard and Bernie Geoffrion. Montreal goalie Jacques Plante had only 17 shots on goal and was beaten on the short side by a nifty individual effort by Dick Duff.

MARCH 11, 1959
Montreal 6 Toronto 2 @ Maple Leaf Gardens

Dickie Moore and Jean Beliveau continued to battle for the point-scoring championship of the NHL as the Canadiens whipped the Leafs 6-2, putting a severe crimp in Toronto's hopes of gaining a playoff berth. Beliveau scored twice while Moore had one and added two assists as Montreal bombed Toronto goaltender Ed Chadwick. The Canadiens, who had already clinched a first-place finish, also got goals from Jean Guy Talbot, Tom Johnson and Claude Provost, while outshooting the Leafs 30-22. A crowd of 13,676 saw George Armstrong and Dick Duff respond for Toronto. Coach Punch Imlach had the Leafs out for a 9 a.m. practice the next morning and threatened to fine any Toronto player $50 by the second if they were late.

MARCH 19, 1959
Toronto 6 Montreal 3 @ The Forum

The Maple Leafs, now in dire straits for every possible point, got a big break when goalie Jacques Plante was unable to play for Montreal due to a painful case of boils on his face. Claude Pronovost played in the Canadiens net for two periods and Claude St. Cyr (only 19 years of age) played the third period as the Leafs poured in goals by Dick Duff (with two), George Armstrong, Bob Pulford, Gerry Ehman and Bert Olmstead (who also got his 30th assist of the season) to salt away the very important win. The Leafs used the line of Pulford, Olmstead and Ron Stewart to go against the Habs' best trio

Jean Beliveau battled with teammate Dickie Moore all season long in 1958–59 for the NHL scoring title. His three-goal performance against the Leafs helped his cause on February 11, 1959, in a 5-2 win by Montreal at the Gardens. However, it was Moore who took the Art Ross Trophy with 96 points to Beliveau's 91 (although the big Canadiens centre did lead the league in goals with 45).

Marcel Bonin — a closer look

In addition to playing professional hockey, Marcel Bonin was well known in his native Quebec for wrestling bears. He first wrestled a bear for $1,000 in Joliette, Quebec, and claimed he knew the muzzled and de-clawed animal very well after having many bouts with his furry opponent. Former boxing heavyweight champion Joe Louis was the referee at the first match (Louis travelled with the bear) and Bonin continued to wrestle in side shows all over the province. Bonin was also known for eating glass and would entertain his teammates with this skill!

Marcel Bonin (#18) has a run-in with Chicago goaltender Glenn Hall during the Stanley Cup playoffs. The 1959 playoffs were the highlight of Bonin's career as he scored 10 goals in 11 post-season games (including the Cup-winning goal). He would only score one more playoff goal in his career. Bonin played on three Cup-winning teams in Montreal and his Canadiens career totals show 68 goals and 205 points in 280 regular-season games. He also played for Detroit and Boston.

of Dickie Moore, Jean Beliveau and Marcel Bonin. The strategy worked and the Leafs went on to clinch a playoff spot on the last night of the season with a 6-4 win in Detroit, while the Habs helped out by beating the fourth-place Rangers 4-2 the same evening. Toronto gained a playoff spot by one point over New York to cap what seemed like an impossible task.

playoffs

SERIES A – MONTREAL VS. CHICAGO

It took the Canadiens six games (and a controversial ending) to subdue a very stubborn Blackhawks team. The Montreal side opened with two wins at home by scores of 4-2 and 5-1. Marcel Bonin scored twice in both games at the Forum. But Chicago won the next two by outscoring the Habs 4-2 and 3-1. Bonin scored in both games. Montreal returned to home ice and won the next game 4-2 on goals by Claude Provost (2), Bernie Geoffrion and the ever present Bonin. Provost, with his second of the game, scored the winning goal in the sixth game at 18:32 of the third period. The goal was scored after referee Red Storey declined to call a trip on the Blackhawks' Bobby Hull by defenceman Al Langlois. NHL president Clarence Campbell was critical of the non-call and the principled Storey resigned, never to referee in the league again. Dickie Moore with two and Doug Harvey also scored in the final game of the series for Montreal.

SERIES B – TORONTO VS. BOSTON

It took the Leafs seven games but they advanced to the finals just as coach Punch Imlach had predicted prior to the start of the series. The series did not start off very well for Toronto, who lost the first two games in Boston by scores of 5-1 and 4-2. But on March 28, 1959, Gerry Ehman scored an overtime winner (his second of the series) to get Toronto a 3-2 win at the Gardens. Ehman scored another goal in the fourth game and Frank Mahovlich scored the overtime winner as the Leafs evened the series. The Leafs scored the winner with the Bruins shorthanded as Jean Guy Gendron was nailed with a five-minute major for cross-checking Ehman. Toronto won the next game in Beantown, as goalie Johnny Bower was outstanding and veteran Bert Olmstead scored once in a 4-1 win. The Leafs could not finish off the Bruins back at the Gardens, as Boston walked away with a 5-4 win, but Ehman was the hero in game seven at the Boston Gardens with a late goal (his sixth of the series) to give Toronto a 3-2 win. The Cinderella Leafs were back in the finals for the first time since 1951.

stanley cup finals

GAME 1 – APRIL 9, 1959 @ THE FORUM
Montreal 5 Toronto 3

The Montreal Canadiens scored two third-period goals to break a 3-3 tie and take the first game of the finals. Marcel Bonin (at 11:59) and Dickie Moore (at 15:02) were the third-period marksmen for the Habs, who were challenged by the upstart Leafs throughout the contest. The Canadiens opened the scoring after just 36 seconds of the first period on a goal by Henri Richard. However, the young Toronto squad responded with two consecutive goals by Dick Duff (a shorthanded effort on a breakaway) and Billy Harris before Ralph Backstrom scored his first-ever playoff goal to tie the game. Andre Pronovost gave Montreal the lead in the second, only to have Ron Stewart tie it for Toronto. The contest featured a fight between Bobby Baun and Henri Richard, and saw Ralph Backstrom and Doug Harvey play very well for the Habs. The game also marked the return to the Montreal lineup of Maurice Richard who had been out with an injury since mid-January. Prior to the start of the series, Toronto coach Punch Imlach had predicted the Leafs would win the Cup in six games, to which Canadiens coach Toe Blake responded, "Imlach was always a good, tough guy behind the bench. It's pretty hard to get hurt there." (*The Montreal Gazette*, April 8, 1959)

"Mental lapses lost the game for us, too. That Harvey is murder unless you play him right. When Doug comes down like he did on the winning goal, you'll seldom see him shoot from the blueline. Let him pull you out of position and he'll set up some other guy here."

Bert Olmstead (*The Montreal Gazette*, April 13, 1959)

GAME 2 – APRIL 11, 1959 @ THE FORUM
Montreal 3 Toronto 1

Once again a pair of third-period goals broke open a tie game and the Montreal Canadiens took the second game of the finals 3-1 over the Maple Leafs. Doug Harvey set up the winner once again, which was scored this time by Claude Provost (who scored twice in the third). Tom Johnson opened the scoring in the game, but the Leafs tied it on a marker by Ron Stewart. Toronto received stellar goaltending from Johnny Bower, who faced 44 shots, but it was not enough to eke out a win. The Leafs complained about tactics used by Harvey (diving to draw a penalty, holding Toronto players), but it was the Leafs who were assessed nine of the seventeen penalties called in the game.

"Yes, Olmstead was the one who taught me a great deal, showed me the inside stuff, the moves to make. Bert knew hockey — every aspect of it."

Frank Mahovlich (Maple Leaf game program, February 23, 1963)

Bert Olmstead
— a closer look

Bert Olmstead of the Leafs battles along the boards with Boston's Leo Boivin (#20) during the 1959 semi-finals between the two clubs. Imlach brought in Olmstead to give the leadership they needed to become a contender. In his first year as a Leaf, Olmstead scored 10 goals and added 31 assists during the season and then chipped in six points in 12 playoff games (including one key goal against the Bruins). When Imlach first took over as coach, he appointed the rugged winger as playing assistant coach, but Olmstead relinquished the title when he felt he was not getting enough say in team matters. He helped Toronto to one Cup (1962) and posted a record of 56 goals and 165 points in 246 games as a Leaf.

Bert Olmstead is one of the few players to have worn both the uniforms of the Canadiens and the Maple Leafs in the six-team era. He also has the distinction of having played his last game in each uniform as a Stanley Cup champion (in 1958 with Montreal and in 1962 with Toronto).

Ticket prices for the first game of the finals at the Forum were $2.25 and $2.00 with $1.75 being charged for general admission (which went on sale at 7 p.m. at the Forum street wicket). Game time was slated for 8:30 p.m.

Toronto's Dick Duff waits for a puck in front of the Canadiens goal occupied by Jacques Plante, while Doug Harvey tries to gather in the loose puck. Duff intercepted a Dickie Moore pass and broke in alone on Plante to score the Leafs' first goal of the finals. Plante faced 24 Toronto shots and Harvey set up the winning goal by Marcel Bonin in the 5-3 Montreal win during the first game of the series.

Canadiens. Toronto opened the scoring on a goal by Billy Harris in the first period, but Marcel Bonin tied it for the Habs. Bert Olmstead gave the Leafs a 2-1 lead in the second, but Dickie Moore tied the game in the third. Toronto defenceman Tim Horton was cut for 12 stitches by the stick of Canadiens forward Bernie Geoffrion, but the hard rock Leaf returned to the game.

GAME 3 – APRIL 14, 1959
@ MAPLE LEAF GARDENS
Toronto 3 Montreal 2 (OT)

A swift-skating Dick Duff crossed the blueline and fired a shot past Jacques Plante for the over-time-winning goal in Toronto's 3-2 victory over Montreal. The goal came at 10:06 of the first overtime period from 45 feet out and appeared to deflect off the skate of Montreal defenceman Tom Johnson. It gave the Leafs some badly needed life in a series that had been dominated by the

"Our guys played their best game of the series so far and they won't stop until they've won that Cup."

Punch Imlach (*The Montreal Gazette*, April 15, 1959)

GAME 4 – APRIL 16, 1959
@ MAPLE LEAF GARDENS
Montreal 3 Toronto 2

In a game that featured no scoring until the third

period, the Canadiens sandwiched three goals around two Leaf markers to take the fourth game of the finals 3-2. Billy Harris opened the scoring for Toronto but Ab McDonald, Ralph Backstrom and Bernie Geoffrion (with a high, hard shot from 25 feet out) scored three consecutive goals in five minutes to seal the win. Frank Mahovlich scored a late goal to make it closer. Geoffrion was the star of the game with his goal and two assists. Speedy forward Bill Hicke made his NHL debut in the game for the Canadiens, who played the contest without Jean Beliveau and Maurice Richard.

The Canadiens, needing just one more win to clinch the Cup, came out and blitzed the Leafs with three straight goals by Ralph Backstrom, Bernie Geoffrion and Tom Johnson. They built up their lead to 5-1 on goals by Marcel Bonin and Geoffrion, but the Leafs refused to quit and scored two goals (by Frank Mahovlich and Bert Olmstead) late in the third. Goalie Johnny Bower was pulled with 2:30 remaining in the game, but the Leafs could only muster a goal by Olmstead. Bob Pulford got the other Leaf goal.

GAME 5 – APRIL 18, 1959 @ THE FORUM
Montreal 5 Toronto 3

The Montreal Canadiens defeated a gritty but outmanned group of Toronto Maple Leafs to capture their fourth straight Stanley Cup with a 5-3 win before 14,790 happy fans at the Forum.

Montreal's Bernie Geoffrion (#5) puts the puck past Toronto goalie Johnny Bower to seal the Canadiens' Stanley Cup victory in the 1959 finals. Toronto defenders Bob Baun and Carl Brewer are trying to help by covering Ralph Backstrom (#6). In the last two games of the series, Geoffrion scored three times (including one game winner) as the Canadiens overpowered the Maple Leafs to win the Stanley Cup.

Last of the Finals — a closer look

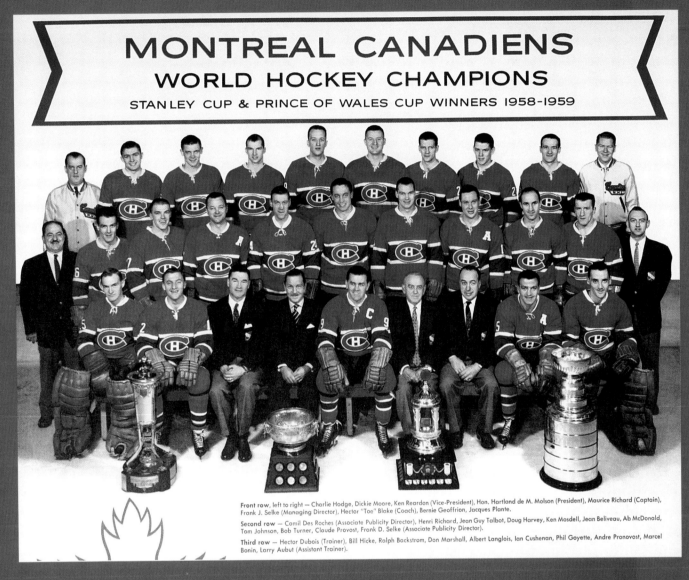

MONTREAL CANADIENS
WORLD HOCKEY CHAMPIONS
STANLEY CUP & PRINCE OF WALES CUP WINNERS 1958-1959

Front row, left to right — Charlie Hodge, Dickie Moore, Ken Reardon (Vice-President), Hon. Hartland de M. Molson (President), Maurice Richard (Captain), Frank J. Selke (Managing Director), Hector "Toe" Blake (Coach), Bernie Geoffrion, Jacques Plante.

Second row — Camil Des Roches (Associate Publicity Director), Henri Richard, Jean Guy Talbot, Doug Harvey, Ken Mosdell, Jean Beliveau, Ab McDonald, Tom Johnson, Bob Turner, Claude Provost, Frank D. Selke (Associate Publicity Director).

Third row — Hector Dubois (Trainer), Bill Hicke, Ralph Backstrom, Don Marshall, Albert Langlois, Ian Cushenan, Phil Goyette, Andre Pronovost, Marcel Bonin, Larry Aubut (Assistant Trainer).

When the game was over, Montreal captain Maurice Richard refused to pose with the Cup (he was dressed for the contest but did not play), so there was no formal presentation. The injured Jean Beliveau and former Canadiens captain Butch Bouchard appeared with the trophy at the south end of the Forum and then Richard and Geoffrion went over and took it from them and brought it over to the gate where the Canadiens went to their dressing room. Richard had an opportunity to get in the game in the third period (and the Forum crowd was anxious to see him play), but he refused, saying that the team did not need him to win.

> *"This is a great team. I'm not just saying they're the greatest but the fellows deserve an awful lot of credit. They did it without two big boys [Beliveau and Richard] against a team that wouldn't quit."*

Toe Blake (*The Montreal Gazette*, April 20, 1959)

Canadiens goaltender Jacques Plante made history
in 1959–60 when he began wearing a face mask
on a consistent basis. He recorded his first shutout
with the mask against the Maple Leafs.

The Leafs–Canadiens Rivalry
1959–60

season summary

To begin the 1959–60 season, the Montreal Canadiens made no major changes. Their club was still loaded with star players in their prime, with the exception of Maurice Richard who was clearly on his last legs. Trouble with nagging injuries and an inability to control his weight would ultimately decide things for the Montreal superstar. It was an agonizing choice for the legend to make, but perhaps it was eased with another championship ring secured by the end of the 1960 playoffs. If Richard was not up to his usual standards, there were many other Canadien players ready to take up the slack. Jean Beliveau finished third in league scoring and Henri Richard earned fifth place among all point-getters, while Bernie Geoffrion finished tenth. Goalie Jacques Plante won his fifth consecutive Vezina Trophy and Doug Harvey took back the Norris Trophy as the best defenceman in the NHL. All of the above-mentioned players made either the first or second all-star team. The only new Hab of note was defenceman J.C. Tremblay, who made his debut with the team (11 games) but did not play in the post season.

The most memorable game of the Canadiens season took place on November 1, 1959, at Madison Square Garden in New York. Plante was struck in the face with a high-rising shot from the stick of the Rangers' Andy Bathgate and had to go off for repairs. Stitched up, swollen and sore, a determined Plante made it clear to coach Toe Blake that he would not go back into the net without a face mask. Blake tried to talk his goalie out of it but Plante's mind was made up. Not wanting to risk using the "house goalie" (there was no back-up on the bench) that the Rangers would provide, Blake relented and hockey history was made. Plante went out and beat the Rangers 3-1 and the mask was here to stay. The crusty Canadiens coach never warmed up to the idea of goalies wearing a mask but Plante and other NHL goalies would win the day.

Montreal defenceman Doug Harvey (#2) won his fifth Norris Trophy in 1959–60 when he scored six goals and 21 assists in 66 games (he added three goals in the playoffs). During his career with the Canadiens, Harvey posted a record of 76 goals and 371 assists in 890 regular-season games. The playoff totals show 59 assists and 67 points in 123 contests. In addition to his superb playmaking skills, Harvey could dish out some punishment, as is evidenced in a game against the Leafs on October 16, 1959, when he cracked the jaw of Ron Stewart.

After their surprising run to the finals in 1959, the Leafs made only a few changes to their team. NHL ironman Johnny Wilson was acquired in a deal, while Gerry James and Gary Edmundson played minor supporting roles with some effectiveness. The big addition for the Leafs came in February when Toronto capitalized on Red Kelly's unhappiness and swung a deal with Detroit. Kelly was supposed to go to New York in a trade but he refused to report and was ready to retire. Leafs coach Punch Imlach dispatched King Clancy to talk with Kelly, and after they agreed to terms, Toronto sent Marc Reaume to the Red Wings in return. It was perhaps the best trade in Leaf history. Imlach had sought Kelly for the purposes of handling Beliveau when the Leafs played the Canadiens and the former all-star defenceman was converted to centre. It did not pay off in 1960, but it would work out very well in the long term for Toronto. The Leafs also got great seasons from Johnny Bower in goal and Allan Stanley, a second team all-star, on defence.

During the season, the Habs pretty much controlled the Leafs with ease (although Toronto did finish in second place) with a 10-3-1 record in the games between the two teams. In the playoffs it was also no contest, with Montreal sweeping to the Cup in eight straight games, including a four-games-to-nothing whitewash of the Maple Leafs in the finals. No NHL team has won five consecutive Stanley Cups since the 1960 Montreal Canadiens.

OCTOBER 16, 1959
Montreal 4 Toronto 2 @ The Forum

In the first meeting between the two teams since their meeting in the finals the previous season, the Habs got off to a quick start and downed the Leafs 4-1 before 13,775 fans. Henri Richard scored just 17 seconds into the contest on a play that was started by Montreal defenceman Doug Harvey, who got the puck to Maurice Richard who passed to Dickie Moore. Moore connected with the Pocket Rocket, who put it away. Jean Beliveau got the second Canadiens score by knocking in Bill Hicke's rebound at 1:59 (Hicke was in the goal crease but the goal stood). Marcel Bonin tipped in a Beliveau shot to make it 3-0 just 21 seconds later. Frank Mahovlich finally got Toronto on the board when he tapped in a Gerry Ehman rebound but Moore scored on a power-play with the Leafs' George Armstrong in the penalty box for high sticking. It stayed that way until Bob Pulford scored early in the third period to make it 4-2. The Leafs enjoyed the better of the play but could not overcome the early deficit. Toronto not only lost the game but forward Ron Stewart suffered a cracked jaw when he took a Doug Harvey elbow to the face. The Leafs had come into the game winners of their last two, while the Canadiens had been walloped 8-4 by Boston in their previous encounter.

OCTOBER 28, 1959
Toronto 1 Montreal 1 @ Maple Leaf Gardens

Dick Duff scored a power-play goal at 5:49 of the third period to lift the Maple Leafs into a 1-1 tie with the Canadiens. Montreal's Jean Guy Talbot was in the penalty box when Duff deked goalie Jacques Plante after taking a nice pass from George Armstrong. The Canadiens had opened the scoring in the first period when 38-year-old captain Maurice Richard scored at 11:06 on passes from Dickie Moore and Henri Richard. The game featured great goaltending from Plante and Johnny Bower. The Leafs were determined to make life miserable for Plante and the Canadiens netminder got run over by Johnny Wilson (Talbot had knocked Wilson into the goalie) while Frank Mahovlich and Bob Pulford body-checked the unsuspecting goaltender.

NOVEMBER 12, 1959
Montreal 3 Toronto 0 @ The Forum

Jacques Plante earned his first shutout of the

Jacques Plante (#1) earned his first shutout wearing the mask against the Maple Leafs (3-0 on November 12, 1959). He started wearing the mask after taking an Andy Bathgate shot in the face during a game in New York on November 1, 1959. After being repaired, Plante refused to go back into the net without the protective gear and coach Toe Blake finally agreed to his goaltender's demand. Plante won that game 3-1 and also won 8-2 in a return match with the Rangers back in the Forum on November 5th and a 2-2 tie with Chicago on the 8th before whitewashing the Leafs. Plante played in 69 games in 1959–60, allowing 175 goals and recording three shutouts.

season and his first while wearing a mask as the Canadiens blanked Toronto 3-0 at the Forum. The Habs were paced by two goals from the stick of Phil Goyette and Dickie Moore added another. Goyette's first goal was actually knocked into the net by Toronto goalie Johnny Bower after misplaying an Andre Pronovost shot. Goyette swiped at the puck and was credited with the goal. His second score was a tip-in off a Claude Provost shot. Moore's goal came as a result of a passout from behind the net by Henri Richard at 9:21 of the third period. A crowd of 14,296 fans saw the Habs run their unbeaten streak to 11 games (eight wins, three ties).

NOVEMBER 21, 1959
Montreal 4 Toronto 1 @ Maple Leaf Gardens

A rare Saturday night contest between the two teams saw the Canadiens beat the Maple Leafs 4-1 at the Gardens on November 21, 1959. Montreal ran its unbeaten streak to 14 on goals by Doug Harvey, Dickie Moore, Jean Beliveau and Don Marshall (into an empty net). Harvey opened the scoring on a screened shot past Toronto goalie Johnny Bower. Bower had a difficult night, giving up a bad goal to Beliveau and then taking a puck in the mouth on a deflected shot by Marshall. He lost one tooth, three were loosened and eight stitches were required to close the wound. After taking the repairs, Bower went back into the goal. (He also played the next night in Boston and won 2-1 despite the badly swollen lips). Beliveau played a feisty game and battled with Dick Duff of the Leafs (stick swinging after a Beliveau elbow) and then rocked Billy Harris with a solid bodycheck. Allan Stanley, who played a superb game, got the only goal for the Leafs.

DECEMBER 1, 1959
Toronto 1 Montreal 0 @ Maple Leaf Gardens

In a thrilling contest played before 14,632 spectators, the Maple Leafs stopped the Canadiens' 18-game unbeaten streak by edging the Habs 1-0. Frank Mahovlich got the only goal of the game at 8:23 of the first period when he backhanded in a Marc Reaume rebound over fallen Montreal goaltender Jacques Plante. It was a physical contest in which the Leafs hit and bumped effectively. Toronto's Larry Regan took five stitches when he was charged by Claude Provost (who was given a five-minute major) of the Canadiens and ended up in the boards. Johnny Bower gained the shutout for the ecstatic Leafs who mobbed him at the end of the game. Plante also played a strong game in the Habs net.

DECEMBER 17, 1959
Montreal 8 Toronto 2 @ The Forum

In a game that featured a record-setting brawl, the Montreal Canadiens whipped the Toronto Maple Leafs 8-2 at the Forum. Jean Beliveau and Marcel Bonin started the onslaught by giving the Canadiens a 2-0 lead and the teams then exchanged a pair of goals in the second (Johnny Wilson and George Armstrong for Toronto; Bill Hicke and Claude Provost for Montreal) before a melee broke out between the two clubs in the same stanza. The fight began when Canadiens defenceman Jean Guy Talbot knocked down Maple Leafs forward Billy Harris. Gerry James came to the aid of Harris by jumping Talbot and that brought Dickie Moore into the fray to even up the sides. Another fight broke out between Beliveau and Toronto rearguard Tim Horton, and the Leafs defenceman twice dropped his taller opponent with a pair of tackles.

Referee Eddie Powers decided to give out penalties to every player on the ice except the goaltenders, a situation no observer at the game had ever seen before in the history of hockey. There was confusion at the timekeeper's box by the unprecedented situation. By the time the game ended, Powers had dished out 24 penalties, including four majors and one misconduct. While Bonin and Toronto's Gary Edmundson staged another fight and Armstrong earned himself a $25 fine and misconduct penalty for coming off the bench to argue a call, the Canadiens got goals from Doug Harvey, Henri Richard, Al Langlois (his first of the season) and Ralph Backstrom in the third period to ice the game for the Habs. The game, played before 13,988 fans, did not finish until 11:19 p.m.

DECEMBER 30, 1959
Montreal 3 Toronto 2 @ Maple Leaf Gardens

All the goals scored in the December 30 contest between the Canadiens and Leafs were scored by centremen as Montreal edged Toronto 3-2. Jean

Johnny Bower

Johnny Bower was the first goaltender to play in 1,000 professional games (not including the playoffs). He set the mark on October 20, 1963, in a game against Detroit. Going into the 1963–64 season Bower had played in 996 pro games, followed by Terry Sawchuk (951), Gump Worsley (837), Glenn Hall (831) and Jacques Plante (741). Bower won major awards in every professional league he played in (NHL, AHL, WHL).

"I'm also sure that if I had to wear a mask in a game I'd be lost. It's a great thing for some goaltenders — but not for me."

Johnny Bower (Hockey 1964, Official Sports Magazine)

Johnny Bower got a measure of revenge against the Montreal Canadiens on December 1, 1959, when he shut out the archrivals 1-0 at the Gardens. Having previously hit the mark with the NY Rangers, in 1959–60 Bower finally re-established himself as a number-one goalie in the NHL, playing in 66 games for Toronto and posting a 2.73 goals-against average with five shutouts. His efforts earned him the J. P. Bickell Cup as the most valuable Leaf for that season; he was informed of the award in a telegram sent to him by Conn Smythe.

Montreal defenceman Albert "Junior" Langlois (#19), shown here battling New York's Andy Bathgate, scored his first goal of the 1959–60 season against the Leafs on December 17, 1959. It was his only goal of the year to go along with 14 assists in 67 games played (he added three assists in the play-offs). Langlois played with the Canadiens between 1957 and 1961, scoring two goals and 31 points in 177 games.

Al Langlois was scouted by assistant general manager Ken Reardon for the Montreal Canadiens. The big defenceman (six foot, 205 pounds) nearly quit the game, but went to Shawinigan (QHL) and then to Rochester (AHL) before joining the Canadiens. He signed his first NHL contract for $7,500 and was teamed with star blueliner Doug Harvey. In later years Langlois felt Reardon was critical of his game and that he was being pulled off the ice every time he made a mistake. Montreal traded the rearguard to New York in 1961 (for John Hanna) and he was reunited there with Harvey to enjoy his best year in 1961–62 with seven goals and twenty-five points.

A CLOSER LOOK

Beliveau (his 21st of the year) opened the scoring for the Habs when he rapped home a Marcel Bonin rebound at 11:38 of the first. Bob Pulford tied it for the Maple Leafs at 1:05 of the second on a short-handed breakaway. But then Henri Richard fired a pair of goals to make the score 3-1 and give the Habs a commanding lead. Richard's first goal came as a result of beating Toronto's Dick Duff to a loose puck and then firing a screened shot past goalie Johnny Bower. The Pocket Rocket added his second of the night at 14:40 of the third period, but the Leafs responded with a late tally by Pulford at 19:48. Time ran out on the Leafs, who played a spirited contest led by their captain George Armstrong, who decked Montreal goalie Jacques Plante. The Canadiens netminder stayed down until his head cleared and he went on to play a stellar game. But it was the Leafs who were very upset by the work of referee Eddie Powers.

JANUARY 14, 1960
Montreal 3 Toronto 1 @ The Forum

The Canadiens recorded another victory against the Maple Leafs with a 3-1 win. Second-period goals by Marcel Bonin and Dickie Moore broke open a scoreless tie to give the home side a 2-0 lead, but Toronto got one back from winger Ron Stewart before the period ended. A third-period marker by Henri Richard at 9:32 gave the Habs some breathing room. Johnny Bower was the best player on the ice of both teams, stopping 36 of 39 Montreal shots on goal (Plante faced only 19 Toronto shots in the contest). The Leaf netminder was run over by Montreal's Doug Harvey and Leaf defenceman Allan Stanley came to the rescue. Andre Pronovost got into a fight with Armstrong in the penalty box after the two were assessed minors. Police and linesmen had to

"I knew I was playing with a master. By watching him I learned how to take the man out, how to hit and when, all the everyday things. If I hadn't played with Doug [Harvey], I probably wouldn't be here."

Al Langlois (*Hockey Annual* magazine, 1963)

break up the scuffle and each player was given a misconduct penalty for their scrap.

FEBRUARY 4, 1960
Montreal 4 Toronto 2 @ The Forum

The Canadiens ran their record against the Maple Leafs to 8-1-1 with a pair of 4-2 wins. The first came at the Forum where 14,954 fans saw the Habs get goals from Jean Beliveau, Dickie Moore (his 20th of the season and 10th on the power-play), Henri Richard and Ralph Backstrom to seal the victory. The win moved Montreal 19 points up on the Leafs in the league standings. Richard's stick accidentally struck Toronto goalie Johnny Bower in the mouth (under his tongue) for six stitches after the Montreal forward collided with the Leafs' Allan Stanley. Bert Olmstead and Bob Baun replied for Toronto.

FEBRUARY 10, 1960
Montreal 4 Toronto 2 @ Maple Leaf Gardens

The Maple Leafs got a big boost from newly acquired Red Kelly (from Detroit) but still lost 4-2 to the mighty Habs, who were without Jean Beliveau, Dickie Moore and Marcel Bonin. Maurice Richard scored twice for the visitors (both set up by brother Henri) while Ralph Backstrom and Claude Provost (into an empty net) got the others. Billy Harris scored Toronto's goals. Goalies Jacques Plante and Johnny Bower both played very well. The contest was witnessed by 14,651 fans who crammed the Gardens to see Kelly make his debut with the Leafs wearing number four. He did not record any points.

FEBRUARY 24, 1960
Toronto 3 Montreal 1 @ Maple Leaf Gardens

The Maple Leafs played perhaps their best game of the season, finally beating the Canadiens 3-1. Toronto built up a 3–0 lead on goals by Ron

Henri Richard

"Henri is a much better all-round player than I ever was. He stickhandles better, controls the puck more and skates faster. He's better in every way except goal scoring."

Maurice Richard (Maple Leaf game program, December 30, 1964)

Henri Richard scored his 200th career goal in his 587th NHL game. He scored 50 against Toronto, 48 against Boston, 40 versus New York, 33 against Chicago and another 29 versus Detroit.

Montreal centre Henri Richard (#16), watched closely by the Leafs' George Armstrong, scored three important goals in two Canadiens wins over the Leafs in December 1959 and January 1960 contests. In the 1959–60 season, Richard would record 73 points (including 43 assists) in 70 games. His goal total of 30 would be the best one-season total of his career.

Montreal goalie Jacques Plante (#1) has to watch Billy Harris of the Leafs at the side of the goal in a game at Maple Leaf Gardens. Plante played his usual great game on February 10, 1960, when the Habs came in for a rare Saturday night contest. Harris was the only Leaf to beat Plante on the night with two tallies. After a career-best 22 goals in 1958–59, Harris could only get 13 in 1959–60, although he did chip in 25 assists. Soon afterwards his playing time was severely reduced by coach Punch Imlach.

Toronto defenceman Allan Stanley (middle of photo) is helping goalie Johnny Bower in front of the Leafs net, with Bob Baun (#21) also looking for the loose puck. Stanley tied a career high with 10 goals in 1959–60 and totalled 33 points to earn a place on the NHL's second all-star team at the end of the season. After stops in New York, Chicago and Boston, Stanley found a home in Toronto, where he played from 1958 to 1968. In 633 games as a Maple Leaf, Stanley scored 47 goals and added 186 assists. He scored an additional 31 points in 82 playoff games.

Stewart, Bob Pulford and Allan Stanley before giving up a late third period goal that ruined a shutout bid by Johnny Bower. Stewart's goal was disputed by Montreal, who claimed the Leaf winger kicked the puck into the net. But it was ruled that the puck had bounced in off Stewart's shin after a Tim Horton blast struck the lucky Leaf for his 13th of the season. Pulford got his goal on a breakaway while the Leafs were down a man; Stanley notched his 10th of the year on the power play by coming in from the point to take a Bert Olmstead pass. Andre Pronovost got the lone Montreal score (another potential goal was disallowed when the goal judge ruled a puck did not cross the goal line) and was also given a major penalty for cutting

Stewart with his stick. Marcel Bonin of the Canadiens had a fight with Gerry James and inflicted a three-stitch cut on his opponent. Both got majors but James claimed he never threw a punch.

MARCH 3, 1960
Montreal 5 Toronto 1 @ The Forum

The Montreal Canadiens clinched another first-place finish (for the 14th time) with a 5-1 win over the Maple Leafs in a game played before 14,715 fans at the Forum on March 3, 1960. Billy Harris actually opened the scoring for Toronto but the Habs scored the next five goals on efforts

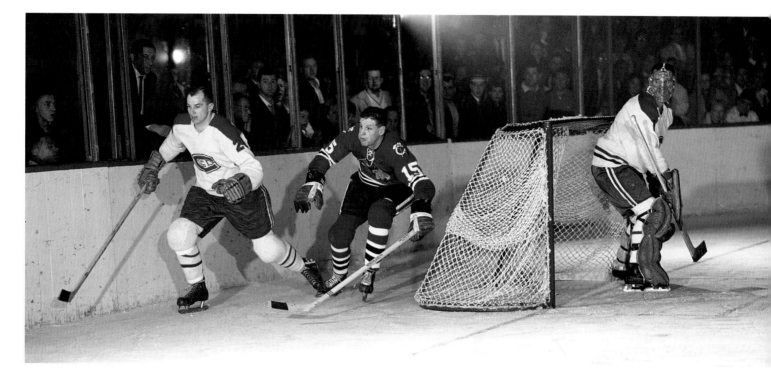

by Don Marshall, Bernie Geoffrion (his 25th of the year), Maurice Richard, Ab McDonald and Dickie Moore (his 21st of the season). Marshall was the best player on the ice and he scored the first Montreal goal by putting in Ernie Hicke's pass by goalie Johnny Bower. The Leafs were without defenceman Allan Stanley and were forced to use Red Kelly on the blueline. Jean Beliveau was out of the Montreal lineup.

Montreal's Don Marshall (#22) tries to escape the checking of Chicago's Eric Nesterenko. Used primarily in a checking role, Marshall was still an effective offensive player for the Canadiens in 1959–60 when he scored 16 times and added 22 assists. His best goal-scoring season as a Hab was in 1957–58 when he potted 22. His career total as a Canadien is 114 goals. He played with Montreal between 1954 and 1963 and totalled 254 points in 585 games.

MARCH 9, 1960
Montreal 9 Toronto 4 @ Maple Leaf Gardens

Bernie Geoffrion scored his 13th career hat trick and Don Marshall scored his fifth goal in as many games as the Habs routed the Maple Leafs 9-4 at the Gardens. The Canadiens basically toyed with the Leafs as Jean Beliveau, Henri Richard (with two), Tom Johnson and Andre Pronovost scored the other Montreal goals. George Armstrong scored two for the Leafs, who also got markers from Red Kelly and Bert Olmstead. The game featured a nine-goal second period (six by the Habs) and three power-play tallies by Montreal to give

them 54 on the year. Montreal goalie Jacques Plante put his mask back on for this game after playing the previous contest against Detroit without his facial protection (at the request of coach Toe Blake). The game also saw a couple of fights take place, one between Bob Turner and Bob Pulford and a renewing of hostilities between Gary Edmundson of Toronto and Pronovost of the Habs.

MARCH 17, 1960
Toronto 6 Montreal 2 @ The Forum

The Maple Leafs got some measure of revenge for some sound beatings they received during the season by beating the defending champions 6-2 at the Forum in the last regular-season meeting between the clubs for the 1959–60 season. It was the first loss on home ice for the Canadiens in 19 starts (14 wins, four ties). Toronto got two goals from Gary Edmundson and singles from Dick Duff, Carl Brewer, Frank Mahovlich and Red Kelly. Marcel Bonin and Bernie Geoffrion scored the Montreal goals. The Canadiens fin-

ished the season with 92 points (40-18-12) and the Leafs were second with 79 (35-26-9).

playoffs

SERIES A – MONTREAL VS. CHICAGO

Montreal made Chicago's stay in the playoffs very brief by sweeping the Blackhawks in four straight.

Jacques Plante (shown here without his mask) had a remarkable season in 1959–60. First, he changed the face of hockey forever by using a goalie mask on a daily basis and then he won the Vezina Trophy (his fifth straight) while earning a place on the second all-star team. He capped it off by recording three shutouts in the playoffs (in eight games) and winning a fifth consecutive Stanley Cup.

Toronto defenceman Carl Brewer battles with Detroit's Gerry Melnyk (#14) for the puck. Brewer was outstanding for the Leafs in the series with Detroit, scoring two goals and two assists. During the regular season Brewer scored four times and added 19 assists to go along with his league-leading 150 penalty minutes. Rookie Melnyk scored three times for the Red Wings in the series against Toronto.

THE NUMBERS

When Maurice Richard retired he held many playoff records including most career goals (82 in just 131 post-season games); most goals in one year (12); most goals in one game (5); most assists in one game (5); consecutive games with a goal (8); most game-winning goals (18); most overtime goals (6); most overtime goals in one year (3); and most three-goal games (7).

Montreal won the first two games at the Forum both by scores of 4-3. The second contest went into overtime but Doug Harvey scored the winner for the Canadiens. The next two games saw Canadiens goalie Jacques Plante record shutouts of 4-0 and 2-0. The line of Don Marshall, Bill Hicke and Ralph Backstrom was especially effective for the Canadiens, who easily advanced to the Stanley Cup finals.

Henri Richard (#16) and his brother Maurice (#9) storm the Toronto net occupied by Johnny Bower. The younger Richard had a big game against the Leafs in the opener of the 1960 finals when he scored once and added three assists in the 4-2 win. Richard led all playoff scorers with 12 points (3 goals, 9 assists) in the 1960 playoffs. The older Richard was playing in his last playoff series and would score his last goal and assist in the games played in Toronto.

SERIES B – TORONTO VS. DETROIT

It took six hard-fought contests but the Maple Leafs eventually advanced to the Stanley Cup finals by beating the Detroit Red Wings four games to two. Detroit actually won the opener

"The Pocket was the difference out there as he has been in so many games this season."

Toe Blake (*The Toronto Star*, April 8, 1960)

2-1 at the Gardens on March 23, 1960, but Toronto came back to win the next game 4-2 on March 26. It took until the third overtime period to win the third game but Frank Mahovlich's winner gave Toronto a 5-4 victory. The Red Wings tied the series with a 2-1 win but Toronto took the series lead for good with another 5-4 victory. A 4-2 win at Detroit on April 3 saw the Leafs wrap up the series on Mahovlich's winning goal.

stanley cup finals

APRIL 7, 1960
Montreal 4 Toronto 2 @ The Forum

The Canadiens opened the finals once again for the second straight year against the Maple Leafs

"It was a long time coming. I got Dickie Moore's rebound and let go a backhander over Bower who was on one knee."

Maurice Richard on his first playoff goal
since 1958 (*The Montreal Gazette*, April 13, 1960)

and skated off with a 4-2 win, with 14,301 fans in attendance. The Habs got goals from Dickie Moore, Doug Harvey, Jean Beliveau and Henri Richard (who also added three assists). The Canadiens roared out of the starting gate and it was 3-0 before the first 12 minutes of the game had passed. Moore scored the opener at 2:27 of the opening stanza on a power-play after the Leafs' Gerry Ehman was penalized. A loose rebound was left near the Toronto net and Moore had an easy time putting the puck past goalie Johnny Bower.

APRIL 9, 1960
Montreal 2 Toronto 1 @ The Forum

The Canadiens got goals from Dickie Moore and Jean Beliveau before six minutes had passed and then held off the Leafs the rest of the way for a 2-1 win and a two-game lead in the series. Larry Regan got the lone Toronto goal; the Leafs felt they had scored another by Johnny Wilson but it was not allowed because referee Eddie Powers did not see the sharp-angled shot cross the goal line. Montreal also had a goal called back (Claude Provost into the empty net) because the clock ran out.

APRIL 12, 1960
Montreal 5 Toronto 2 @ Maple Leaf Gardens

Even though they were back on home ice, the Maple Leafs were still no match for the mighty Canadiens, who easily won the game 5-2. Showing too much speed, finesse and puck control, and with

---

Toronto's George Armstrong (#10) tries to put the puck past Jacques Plante in the Montreal net with Al Langlois (#19) and Dickie Moore (#12) doing their best to stop the Leaf captain. Armstrong set up the only goal the Leafs scored on April 9, 1960, in the second game of the finals that was credited to Larry Regan. Armstrong first joined the Leafs as a 19-year-old when he played two games for the team in the 1949–50 season. He scored his first NHL goal against the Canadiens on February 9, 1952, when he beat goalie Gerry McNeil.

great goaltending, the Canadiens got goals from Don Marshall, Phil Goyette (with two) and Henri and Maurice Richard (a sweeping backhander for his final post-season goal) to pull away from the Leafs and take a commanding 3-0 lead in the series. Johnny Wilson and Bert Olmstead got the Leaf goals to make it more respectable. Marshall got the opener for the Habs by taking a Bill Hicke pass, faking Leaf defenceman Bob Baun to his knees and then whipping a shot past Johnny Bower.

APRIL 14, 1960
Montreal 4 Toronto 0 @ Maple Leaf Gardens

Jacques Plante made 30 saves and survived a Bob Pulford elbow to record a 4-0 shutout as the Montreal Canadiens won their fifth straight Stanley Cup. As in all the games in this series, the Leafs were quickly down 2-0 after goals by Jean Beliveau and Doug Harvey. The Leafs played hard but could not beat Plante in the Canadiens goal despite their efforts to rattle the "Masked Marvel." Harvey showed the Leafs that the Habs were not going to be pushed around by decking Toronto captain George Armstrong with a solid bodycheck. Henri Richard in the second, and Beliveau in the third, rounded out the scoring. Maurice Richard earned an assist on his brother's goal for his final NHL point. At the end of the game, the Stanley Cup was presented to Maurice Richard who accepted the trophy as team captain. The rest of the team skated off the ice and Richard posed for pictures with Plante and the silver trophy near centre ice.

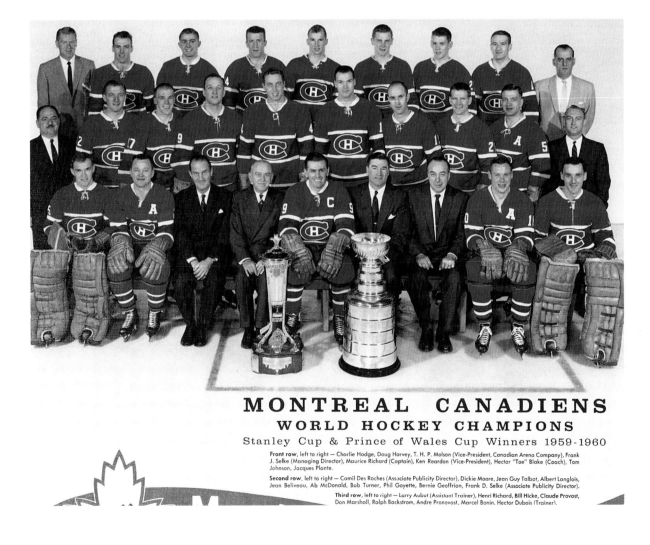

MONTREAL CANADIENS
WORLD HOCKEY CHAMPIONS
Stanley Cup & Prince of Wales Cup Winners 1959-1960

Front row, left to right — Charlie Hodge, Doug Harvey, T. H. P. Molson (Vice-President, Canadian Arena Company), Frank J. Selke (Managing Director), Maurice Richard (Captain), Ken Reardon (Vice-President), Hector "Toe" Blake (Coach), Tom Johnson, Jacques Plante.

Second row, left to right — Camil Des Roches (Associate Publicity Director), Dickie Moore, Jean Guy Talbot, Albert Langlois, Jean Beliveau, Ab McDonald, Bob Turner, Phil Goyette, Bernie Geoffrion, Frank D. Selke (Associate Publicity Director).

Third row, left to right — Larry Aubut (Assistant Trainer), Henri Richard, Bill Hicke, Claude Provost, Don Marshall, Ralph Backstrom, Andre Pronovost, Marcel Bonin, Hector Dubois (Trainer).

Toronto's Frank Mahovlich (left) and Montreal's Bernie Geoffrion (right) battled all season long in 1960–61 to break the one season goal-scoring record of Maurice Richard. Mahovlich would fall a little short with 48 while Geoffrion would tie the mark with 50 goals.

The Leafs–Canadiens Rivalry
1960–61

season summary

The 1960–61 season could be summarized as the year of the great chase and the great disappointment. Bernie Geoffrion of the Canadiens and Frank Mahovlich of the Maple Leafs staged a year-long battle for the goal-scoring lead and for Maurice Richard's NHL record of 50 goals in one season. Actually, it was Dickie Moore of the Canadiens who was dueling with Mahovlich in the early stages, but as he faded and as Geoffrion returned from injury, the race between the two hard-shooting wingers was on until the final three games of the season. As Geoffrion gathered steam, he passed a worn-out Mahovlich in goals scored and on March 16, 1961, in a game against the Maple Leafs, the Canadiens did everything they could to get "Boom-Boom" the goal he needed. He finally got it in the third period of a 5-2 win and Mahovlich was unable to get going again, finishing with 48. For a while it appeared Mahovlich might score many more than 50 but the scrutiny was too intense for a youngster who was just getting his career started. The savvier Geoffrion was better suited to the task and eventually tied the record.

Going into the regular season, the Habs were still heavy favourites to repeat as Stanley Cup champions, since most of their team was back in uniform. Rocket Richard had retired, but they added Gilles Tremblay and Guy Gendron (acquired in a deal) up front to help with the scoring. Goalie Charlie Hodge was brought in to assist Jacques Plante in the nets, while J.C. Tremblay and Jean Gauthier got some playing time on the blueline. Ab McDonald was dealt away to Chicago.

The Canadiens had a little more trouble than usual in defending their first-place status but still wound up on top of the heap with 92 points (41-19-10) to Toronto's 90 (39-19-12). The Canadiens and Leafs jockeyed for first place all season long and the battle may have worn both teams out. The Blackhawks, who finished with 29 wins, took out the mighty Canadiens in six games as the young and very talented Blackhawks squad matured at playoff time to end the Montreal dynasty.

For the Maple Leafs, their rebuilding program was just about complete with the addition of two super rookies in Dave Keon and Bob Nevin. Both players could score goals (Keon got 20 and Nevin put in 21) and make a good play. Nevin played alongside Mahovlich when the big winger was going for 50 goals. In addition, Punch Imlach added speedy forward John MacMillan in a utility role and defenceman Larry Hillman as insurance. Things came apart for the Leafs when goalie Johnny Bower was hurt in February in a game against the Red Wings when he was run over by Detroit defenceman Howie Young. Bower recovered in time for the playoffs but Imlach felt he was not the same and the Wings staged a major upset in five games.

Despite the post-season disappointments, the two teams took most of the major awards. Geoffrion took the Art Ross (with 95 points) and Hart trophies while Doug Harvey reclaimed the Norris. Keon walked off with the Calder, Bower took the Vezina and Red Kelly won the

Lady Byng for the Maple Leafs. They also dominated the all-star teams, with Bower, Geoffrion, Mahovlich and Jean Beliveau on the first team and Moore, Henri Richard and Allan Stanley on the second team. By the end of the 1960–61 season it was the Leafs who were ready to win a Stanley Cup and the Canadiens who would need to rebuild their club for the future.

OCTOBER 6, 1960
Montreal 5 Toronto 0 @ The Forum

The opening game of the 1960–61 season for both teams proved to be a laugher for the Canadiens, who beat the Maple Leafs 5-0 before 13,747 fans. The Habs certainly showed no signs of missing the now-retired Maurice Richard, as brother Henri paced the team with two goals. Marcel Bonin, Bernie Geoffrion and Bill Hicke got the other goals while Jacques Plante posted the shutout by making 19 saves. The Canadiens netminder made his toughest save off Leaf rookie Bob Nevin but otherwise had an easy time in the nets. Toronto's George Armstrong high sticked Montreal's Phil Goyette into the boards and was given a five-minute major in the first period. Montreal scored twice while Armstrong was off and the Leafs never recovered.

OCTOBER 19, 1960
Toronto 3 Montreal 1 @ Maple Leaf Gardens

A 3-1 Toronto win was overshadowed by a nasty third-period fracas between Frank Mahovlich of the Leafs and Henri Richard of the Canadiens.

"But in his last season or two, I gave him many passes and he couldn't do anything with them. His reflexes were much slower. He always trailed the play. He could still put the puck into the net but he couldn't keep up with me and Dickie Moore."

Henri Richard on the retirement of his brother Maurice (*Hockey Illustrated*, January 1963)

The Canadiens accused the big Maple Leaf winger of deliberately shooting the puck at Richard causing an eight-stitch cut above Richard's right eyebrow. Referee Eddie Powers ruled that it was an accident and no penalty was assessed on the play. Mahovlich claimed it was a clearing attempt that just happened to catch Richard in the face. The Montreal bench was furious and coach Toe Blake refused to ice a team for a few minutes. Montreal winger Dickie Moore tried to get at Mahovlich but was restrained by Bert Olmstead of the Leafs. The Habs called the Big M many other names after the game, as they were still very frustrated by Mahovlich's actions and the lack of a penalty. The Leafs got goals from Gerry Ehman, Bob Pulford and Bob Nevin while Richard got the lone Canadiens marker. Pulford's goal broke up a 1-1 tie and Nevin put in a Mahovlich rebound after the latter had burst through the Canadiens defence to give Toronto an insurance marker.

NOVEMBER 3, 1960
Montreal 3 Toronto 1 @ The Forum

The Montreal Canadiens used a first-period hat trick by Jean Beliveau to cruise past the Maple Leafs 3-1 on November 3 at the Forum. Before the largest crowd of the season (14,747), the Habs broke open the scoring at 1:11 of the first period when Beliveau slapped home a shot past goalie Johnny Bower. Beliveau got his next two on the power-play and the Leafs were only able to get one back in the third by Bob Nevin. In this game it was the Leafs who were upset with referee Eddie Powers for what they thought was inconsistent officiating.

NOVEMBER 19, 1960
Toronto 6 Montreal 3 @ Maple Leaf Gardens

The Leafs got even with the Canadiens on November 19 by pounding out a 6-3 win. In front of 14,720 fans (a new attendance record)

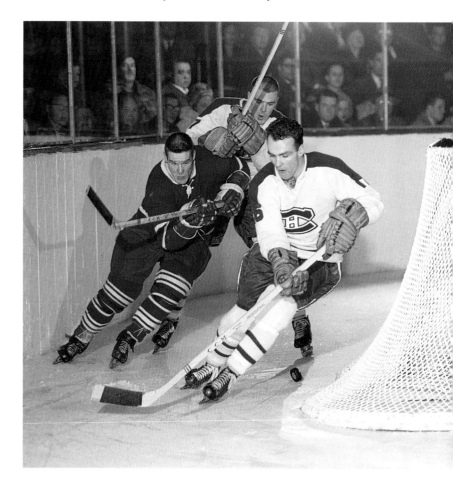

Montreal's Henri Richard (#16) circles the net with Toronto's Tim Horton in hot pursuit. Richard scored the only Canadiens goal in a 3-1 loss to the Leafs on October 19, 1960, and suffered a nasty gash when struck in the face by a Frank Mahovlich clearing attempt. The Canadiens demanded that the Leaf player be penalized but the referee refused to do so. It would set up some further bad blood between the two teams in the 1960–61 season.

on a Saturday night, the Leafs were in total control of the game and got two goals from winger Ron Stewart. Frank Mahovlich scored his 14th marker of the season while Dick Duff, rookie Dave Keon and Eddie Shack got the others. Montreal's Don Marshall opened the scoring but Toronto then reeled off four straight goals to take command. Marcel Bonin and Bernie Geoffrion also scored for the Habs.

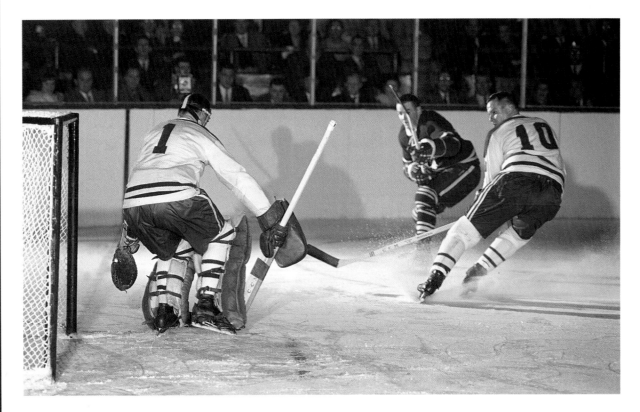

Toronto's Dave Keon (taking a backhand shot) tries to put a puck past Montreal goalie Jacques Plante (#1) while contending with defenceman Tom Johnson (#10). Keon scored his first goal against the Canadiens on November 19, 1960, when he picked up a loose puck and put it past Plante. A native of Noranda, Quebec, Keon was not expected to make the Leaf team in 1960 but he played too well in the exhibition season to keep him off the team. As a rookie, he would score 20 goals and add 25 assists to win the Calder Trophy, edging out teammate Bob Nevin for the award.

DECEMBER 1, 1960
Montreal 6 Toronto 3 @ The Forum

Henri Richard was the centre of attention once again as he scored twice and sought revenge on Frank Mahovlich in a 6-3 Montreal win over Toronto. The Pocket Rocket opened the scoring by popping in a pair for the Habs, who built up a 4-1 lead in the second period only to see the Leafs get goals from Eddie Shack and Mahovlich (his 17th of the season) to cut the lead to one. Goals by Dickie Moore and Marcel Bonin (his second of the night) finished off the Leafs' chances for a comeback.

With the game well in hand, Richard and Mahovlich squared off at 16:22 of the third period (after a previous scuffle in the early part of the period during which the Canadiens centre charged the Big M and then refused to go to the penalty box). The feisty Canadien high sticked Mahovlich and then started swinging at his larger foe. Moore snuck in a punch at the Leaf player but was quickly grabbed by Toronto's Bob Pulford and they would eventually draw majors. Bonin and Carl Brewer tangled, as did Tom Johnson and Bobby Baun of the Leafs. In total, Richard got a major, two minors and two misconducts in the game (which cost him $50) but a message was delivered. Guy Gendron for Montreal and Allan Stanley for Toronto got the other goals in the game. The Canadiens now had scored 23 power-play goals on the season.

For the remarks at left, the League office fined the Leafs coach $200.

DECEMBER 7, 1960
Montreal 6 Toronto 2 @ Maple Leaf Gardens

An injury-riddled Toronto lineup was no match for a surging Montreal squad that won its sixth straight contest 6-2 at the Gardens on December 7. Henri Richard once again led the way with one goal and two assists for the Canadiens, and Bernie Geoffrion scored his 270th and 271st career goals to pass Howie Morenz (his late father-in-law) on the all-time NHL goal scoring list. Dickie Moore had his 23rd of the season and Guy Gendron (acquired in a deal with Boston for Andre Pronovost) also notched a Hab marker. Eddie Shack and Bert Olmstead replied for the Leafs. Toronto suffered another injury during the game when defenceman Allan Stanley had his jaw fractured and cut by the skate of Montreal's Bill Hicke. The Canadiens winger felt so badly about the accident that he went into the Leafs dressing room to apologize. Stanley told him to forget about it. Stanley joined Ron Stewart, Tim Horton, Larry Regan and Carl Brewer on the Leafs injury list.

Montreal's Dickie Moore (#12) takes the puck away after Toronto's Bob Nevin had taken a spill with the aid of Jean Guy Talbot of the Canadiens (#17). The 1960–61 season was the last great year for Moore in a Canadiens uniform. He finished with 35 goals and 69 points (his third-highest career total). Moore's best season came in 1958–59 when he won his second Art Ross Trophy with an NHL-record 96 points. His Montreal career statistics show 254 goals and 594 points in 654 games. Moore was just as sharp in the playoffs with 38 goals and 94 points in 112 games. Nevin scored 25 times as a rookie with the Leafs in '60–61.

"I'll tell you, these two goals, they mean the most to me. My wife will be mad maybe, but that's okay."

Bernie Geoffrion (*The Toronto Star*, December 8, 1960)

THE NUMBERS

Dickie Moore once also set an NHL record by scoring a playoff goal after just 10 seconds from the start of the game against the Boston Bruins on March 25, 1954. In the 8-1 Canadiens romp, Moore scored two goals and added four assists to set another playoff game record for most points in a post-season game by one player (both marks have since been surpassed).

DECEMBER 15, 1960
Toronto 4 Montreal 2 @ The Forum

A still-depleted Toronto team found themselves down 2-0 to Montreal but then scored four unanswered goals to take a 4-2 victory at the Forum on December 15. Minus five regulars, including wingers Dick Duff and George Armstrong, the Leafs gave up goals by Bernie Geoffrion and Dickie Moore before mounting a comeback in front of 14,385 surprised fans. Bob Nevin scored the winner after Bob Pulford and Billy Harris had tied the score for the visitors. Nevin's goal came after some hard work by teammate Frank Mahovlich, who tied up goalie Charlie Hodge and defencemen Doug Harvey and Al Langlois. Nevin calmly lifted the puck over the fallen group of players and gave the Leafs the lead at 14:16 of the third period. Mahovlich then scored an empty net goal (his 27th) to secure the win and give him a two-goal edge in leading the NHL (Moore was second with 25). The loss snapped Montreal's eight-game winning streak.

DECEMBER 28, 1960
Montreal 4 Toronto 1 @ Maple Leaf Gardens

The Maple Leafs were brought back to earth with a thud when the Canadiens stopped their unbeaten streak at seven games when the Habs won 4-1 at the Gardens on December 28. Montreal netminder Charlie Hodge had a big game in goal for the Habs and teammates Bill Hicke, Guy Gendron, Bernie Geoffrion and Ralph Backstrom provided all the goals. Hicke opened the scoring at 5:24 of the first period

when he took a Marcel Bonin pass and put a shot past Leaf goalie Johnny Bower. Gendron put in a rebound off the glass from a shot by rookie call-up Jean Gauthier for the Canadiens' second goal. Geoffrion let one of his bullets go for the third Montreal goal while Toronto's Allan Stanley was serving a penalty. The goal was Geoffrion's 26th of the year. The Leafs' Frank Mahovlich was held off the score sheet and his goal total remained a league-best 31. Eddie Shack got the lone Leafs goal.

JANUARY 12, 1961
Montreal 6 Toronto 2 @ The Forum

The Canadiens handed the Leafs their worst loss of the season so far with a 6-2 thumping at the Forum on January 12. The win moved the Habs four points up on the Leafs for first place in the NHL and it was accomplished without star defenceman Doug Harvey, who was nursing a bad shoulder (his place was taken by J.C. Tremblay). Bill Hicke, who had two, Jean Guy Talbot, Dickie Moore, Bernie Geoffrion and Guy Gendron paced the six-goal attack. Geoffrion's goal was his 27th of the season and was the seventh tally against Toronto goaltender Johnny Bower. The Leaf goalie fell into second place in the Vezina Trophy race when he let the six shots get past him. Only Dick Duff and a very late goal by Billy Harris beat Montreal's Charlie Hodge.

JANUARY 25, 1961
Toronto 5 Montreal 3 @ Maple Leaf Gardens

Frank Mahovlich broke a Maple Leaf club record for most goals in one season when he scored his 38th and 39th goals of the 1960–61 campaign as the Leafs defeated the Habs 5-3. Going into the contest, Mahovlich shared the team mark with Gaye Stewart (who set his record of 37 back in the 50-game 1945–46 season) and Tod Sloan (who equalled the mark in the 70-game 1955–56

Montreal's Bernie Geoffrion had a bonus in his 1960–61 contract that paid him $100 for every goal he scored above 20. He finished the season with 50 goals for a bonus of $3,000.

VALUE DAYS

Bill Hicke

Montreal's Bill Hicke (#8) puts a shot past Toronto netminder Johnny Bower. Hicke scored 18 goals and 45 points for the Canadiens in 1960–61, while Bower won his first-ever Vezina Trophy by allowing only 145 goals in 58 games played for the Leafs in the same season.

THE NUMBERS

The Montreal Canadiens saw Bill Hicke as a top prospect when he put together 52- and 54-goal seasons for the Regina Pats junior team. He then had an award-winning season in Rochester of the American Hockey League while posting the top point total of 97 (41 goals, 56 assists). The Habs even had visions of Hicke replacing the goals normally scored by Maurice Richard, but the industrious winger could only put up decent years of 18, 22 and 17 goals. Although he was on the small side, Hicke had good speed and a decent shot. By 1964–65 he was splitting his playing time between Montreal and the AHL before he was dealt to the New York Rangers for Dick Duff in what turned out to be a great deal for the Canadiens. Hicke did have good years with California in the post-expansion era (46 goals in his first two years with the Seals).

season). The Big M set his mark after just 47 games and his second of the game was also his 100th career goal. On his first goal, Mahovlich put in a rebound off an Allan Stanley shot and his second tally saw him whip a Bob Nevin pass behind Montreal goalie Charlie Hodge.

The game also featured the first-ever NHL goal by the Canadiens J.C. Tremblay, who opened the scoring by lofting a 90-foot shot past Johnny Bower (blooper goals would become a specialty for the Montreal defenceman). The Leafs tied it on a goal by Dick Duff, only to have Ralph Backstrom give the Habs another lead. Mahovlich then sandwiched his goals around another tally by teammate Bert Olmstead to give the Leafs a 4-2 lead. Jean Guy Talbot made it 4-3 before Red Kelly scored into the empty net.

Montreal coach Toe Blake shoved goal judge Alf Jones when it was ruled that a Phil Goyette shot did not enter the Leaf net on a play that would have tied the game 3-3. The Canadiens claimed the puck was at least four inches over the line before Bower pulled it back, but Jones said he had a clear view and the puck never crossed the red line. The Leafs moved to within two points of the first-place Habs, who were without Bernie Geoffrion, Jean Beliveau and Doug Harvey for this contest.

Toronto owner Conn Smythe suggested that the Maple Leafs would agree to play a team from Russia in Moscow if $250,000 were on the line. The idea received support from coach and manager Punch Imlach during the 1960–61 season.

Frank Mahovlich (centre) poses with George Armstrong (left) and Bert Olmstead. Mahovlich appeared to be a cinch to score 50 or more goals in 1960–61 but he tired and came up just short with 48. It was still his best year with the Leafs and his 84-point total placed him third in league scoring. His 131 penalty-minute total—showing an aggressiveness coach Punch Imlach thought the winger should display more often—also marked his highest total in his career with Toronto.

FEBRUARY 15, 1961
Montreal 3 Toronto 1 @ Maple Leaf Gardens

Montreal goalie Jacques Plante served notice that he was back in top form as the Habs downed the Maple Leafs 3-1 at the Gardens. Dave Keon of Toronto opened the scoring for the Leafs but Plante robbed Bob Nevin to keep the Habs down by just one. Marcel Bonin tied it up before the first period ended with assists to Dickie Moore and Jean Beliveau. In the second period, with the score still tied, the Habs were down two men for 66 seconds, but Plante made great saves on Dick Duff and Billy Harris to keep the score even. Beliveau scored to make it 2-1 just before the end of the second stanza and Don Marshall scored into an empty net to give the Montreal club the insurance marker. Gerry McNamara played well in goal (in his first NHL game) for Toronto, replacing the injured Johnny Bower. The win moved Montreal to within four points of the first-place Leafs with two games in hand. The loss was the first for the Leafs in nine games.

FEBRUARY 23, 1961
Toronto 4 Montreal 2 @ The Forum

The Leafs were missing coach Punch Imlach for this contest but still came up with a 4-2 win at the Forum. Imlach missed the game when his plane was grounded in Pittsburgh when he was on his way home from a three-day holiday. King Clancy took over behind the bench and saw the Leafs get two goals from Red Kelly and

singles from Dick Duff (who was later tossed from the game for arguing a penalty too strenuously) and Bob Nevin to get the win. Nevin's goal at 17:35 of the third period proved to be the winner, but it was hotly disputed by the Canadiens when the goal judge didn't put the red light on. The Habs stormed around referee Eddie Powers, who would not change his mind about the goal. Jean Guy Talbot of the Canadiens was given a 10-minute misconduct, and when he continued to rant in the penalty box, a game misconduct. The capacity crowd of 15,000 littered the ice with everything they could get their hands on, including rubber boots and programs. Powers needed a police escort to get to the dressing room at the end of the game, although he was still hit in the face with a flying rubber. Gerry McNamara recorded his first win as the Leaf goalie.

MARCH 1, 1961
Toronto 3 Montreal 1 @ Maple Leaf Gardens

Showing their excellent team speed, the Leafs led by Frank Mahovlich and rookie goaltender Cesare Maniago beat the Canadiens 3-1 to give them a four-point lead over their hated rivals in the race for first place. Mahovlich opened the scoring in the game with his 46th of the season

"We are not going to roll over and play dead now. The Canadiens still have to catch us."

Punch Imlach (*The Toronto Star,* February 16, 1961)

"They blew their big chance tonight. Tell Punch they won't get another one."

Marcel Bonin on the Leafs' chances of finishing first (*The Toronto Star,* February 16, 1961)

Gerry McNamara's career in net with Toronto consisted of only seven appearances (2-2-1 record) but he is only one of three men to have played for the Maple Leafs and gone on to be the general manager of the team. The other two are Hap Day and Pat Quinn.

Montreal's Bernie Geoffrion (#5) tries to score on Leafs goalie Johnny Bower with the help of teammate Ralph Backstrom (#6) while being checked by Toronto's Eddie Shack. Bower was injured and unable to play the night of March 16, 1961, when Geoffrion scored his 50th of the year to tie the record of Rocket Richard for most goals in one season. The man nicknamed "Boom-Boom" scored 10 of his 50 goals against the Leafs in 1960–61 and eight of them came at the expense of Bower (two beat Maniago). Geoffrion had the most success against the New York Rangers (16 goals against) and the Boston Bruins also allowed 10. He scored nine against Detroit and five versus Chicago. Geoffrion could not get a goal in the last two games of the season to pass the 50-goal plateau.

when he combined with linemates Red Kelly and Bob Nevin before ripping a shot past Montreal goalie Jacques Plante early in the second period. Ron Stewart then scored a pair of goals, including what proved to be the winner, for the Leafs before Bernie Geoffrion notched a tally (his 41st) for the Habs. Maniago was named the first star of the game for the second time in the three contests he started, and was especially good in robbing Montreal's Don Marshall in close in the scoreless first period. Jean Beliveau tried to ruffle the unflappable Leaf goalie in the third period but Maniago shoved right back. A crowd of 14,384 roared its approval as the Leafs held on to first place with only seven games to play.

Toronto's Tim Horton fights off Montreal's Gilles Tremblay in a race for a loose puck. Horton's great play in the 1962 playoffs (3 goals, 13 assists) helped the Maple Leafs to secure their first Stanley Cup in eleven years.

Detroit goalie Terry Sawchuk makes a save on Toronto's Frank Mahovlich during their playoff series in 1961. Sawchuk had a 2-0 shutout in the third game of the series and gave the Red Wings a lead in the series they would never relinquish. His superb goaltending ensured a major upset for the Detroit team over a highly favoured Toronto club. Mahovlich had one goal and one assist in the five-game series.

MARCH 16, 1961
Montreal 5 Toronto 2 @ The Forum

The final meeting between the Canadiens and the Maple Leafs was loaded with drama as two players were vying for a 50-goal season. When the smoke had cleared, 15,011 fans at the Forum witnessed hockey history and went a little wild as Bernie Geoffrion of the Canadiens scored his 50th of the year when he beat goalie Cesare Maniago in the Toronto net. Frank Mahovlich of the Leafs was held off the score sheet in his attempt to get to 50 goals. He would only add one more goal to his total of 47 before the season ended. Maniago held the Leafs in the game for the longest time. Leaf rookie Dave Keon scored his 20th of the season to tie the game at 1-1 after Guy Gendron had opened the scoring. Third-period goals by Bill Hicke and Henri Richard gave the Habs a 3-1 lead before Eddie Shack made it a closer game at 3-2. However, goals by Ralph Backstrom and Geoffrion salted the game away for Montreal. Jean Beliveau set a new NHL mark by recording his 58th assist of the season beating the previous mark of 56 held by Bert Olmstead, now with Toronto. The win gave the Canadiens a three-point lead on the Leafs with both teams having just two games to play.

playoffs

SERIES A – MONTREAL VS. CHICAGO

For the third straight season the Canadiens and the Blackhawks would meet in the first round of the playoffs, this time with a different result. The series started in familiar fashion as the Habs took the first game 6-2 at the Forum on March 21, 1961. Six different players did the scoring for Montreal. The second game, however, saw Chicago win 4-3 with former Canadien Eddie Litzenberger getting the winner. The teams split the next two games of the series, with Chicago winning an epic in the third game 2-1 on Murray Balfour's overtime marker in the third overtime period. Canadiens coach Toe Blake was so incensed at a penalty given to Dickie Moore (Chicago scored on the power-play) that he came on to the ice at the end of the game and punched referee Dalton McArthur. His actions would cost him a fine of $2,000. Montreal bounced back to take game four 5-2 to even the series at two games each. Blackhawks goalie Glenn Hall posted a 3-0 shutout in the next game at the Forum and then another 3-0 blanking at the Stadium to wrap up the series for Chicago on April 4, 1961.

SERIES B – TORONTO VS. DETROIT

The Maple Leafs had finished 24 points ahead of the Red Wings and expected little trouble from the Motowners. Toronto took the first game at the Gardens on March 22, 1961, by a score of 3-2. It took an overtime winner from George Armstrong to get the Leafs a victory. It would be the last Maple Leaf win as Detroit won the next four games by scores of 4-2, 2-0, 4-1 and 3-2. The last contest of the series was played on April 1, 1961, and it marked the 100th playoff game for Gordie Howe.

Chicago's Ken Wharram (#17) battles for position with the Canadiens Tom Johnson (#10). Wharram was named the first star of the game in the second contest between the Blackhawks and Canadiens in the 1961 playoffs. The speedy Blackhawk winger scored one goal in that game and had eight points in twelve games as Chicago won the Stanley Cup in six games over Detroit. Johnson had one assist in the six-game series.

The Leafs–Canadiens Rivalry
1961–62

The Maple Leafs and Canadiens experienced a role reversal to start the 1961–62 season. Usually it was Toronto making most of the changes, but this year it was the Montreal club that decided to make more moves. The biggest change was the dealing of Doug Harvey to the New York Rangers. The Habs had come to view Harvey as a malcontent and had been looking to get rid of him for some time. In exchange for Harvey, Montreal landed tough defenceman Lou Fontinato and started a major revamping of their blueline. Al Langlois was also sent to the Rangers and Bob Turner was dealt to Chicago. Al MacNeil was taken from Toronto in the intra-league draft to play defence and J.C. Tremblay was given a permanent spot in front of goalie Jacques Plante, who was returning for his tenth season (he would be backed up by Cesare Maniago, as Charlie Hodge was back in the minors). All of the Montreal forwards returned as Bobby Rousseau and Gilles Tremblay both landed full-time roles (70 games each). Gordon "Red" Berenson made his first NHL appearance in 1962, while Jean Gauthier and Bill Carter also played briefly for the Habs.

Punch Imlach made few changes with his Leafs but did talk goalie Don Simmons out of retirement to back up Johnny Bower. Simmons, acquired from the

Boston Bruins, would play in Rochester of the American Hockey League and be available should anything happen to Bower. Defenceman Al Arbour would be selected in the intra-league draft from the Chicago Blackhawks to act as the fifth defenceman, while Larry Regan and Gerry Ehman would find themselves in the minors. During the season the Leafs would add veteran forward Eddie Litzenberger from Detroit on waivers. Litzenberger had captained the Blackhawks to the Cup in 1961 but was deemed to be too slow and a little old, making him just the type of player Imlach valued very highly. A few new players made appearances for the Leafs (such as Les Kozak, Larry Keenan, Alex Faulkner and Arnie Brown), but mostly it was the same crew as the previous season.

The Leafs and Canadiens staged a back-and-forth struggle for first place all season long. But led by the stellar work of goalie Jacques Plante, the Habs once again finished on top, with a 42-14-14 record and 98 points. Plante was the best goalie and was named as the NHL's top player. Rousseau was named rookie of the year for his performance, which included 21 goals and 24 assists. Ralph Backstrom (65 points) and Claude Provost (63 points) led the Canadiens in scoring, which was unusual considering their bevy of well-known stars, but injuries and slumps took their toll. However, the Canadiens proved during the 1961–62 season that a team could still win while starting to rebuild. The playoffs were another matter as the Chicago club once again eliminated the Habs in six games.

Toronto finished comfortably in second place with 85 points (37-22-11) but had a very difficult time during the season with the Canadiens. The Leafs beat the Habs only four times all season long (another three were ties) and it seemed a playoff meeting between the two rivals did not augur well for the Maple Leafs. But there was no need to worry as the Leafs got past a stubborn New York squad (led by player-coach Harvey) in the first round of the post season and then fought off a determined Chicago team to finally

reclaim the Stanley Cup. It was their first championship since 1951.

NOVEMBER 1, 1961
Toronto 3 Montreal 2 @ Maple Leaf Gardens

The first game of the season between the two Canadian teams went to the Maple Leafs, who eked out a 3-2 victory. Bob Pulford, Frank Mahovlich and Bob Nevin scored for the Leafs, while Claude Provost (with his 100th career goal) and Marcel Bonin replied for the Canadiens. The game featured some great penalty killing by the Leafs, who withstood a two-man disadvantage for 46 seconds, and then killed off a five-minute major to defenceman Tim Horton who had clipped Provost with a high stick. Dave Keon (who played 28 minutes in this game), Carl Brewer, Al Arbour and Pulford were prominent penalty killers for Toronto and received a rousing ovation from the 13,601 fans in attendance. Montreal had come into the game undefeated with seven wins and one tie but were missing Jean Beliveau and Dickie Moore for this contest. Jacques Plante was outstanding in the Habs net but could not stop Mahovlich's game winner when the Leaf winger put in Red Kelly's rebound while he was down. Toronto forward Eddie Shack and Montreal defenceman Lou Fontinato (one-time teammates on the New York Rangers) began a feud that would last the entire season.

NOVEMBER 9, 1961
Montreal 5 Toronto 2 @ The Forum

The Canadiens quickly got revenge for their loss to the Leafs by beating Toronto 5-2 eight days after their first meeting. Claude Provost, riding a hot scoring streak, scored three goals to lead the Habs, and Gilles Tremblay and Bill Hicke scored singles. Provost, using a shorter stick on a tip from Gordie Howe of Detroit, was

Montreal's Lou Fontinato (#19), Gilles Tremblay (#21) and goalie Jacques Plante defend against the Leafs' Red Kelly and Frank Mahovlich during a game at the Forum. Fontinato was acquired in the deal that sent the legendary Doug Harvey to the New York Rangers. He was brought in to bring some toughness to the Canadiens defensive corps. His first season in Montreal saw "Leapin Louie" score two goals and add thirteen assists while racking up a league-high 167 minutes in penalties in 1961–62. Kelly (with 22) and Mahovlich (with 33) combined to score 55 goals in '61–62.

unexpectedly scoring at a much faster pace than usual (13 goals in 12 games). It also helped that he was now playing with Henri Richard and that his contract called for him to receive a bonus when he scored his 16th of the year. Al MacNeil (a one-time Leaf defenceman) dished out some good bodychecks for the Canadiens. Red Kelly and Frank Mahovlich scored the two Toronto goals. Maple Leaf goalie Johnny Bower was so upset with the way his team played in front of him (he faced 22 shots in the second period and gave up three goals) that he suggested Gerry Cheevers be called up from the minors to take his place.

"My style is to play the man rather than the puck and I'm not afraid to open up and slam a few guys when we're ahead in the score."

Lou Fontinato (*Hockey Annual* magazine, 1963)

Toronto's Eddie Shack has beaten Montreal's Lou Fontinato to the Montreal goal occupied by Jacques Plante. Shack scored an important goal in a November 15, 1961, victory over the Habs. The Leafs acquired Shack in a deal with the New York Rangers (for Johnny Wilson and Pat Hannigan) in November 1960, and he scored fourteen goals in fifty-five games for Toronto in 1960–61. In 1961–62, Shack played in only forty-four games and scored seven goals.

NOVEMBER 15, 1961
Toronto 3 Montreal 2 @ Maple Leaf Gardens

Just when it looked like the Maple Leafs were going down to defeat, Eddie Shack scored the goal that tied the game and inspired the Leafs to a 3-2 win over the Canadiens. Montreal had taken the lead early in the third period on a goal by Gilles Tremblay that made the score 2-1. Less than four minutes later, Shack grabbed the puck and charged down the right wing before outsmarting defenceman Lou Fontinato of the Canadiens with a clever move and driving to the net occupied by goalie Jacques Plante. The masked netminder stopped Shack's shot but the two fell down in a heap and eventually the Leaf winger swept the puck home with help from teammates Bert Olmstead and Bob Pulford. Olmstead then scored the winner just 17 seconds after Shack's goal to give the Leafs the lead for good. Shack, who was named as the first star of the game, and defenceman Carl Brewer led the Toronto team in hits, while Al MacNeil rocked a few Leafs with solid belts. Dave Keon scored the opener for the home team but Bernie Geoffrion tied it for the visitors. The win moved the Leafs into second place, just one point behind the Canadiens.

NOVEMBER 29, 1961
Toronto 2 Montreal 2 @ Maple Leaf Gardens

The main story of the 2-2 tie between the Leafs and Canadiens on November 29 was another

---

Toronto's Bob Nevin (#11) tries to get the puck past Montreal goalie Jacques Plante after taking a pass from Red Kelly who is being checked by J.C. Tremblay (#3). Nevin's goal total dropped to 15 in his second season (after 21 as a rookie), but he still managed to add 30 assists in the 1961–62 season. He would add six points in twelve playoff games. Tremblay played his first full year in the NHL in '61–62 and scored three goals with seventeen assists in seventy games.

key injury suffered by the Montreal squad. Already missing Jean Beliveau with a knee injury and having Dickie Moore just back from the infirmary (leg), the Canadiens suffered a big loss on the defence when Tom Johnson took a stick in the eye and would be lost to the team for an indefinite period. (Johnson's role was much more vital this year with the loss of Doug Harvey to the Rangers.) Otherwise, the contest featured great goaltending by Johnny Bower and Jacques Plante, along with more hostilities between Leafs winger Eddie Shack and Canadiens bruising defenceman Lou Fontinato. Shack actually set up the tying goal by centring a pass to Bob Pulford in the third period after he took a Bert Olmstead pass and breezed by defenceman Jean Guy Talbot in the Montreal end. Marcel Bonin had opened the scoring for the Habs but Bob Nevin tied it for the Leafs after he combined with Red Kelly around the Canadiens net.

The other teams have to watch Shack. He's about as good a hockey player as we have right now and can nearly always move the puck into their end. He's twice the player Fontinato is and I'd sooner have him playing hockey than chasing that guy. Let Fontinato chase him and Shack will eat him one of these nights.

Punch Imlach (The Toronto Star, November 30, 1961)

Fontinato scored the second Montreal goal on a screened shot from the point but the Leafs evened the score before 13,711 fans who saw an entertaining game.

NOVEMBER 30, 1961
Montreal 1 Toronto 1 @ The Forum

In the second game of back-to-back contests it was the goalies who once again stole the show. Jacques Plante made 32 saves and Johnny Bower turned back 31 Montreal efforts as the clubs played to a 1-1 tie. The point earned by each team left them tied for first place in the league standings with 29 points apiece.

The crowd of 14,568 appreciated the efforts of the two netminders as the game remained scoreless after two periods. Bernie Geoffrion finally broke through to give the Habs a 1-0 win but Bert Olmstead quickly tied it for the Leafs just 30 seconds later at 11:59 with a rising shot that went over Plante's shoulder. Bower made great saves against Moore and Don Marshall, while Plante looked sharp in stopping Frank Mahovlich, Allan Stanley, Dick Duff and George Armstrong scoring efforts. The Canadiens called up Jean Gauthier from Hull-Ottawa of the EPHL to replace Tom Johnson.

DECEMBER 7, 1961
Montreal 4 Toronto 1 @ The Forum

Quick thinking by Montreal coach Toe Blake

got the Canadiens going after they were down 1-0 to the Maple Leafs and wound up with a 4-1 victory. Blake replaced Jean Beliveau with Ralph Backstrom between wingers Bernie Geoffrion and Don Marshall to ignite the Habs. The move paid immediate dividends as Backstrom scored at 19:37 of the second period to tie the score 1-1. (Bob Pulford had opened the scoring for Toronto earlier in the second stanza.) Then, early in the third, Marshall and Backstrom scored 35 seconds apart and the Leafs never recovered. Gilles Tremblay scored the other Canadiens goal less than two minutes later. The Montreal crowd of 15,086 screamed with delight as the Habs pumped their goals past Toronto netminder Don Simmons and increased their first-place lead on the Leafs to four points. Jacques Plante was once again outstanding in the Montreal goal.

JANUARY 3, 1962
Toronto 3 Montreal 1 @ Maple Leaf Gardens

Dave Keon scored two goals, including the game winner, as the Maple Leafs beat the Canadiens 3-1 at the Gardens. Playing despite a heavily taped leg (to protect an injury), Keon's trademark skating was not hampered in any way and he buzzed around the Montreal end all night long. Dick Duff opened the scoring for the Leafs when he backhanded a perfect Tim Horton pass past goalie Jacques Plante. Keon then scored a pair and had a great chance for a hat trick but was stopped by Plante on a penal-

"I suppose you think I'm a genius. If we lost, I'd be a bum for breaking up that line … I still say our big man was Jacques Plante. He played tremendous goal. He kept us in there while this young team was jelling and still is playing like a Vezina Trophy winner."

Toe Blake (*The Toronto Star*, December 8, 1961)

Jacques Plante (#1) makes a stop against Norm Ullman (#7) of the Detroit Red Wings with Lou Fontinato (#19) and J.C. Tremblay (#3) looking on. Plante was named the winner of the Hart Trophy for his outstanding performance in 1961–62. He played in all 70 games for the Canadiens and allowed only 166 goals against and won 42 times. Plante also earned his sixth Vezina Trophy and a place on the first all-star team.

ty shot. After consulting with Leaf netminder Johnny Bower, Keon decided to shoot high. He beat Plante with the shot, only to have it hit the post two inches below the crossbar. The penalty shot was awarded by referee Eddie Powers after Montreal's Ralph Backstrom hooked Keon from behind (the NHL had revised and clarified the penalty shot rule to start the 1961–62 season but to this point only two had been called). Bower lost his shutout bid with only 11 seconds remaining on a goal by Marcel Bonin.

JANUARY 11, 1962
Montreal 4 Toronto 2 @ The Forum

Jacques Plante was once again outstanding in the Canadiens net as the Habs regained first place with a 4-2 win over the Leafs at the Forum before 14,959 fans. Plante made a total of 39

saves in the game and kept the Toronto club off the scoreboard until 12:58 of the third period when Dave Keon scored and then Bert Olmstead added another at 14:06. Montreal built up a 4-0 lead on goals by Dickie Moore (on a power-play with Carl Brewer off for the Leafs), Bobby Rousseau, Henri Richard and Don Marshall. Plante was at his best in the first period when he stopped Bob Pulford on a breakaway and fol-

"That was the biggest win of the season for us. I went to bed thinking we were tied with the Leafs because someone gave me the Toronto–Boston score as 3-3 [from the previous evening]. I woke to find us in second place. Now we are back on top, the only place to be."

Jacques Plante (The Toronto Star, January 12, 1962)

Jean Guy Talbot

Montreal defenceman Jean Guy Talbot (#17) has his best NHL season in 1961–62 when he scored five goals and added forty-two assists. Talbot shouldered a big load in '61–62 with Doug Harvey no longer there and Tom Johnson out with an eye injury. He was named to the NHL's first all-star team at the end of the season for his great play. His career numbers in Montreal show 36 goals and 209 assists in 791 games played and seven Stanley Cups to his credit as a Canadien.

A CLOSER LOOK

Jean Guy Talbot started out as a goalie in midget hockey until one game when he allowed 22 goals and never returned to the nets. He became a defenceman and although he was not a goal scorer, he could rush and handle the puck effectively. Talbot played his first game for the Canadiens in 1954–55 and then won five straight Stanley Cups with the team. He was the only holdover defenceman from the Fifties to stay with the club during the Sixties as the team rebuilt their blueline with newcomers like Jacques Laperriere, J.C. Tremblay, Terry Harper and Ted Harris. Talbot's veteran leadership helped the team to Cups in 1965 and 1966.

lowed that up with stops on Dave Keon, Eddie Litzenberger (twice) and Frank Mahovlich.

FEBRUARY 1, 1962
Montreal 5 Toronto 2 @ The Forum

Goalie Jacques Plante held the Canadiens in the game during the first period and the Canadiens came to life in the second on their way to a 5-2 win over the visiting Leafs on February 1 before the largest crowd (15,266 fans) of the season at the Forum. Plante was nursing a tender ankle (with Cesare Maniago ready to replace him if needed), but held the Leafs scoreless in the opening frame when they clearly outplayed the Canadiens. He made four good saves on Dave Keon shots alone and then got help from Gilles Tremblay and Jean Beliveau as the Canadiens took the lead 2-0. Don Marshall got a goal early in the second to make it 3-0 but Keon (with his 20th) and Frank Mahovlich (with his 26th) scored within 18 seconds to suddenly make it close. However, third-period tallies by Bernie Geoffrion (his first goal since December 17) and Henri Richard pulled the Canadiens away.

The Habs now had a six-point lead on the Leafs with 22 games to play and felt they could hold off the Toronto club, which had injuries to Dick Duff, Eddie Shack, Bob Baun and Red Kelly to contend with. Leafs goalie Johnny Bower was also cut for six stitches by an errant stick while the Habs were scoring their fourth goal and still faced 21 shots in the third.

FEBRUARY 10, 1962
Montreal 4 Toronto 2 @ Maple Leaf Gardens

Before a Saturday night crowd of 14,672 fans at the Gardens, the Montreal Canadiens moved their first-place lead to seven points with a 4-2 win over the Maple Leafs. The Canadiens completely dominated the contest and got opening period goals by Don Marshall and Jean Guy Talbot to take the lead. Talbot's goal came on a

blast from the point with Bob Nevin in the penalty box for the Leafs. Allan Stanley scored late in the first to make it 2-1, but a Bobby Rousseau marker in the second gave the Habs their two-goal lead back. Kelly got one back for Toronto in the third but Ralph Backstrom finished off any Leaf hopes with a goal at 6:17 of the final period. The slumping Leafs are all but out of the first-place race at this point and still have a difficult time beating Montreal goalie Jacques Plante.

Toronto's Tim Horton looks to get back to his position on defence after a foray into the Montreal end where he encountered Tom Johnson (#10) and Jacques Plante (#1) of Montreal. The Leaf rearguard had goals in consecutive games against the Habs on February 21 and March 8. Horton had a good season for the Leafs in 1961–62 when he scored 10 goals and had 38 points. He saved his best for the 1962 playoffs when he set two records for defencemen: most points (16) and most assists (13) in one playoff year.

FEBRUARY 21, 1962
Montreal 4 Toronto 2 @ Maple Leaf Gardens

The Maple Leafs played another poor game against the Montreal Canadiens in front of 13,750 disgruntled fans and dropped a 4-2 deci-sion. The Canadiens were glad to see defence-man Tom Johnson back in their lineup and got an early goal from Jean Beliveau at 2:47 of the first period with Allan Stanley of Toronto in the penalty box. Stanley tied it for the Leafs by fin-ishing off a passing play with Tim Horton, but then the Canadiens reeled off three straight from the sticks of Dickie Moore, Henri Richard and Ralph Backstrom (his 25th of the year). Horton let go a slap shot that eluded Jacques Plante to finish the scoring. Linesman George Hayes was knocked out cold when he struck his head at the Montreal bench with 39 seconds to go in the second period. He came back for the third period.

MARCH 8, 1962
Montreal 1 Toronto 1 @ The Forum

A bitter contest between the Canadiens and Maple Leafs at the Forum ended up in a 1-1 tie. Referee Frank Udvari called 18 minors in the contest as he tried to keep control of the game. Leaf defenceman Tim Horton opened the scoring on a Toronto power-play when he beat Jacques Plante with a screened backhanded shot in the first period. It stayed that way until Bernie Geoffrion tied it for the Canadiens at 11:26 of the third period. Montreal took advantage of an Eddie Shack miscue to turn the puck up the ice and it led to Geoffrion's tally to even the game. Bob Nevin had a great chance to score the winner in the third period but was foiled by Plante and defenceman Lou Fontinato, who made separate stops on the Leaf winger. The Montreal crowd of 15,257 grew angry at Udvari when he gave Moore a 10-minute misconduct in the second period and when coach Toe Blake questioned a call in the third. The fans showered the ice with enough rubber boots to open a store, joked the Canadiens mentor after the game.

MARCH 14, 1962
Toronto 5 Montreal 2 @ Maple Leaf Gardens

The Maple Leafs beat the Canadiens for just the fourth time this season with a 5-2 win on March

14. With Don Simmons in goal, the Leafs got goals from Dave Keon, Bob Pulford, Bob Nevin and Eddie Litzenberger to make up for Montreal's opening goal by Gilles Tremblay just 33 seconds after the game started. The Leafs now had seven wins and one tie in their last eight starts. The turning point of the contest came when the Habs had a two-man advantage for a full two minutes but could not score a goal. The Leafs got a shorthanded goal from Keon and a power-play marker by Litzenberger. The Canadiens went into the contest without Don Marshall and Henri Richard, who had a broken arm and would be lost for the year. The win gave the Leafs some hope of finishing first and a major confidence boost as they headed toward the playoffs.

MARCH 22, 1962
Montreal 4 Toronto 1 @ The Forum

The Montreal Canadiens rebounded on home ice in their next meeting with the Leafs by winning 4-1 on March 22. Jean Beliveau (who was not originally going to play because of a shoulder injury) had four points on the night including the winning goal (his 18th) for the Habs, who came from behind to beat the Leafs. Gilles Tremblay scored two in the contest to bring his total to 31. Defenceman Al MacNeil got the other Montreal goal. Toronto's only score came from the stick of Bob Pulford who opened the scoring in the game. With the team securely in first place (they had clinched the title on March 17 with a 2-0 win over the New York Rangers), the Canadiens were now focusing on the Vezina Trophy for goalie Jacques Plante; he had a 12-goal lead on Toronto's Johnny Bower after this game. Plante had a run-in with Toronto's Bobby Baun who charged into him after stopping a shot. The loss meant the Leafs did not win all year at the Forum.

Gilles Tremblay

As a rookie with Montreal in 1960–61, Gilles Tremblay earned about $7,000. In his second season (when he scored 32) he was paid $7,500, a very good bargain when the words of general manager Frank Selke are considered: "I wouldn't trade Gilles for Frank Mahovlich even up. He may not score as many goals as the Big M but he is far more valuable to his team. He kills penalties, checks … is seldom out of position and gets big goals." (*The Toronto Star*, March 23, 1962)

VALUE DAYS

Montreal's Gilles Tremblay (#21) is watched closely by a host of Maple Leaf players, the closest to him being George Armstrong. The 1961–62 season was the best for the smooth-skating Tremblay in terms of goals (32) and points (54). It came at a good time for the Canadiens, who hoped the solidly built youngster with a good shot could offset the decline in Dickie Moore and Marcel Bonin's production. The winger would go on to play his entire career in Montreal and record 168 goals and 330 points in 509 games. Tremblay added 23 points in 48 playoff games.

playoffs

SERIES A – MONTREAL VS. CHICAGO

For the fourth straight year the Canadiens met the Blackhawks in the first round of the play-offs. Montreal was out for some revenge for last year's loss to Chicago, but it was not meant to be. The Canadiens started out well by winning the first two games by scores of 2-1 and 4-3. Dickie Moore was prominent in both games and totalled three goals in the two contests. It was a different story in Chicago as the Blackhawks won both games in the Stadium by scores of 4-1 and 5-3. Sensing the Habs were once again on

Chicago's Bill Hay (#11) and Bobby Hull (#7) storm the Montreal net defended by goalie Jacques Plante (#1) and defenceman Tom Johnson (#10). Hay (3) and Hull (4) combined to score seven goals in the six-game series during the 1962 playoffs that saw the third-place Blackhawks knock off the first-place Canadiens.

the ropes, the Blackhawks won the next two by scores of 4-3 in Montreal on April 5, 1962, and 2-0 back in Chicago on April 8, 1962. Ken Wharram scored goals for Chicago in each of the last two games. The defending Cup champions were back in the finals awaiting the winner of the Toronto–New York series.

SERIES B – TORONTO VS. NEW YORK

The young New York squad gave the Toronto team all they could handle in the six-game series that was won by the Leafs. The Maple Leafs won the first two at home by scores of 4-2 and 2-1, but were rudely awakened when the Rangers came back strong on home ice to win 5-4 and 4-2 to even the series. On April 5, 1962, the Leafs went into double overtime at home to beat the Rangers 3-2 on a goal by Red Kelly. Two nights later, still on home ice because Madison Square Garden was not available, the Leafs demolished the Ranger squad 7-1 to clinch the series.

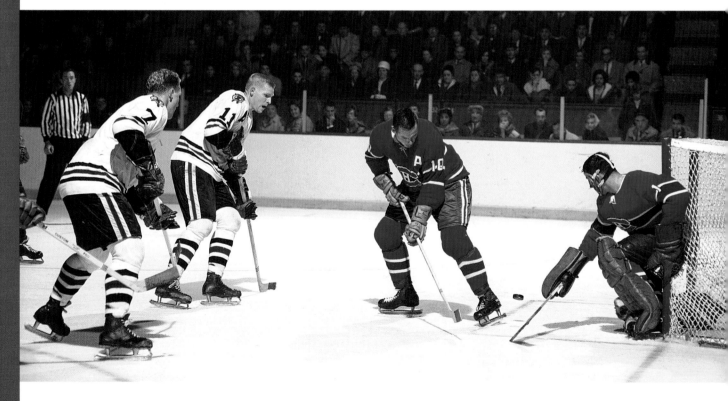

During the 1962 playoffs, Montreal fan Ken Kilander, a 25-year-old, stole the Stanley Cup from its glass case display at the Chicago Stadium. Kilander often travelled with the Canadiens on the road, sometimes playing piano in local bars for $20 a night to help pay for his expenses (he was a lifeguard during the summer). The Rangers manager, Muzz Patrick, banned him when the attempt to steal the Cup became known, but later relented by putting Kilander on probation and forbidding him to wear his Canadiens jacket. Kilander was stopped before he left the Stadium with the precious silverware.

Johnny Bower stops Chicago's Stan Mikita at his doorstep during the Stanley Cup finals. The Blackhawks superstar would lead all playoff scorers in 1962 with twenty-one points in twelve games (six goals, fifteen assists) and would notch three goals in the finals—all against Bower. After many years of waiting, Bower would finally get his name on the Cup, but in a twist of irony, he was unable to play in the clinching game for the Leafs because of an injury. Reserve goaltender Don Simmons would ensure a six-game victory by the Leafs.

Toronto's Red Kelly battles with New York's Doug Harvey along the boards for a loose puck. Kelly scored his most important goal as a Leaf when he beat Gump Worsley in the second overtime period of the fifth game of the 1962 semi-final series. The loss demoralized the New York club and the Leafs went on to win the series in six games. Kelly had three goals and four assists in total against the Rangers as the Leafs made another trip back to the finals.

"It was a big win for us. I passed the puck to Frank Mahovlich near the blueline and he took a shot that Gump lost control of. As soon as I passed the puck to Frank, I went as fast as I could for the net. [Worsley] lost the puck when he fell down. He thought he was lying on it but I was on him so fast that I spotted it lying beside his shoulder and tapped it in."

Red Kelly describing his overtime-winning goal against the Rangers in 1962 (Maple Leaf game program, April 18, 1967)

stanley cup finals

TORONTO VS. CHICAGO

The Stanley Cup finals opened in Toronto on April 10, 1962, and the Leafs won the first game 4-1 over the defending champions. Bobby Hull opened the scoring for the Blackhawks, but some shoddy defensive work and unnecessary penalties gave the Leafs the chance to score four times. Frank Mahovlich and Dave Keon gave the Leafs the lead and tallies by Tim Horton and George

The playoff performance of Frank Mahovlich in 1962 certainly caught the eye of the Chicago Blackhawks, who were dethroned by the Maple Leafs as Cup champions. Chicago owner Jim Norris thought having Mahovlich and Bobby Hull on the same team would make the Blackhawks invincible, especially if he would not have to give up any players in return. During the All-Star Game festivities at Toronto on October 4, 1962, the Blackhawks owner probed the Leaf ownership as to the Big M's availability. Harold Ballard, acting on behalf of the Maple Leafs, got Norris to bid one million dollars for the rights to Mahovlich. Norris had started at $250,000 and kept raising the amount until Ballard "accepted" as a representative of the Leafs ownership. Although all parties involved in the transaction had been drinking, Norris still managed to peel off $1,000 in cash as a deposit. Toronto coach and general manager Punch Imlach, sensing too much alcohol had been consumed, refused to shake hands on any deal. The next morning a cheque was sent to Maple Leaf Gardens for one million dollars in Canadian funds "for payment in full for player Frank Mahovlich." Ballard still wanted to accept the deal—it would help to pay off the purchase of the team made recently in November 1961 by himself along with partners Stafford Smythe and John Bassett and he believed the Leafs would have a hard time signing Mahovlich to a new contract— but at the urging of a few people, especially former owner Conn Smythe, the deal was nixed and the cheque was returned to Norris, who was understandably furious. Mahovlich was given the contract he asked for as a result of all the shenanigans.

Frank Mahovlich

Toronto's Frank Mahovlich is surrounded by a group of Blackhawks in front of Chicago goalie Glenn Hall. Mahovlich had twelve points (six goals, six assists) in twelve playoff games in 1962, but saved his best for the final two games of the series against Chicago when he scored twice in the fifth game and then set up Bob Nevin to tie the score in the

Armstrong added to the margin of victory. The second game was closer, but the Leafs still prevailed to win 3-2. Stan Mikita scored twice for Chicago to tie the game at 2-2 after Billy Harris and Mahovlich had given Toronto a 2-0 lead. Armstrong scored the winner.

Back home the Blackhawks evened the series with 3-0 and 4-1 victories as they used their physical play to great advantage. The fifth game was back in the Gardens on April 19 and the Leafs got great efforts from Bob Pulford (three goals) and Mahovlich (two goals) to win 8-4. Don Simmons was now in goal for the Leafs with Bower injured and unable to continue after the fourth game. The wait for a Cup (since 1951) finally ended for the Leafs on April 22 in Chicago when a couple of late goals by Bob Nevin and Dick Duff wiped out a 1-0 Blackhawk lead. The winning goal was set up by Tim Horton, who found Duff open in front of the net at 14:14 of the third period.

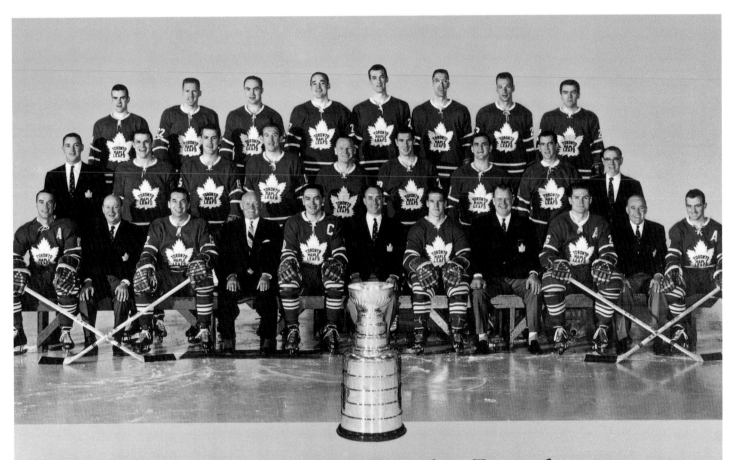

Toronto Maple Leafs
WORLD CHAMPIONS & STANLEY CUP WINNERS 1961-62

Front row, left to right — Bert Olmstead; George (Punch) Imlach, Manager and Coach; Ron Stewart; Conn Smythe; George Armstrong, Captain; Stafford Smythe, President; Tim Horton; Harold Ballard, Executive Vice-President; Frank (King) Clancy, Assistant Manager-Coach; Dick Duff.

Centre row, left to right — Bob Haggert, Trainer; Carl Brewer; Bill Harris; Bob Nevin; Johnny Bower; Bob Pulford; Bob Baun; Don Simmons; Tom Nayler, Assistant Trainer.
Back row, left to right — Dave Keon; Larry Hillman; "Red" Kelly; Frank Mahovlich; Eddie Litzenberger; Al Arbour; Eddie Shack; John MacMillan.

Maple Leafs defenceman Kent Douglas (#19) and forward Bob Nevin (#11) provide close coverage on the Canadiens centreman Henri Richard. A long-time minor leaguer, Douglas surprised everyone by winning the Calder Trophy as the NHL's top rookie in 1962–63. He was the first blueliner to win the award.

The Leafs–Canadiens Rivalry
1962–63

As defending Stanley Cup champions, the Maple Leafs decided to stick with their entire roster and there was only one new face added. Kent Douglas was acquired in a trade to help out on the blueline and the rookie defenceman rewarded the Leafs with a Calder Trophy-winning season. This would be the only year Douglas shone for the Leafs as his star quickly declined, but he certainly contributed well in '62–63. The only other major change for Toronto was the loss of forward Bert Olmstead to retirement. Forced to protect some younger prospects in the June draft, Olmstead was grabbed by the New York Rangers when Punch Imlach reluctantly left the veteran available. A bitter Olmstead chose to retire instead of report to the Rangers, and he never played again. Back-up goaltender Don Simmons saw action in 28 games and Bronco Horvath was picked up in mid-season to make a small contribution. Norm Armstrong, Rod Seiling, Andre Champagne and Jim Mikol were also newcomers to the team in minor roles.

In Montreal, the rebuilding process continued as Terry Harper, Jacques Laperriere and Claude Larose made their first appearances in the Canadiens line-up. Forward Marcel Bonin was deleted and defenceman Al MacNeil was sent to Chicago. Goalie Cesare Maniago was brought in to give Jacques Plante some time off, while defencemen Tom Johnson and Lou Fontinato suffered serious injuries during the season. Neither would play for the team again, and in Fontinato's case, his career was ended. Blueliner Jean Gauthier played in 65 games for the Habs and Red Berenson made 37 appearances as a forward. Bill McCreary, Gerry Brisson and goalie Ernie Wakely also played some games for Montreal. Captain Jean Beliveau scored his 300th career goal during the season.

As expected, the Leafs finished in first place in the regular season with a 35-23-12 record to edge Chicago by one point for the Prince of Wales Trophy (their first in 15 seasons). Montreal dropped to third place (with 79 points) but only three points out of first. The Leafs clinched first place late in the season when they earned a 3-3 tie with the Habs on March 20, 1963. Dave Keon (the Lady Byng Trophy winner) scored the game-tying goal with only eight seconds to play to clinch the regular season title for Toronto. The teams played many good games during the season series (won by the Leafs 6-4-4) and then met during the playoffs. Although four of the five post-season games were close, the Canadiens did not seriously challenge the Leafs. Goalie Johnny Bower posted two shutouts and Keon was once again his usual self, skating circles around the opposition.

In the finals, it was much the same story as the Leafs made short work of the Detroit Red Wings (who had upset the Chicago Blackhawks in the other semi-final). Toronto won the first three games of the series before Detroit won the fourth. A close game in the fifth contest was clinched by two goals from the stick of Keon, giving the Leafs a 3-1 win and their second straight Cup. It was the first time they had won the Cup on home ice since 1951. Dick Duff, Allan Stanley, Red Kelly, George Armstrong and Eddie Shack all played well for the Leafs in the playoffs. Carl Brewer, who suffered a broken arm in the last game of the finals, and Frank Mahovlich were named to the first all-star team at the end of the season. Tim Horton of Toronto

and Henri Richard of Montreal were both named to the second team.

OCTOBER 18, 1962
Montreal 4 Toronto 2 @ The Forum

The Montreal Canadiens overcame a 2-0 first-period lead by the Toronto Maple Leafs to score four straight times and beat the Stanley Cup champions 4-2 at the Forum before 14,132 fans. Dick Duff opened the scoring for the Leafs on a Toronto power-play by tipping in Tim Horton's shot from the point. Leafs rookie defenceman Kent Douglas scored the second goal (his first in the NHL) when he unleashed a slap shot from the point that got past Canadiens goalie Cesare Maniago, who was replacing an injured Jacques Plante. Although the Leafs thoroughly outplayed the Habs in the first period, the hometown team came back to score twice in the second (Henri Richard, Jean Beliveau) and twice more in the third (Bernie Geoffrion, Ralph Backstrom) to win their second game of the season. Richard was on a breakaway when he fired a 30-footer into the far corner of the net past Johnny Bower in the Leaf goal. Beliveau's goal tied the game when his shot banked off Leaf defenceman Bobby Baun and into the Toronto net. Geoffrion finished off a passing play with Gilles Tremblay for his goal while Backstrom slapped a 40-foot blast for a goal.

OCTOBER 31, 1962
Montreal 4 Toronto 3 @ Maple Leaf Gardens

A late rally by the Maple Leafs fell short as the Canadiens hung on to win 4-3 in front of 14,003 fans at the Gardens on October 31. The Habs built up a 4-1 lead on goals by Claude Provost, Gilles Tremblay, Tom Johnson and Bernie Geoffrion after Toronto's George Armstrong had given the Leafs a 1-0 lead. Third-period goals by Billy Harris and Dave Keon brought the Leafs closer, but Montreal

"Johnny Bower has slowed down. His reflexes are not what they used to be. I try to keep my shots low at him ... Bower was in net when I got my first hat trick in the NHL last December [1961]."

Claude Provost (Hockey Illustrated, December 1962)

goalie Cesare Maniago shut the door the rest of the way. The Leafs pulled their goalie with 43 seconds to play and Maniago was forced to make a brilliant stop on Keon. The game featured a couple of fights for Leaf rookie Kent Douglas, who took on Bill Hicke and Geoffrion in separate battles. Geoffrion's goal came on a backhander just 33 seconds into the third period and proved to be the 62nd career game winner for the great Canadiens winger.

Toronto's Eddie Shack (#23) is checked behind the net by Montreal's Claude Provost (#14). In 1962–63, Shack scored 16 goals and 25 points (his best totals to that point in his career) while recording 97 penalty minutes. Provost saw his goal production slip down to 20 in 1962–63 after a career-high 33 tallies the previous season, although he did have 30 assists. The lantern-jawed Provost (nicknamed "Joe") played his entire career (1,005 games) for the Canadiens between 1955 and 1970 and finished with 254 goals and 589 points in the regular season. He added 25 goals and 63 points in 126 playoff games.

NOVEMBER 1, 1962
Toronto 3 Montreal 1 @ The Forum

For the first time in two seasons the Maple Leafs finally won a game at the Forum with a 3-1 victory. The Leafs put together a solid 60-minute effort to win the contest with goals from Red Kelly, Dave Keon and Eddie Shack. The Toronto club pelted 37 shots at goalie Cesare Maniago in the Canadiens net and got a good effort from netminder Johnny Bower, who was only beaten by a

Gilles Tremblay shot. The best goal of the night belonged to Keon who converted a perfect pass from Dick Duff to score the game winner. The best Leaf on the night was defenceman Carl Brewer, who played well defensively and was involved in the action with three penalties to his credit. Montreal fans became so incensed with the Leaf rearguard that they threw rubber boots and programs onto the ice on two separate occasions.

NOVEMBER 14, 1962
Toronto 4 Montreal 2 @ Maple Leaf Gardens

Third-period goals by Bob Pulford and Billy Harris restored a two-goal Toronto lead and gave the Maple Leafs a 4-2 win over the Canadiens. Pulford's tally came after just 21 sec-

---

Toronto's Billy Harris reaches high to grab a loose puck against Montreal defenceman Jacques Laperriere (#2). Harris scored a beautiful goal in the Leafs 4-2 win over the Habs on November 14, 1962. It was only one of eight goals Harris scored for Toronto in 1962–63 in 65 games played. He added a respectable 24 assists in a season that saw him get little ice time as a utility player. Harris played in Toronto between 1955 and 1965 and recorded 287 points (181 assists) in 610 games. Laperriere began his NHL career in 1962–63 when he played in six games (two assists) for Montreal and in all five playoff contests (one assist).

onds of the final stanza when he put in his own rebound, as the Montreal defence could not find the loose puck. The score remained 3-2 until 41 seconds remained in the contest when Harris completed a beautiful play for his goal. The Leaf centre took the puck past Montreal defenceman Jean Gauthier, moved in on goalie Jacques Plante and made a pretty deke before putting the puck in the net. Both Plante and Toronto netminder Johnny Bower faced 30 opposition shots and had to make difficult saves to keep the game close. Bower was playing for the first time in three games and was not expected to play in this game, but back-up Don Simmons came down with the flu just before game time, forcing Toronto's number-one goalie back into the nets. Dave Keon and George Armstrong scored the Leafs' other goals, while Henri Richard and Bernie Geoffrion scored for the Habs to tie the game 2-2.

Ron Stewart — a closer look

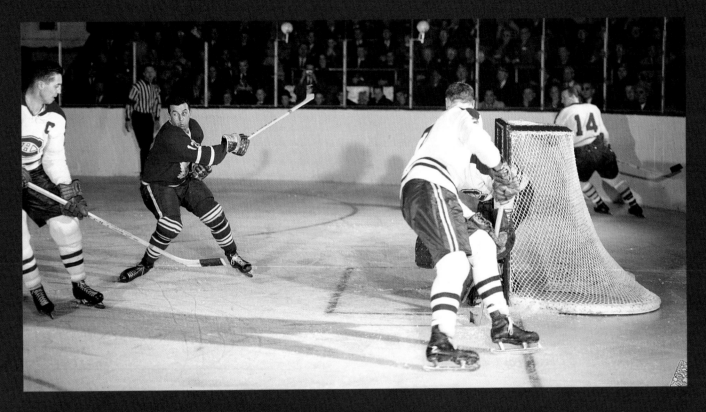

Toronto's Ron Stewart (#12) had a couple of good games against Montreal in the 1962–63 season (including a game-winning goal on December 5). The smooth-skating veteran chipped in with sixteen goals in the regular season and then added four more in the playoffs in help-ing the Leafs to a second straight Cup. Stewart played for the Maple Leafs between 1952 and 1965 and amassed 368 points (including 186 goals) in 838 games. He contributed 10 goals and 28 points in 82 playoff appearances.

During the 1962 Stanley Cup finals, Ron Stewart suffered cracked ribs in an auto mishap. He had borrowed teammate Bert Olmstead's station wagon and was visiting family in Barrie, Ontario, when the accident occurred. The car hit a patch of snow and ice causing it to roll over. The vehicle was a write-off but Stewart was able to walk away with damaged ribs. Amazingly, the Leafs were able to keep the injury a secret until the finals were over, something that would be impossible to do today.

NOVEMBER 29, 1962
Toronto 4 Montreal 4 @ The Forum

A three-goal outburst during a 2:48 span in the third period lifted the Canadiens into a 4-4 tie with the Maple Leafs on November 29. Goals by Bernie Geoffrion, Gilles Tremblay and Claude Provost erased a 4-1 lead the Leafs had built up going into the final period. After Henri Richard had scored to give the Habs the lead, Toronto responded with two goals by Frank Mahovlich and singles by Ron Stewart and Eddie Shack for what seemed to be a commanding lead. The 14,254 fans in attendance at the Forum began to cheer the Leafs in the second period but changed their tune after the Montreal lightning attack in the third. Mahovlich got his first on the power-play when he tipped in a Kent Douglas shot. His second goal featured a typical rush by the Big M as he swept by Montreal defenceman Jean Gauthier (filling in for an ailing Jean Guy Talbot) before firing a shot past Jacques Plante in the Canadiens goal. Stewart steered a Bob Pulford shot into the net for his marker, while Shack scored on his one and only appearance on the ice. Montreal's rally culminated when Provost backhanded a shot past goalie Don Simmons after he corralled a pass from Don Marshall.

DECEMBER 5, 1962
Toronto 2 Montreal 1 @ Maple Leaf Gardens

A tight-checking game with excellent goaltending at either end marked the Leafs' 2-1 win at the Gardens. Jacques Plante faced 32 shots in the Montreal net and allowed goals by Frank Mahovlich (his 14th) and the game winner by Ron Stewart. Johnny Bower was equally sharp in the Leafs net with 31 shots coming his way and only a Bernie Geoffrion power-play marker beating him. Geoffrion hurt his wrist after colliding with Bower as he scored his goal and missed the rest of the game (X-rays revealed a broken bone in his right wrist). After the Canadiens tied the score, Stewart scored his goal just a minute later when defenceman Carl Brewer sprung him into the clear with a cross-ice pass. Stewart drove the puck into the open side of the net to give the Leafs the lead and send 14,086 fans home happy. The win gave the Leafs sole possession of second place in the league standings behind Chicago.

DECEMBER 20, 1962
Montreal 4 Toronto 4 @ The Forum

A late-game stick incident marred a 4-4 tie between the Canadiens and Leafs at the Forum on December 20. Leaf defenceman Carl Brewer caught Montreal forward Bobby Rousseau with a high stick at 19:02 of the third period, cutting the Canadiens player for four stitches. The Leaf rearguard was given a five-minute major and Rousseau left the game bleeding from the cut over his eye. The 13,588 fans on hand for the contest littered the ice with debris and a few made menacing gestures at the Leaf players still on the bench. Assorted items, like game programs, were tossed at the Toronto players, who threw them back. Montreal police were forced to protect the Leaf bench area until the end of the game. The Leafs got goals from Dick Duff (with two), Frank Mahovlich and Eddie Litzenberger, while Henri Richard, Gilles Tremblay, Bernie Geoffrion and Bobby Rousseau gave the Canadiens theirs. Rousseau's third-period tally evened the score at 3-3. Duff's second on the night gave the Leafs a 4-3 lead but Geoffrion beat Brewer to a loose puck before beating goalie Johnny Bower in close to once again even the score in the 15th minute of the final period.

JANUARY 17, 1963
Montreal 6 Toronto 4 @ The Forum

A goal by veteran Dickie Moore broke a 3-3 tie in the third period and helped the Canadiens to a 6-4 win over the Maple Leafs on January 17. Moore took a pass from Henri Richard and

Toronto defenceman Carl Brewer (#2) helps partner Larry Hillman (#22) defend against Bobby Rousseau (#15), Henri Richard (#16) and Gilles Tremblay (#21) at the Forum. Brewer caused a major ruckus at the Forum on the night of December 20, 1963, when he cut Rousseau with his stick. The Leafs defenceman was no stranger to trouble, having led the league in penalty minutes (in 1959–60 with 150) and in 1962–63 he had 168 minutes in penalties to go along with two goals and 25 assists. Brewer was prominent in games against the Canadiens all season long with many feisty battles.

handcuffed goalie Don Simmons with a shot from about 30 feet out to give the Habs the lead for good. Claude Provost (33 seconds after Moore's tally) and Bobby Rousseau scored insurance goals for Montreal, who allowed the Leafs only one third-period goal by Dave Keon. Gilles Tremblay, Ralph Backstrom and Henri Richard had scored earlier for the Canadiens, while the Leafs were led by goals from George Armstrong, Eddie Litzenberger and Bob Nevin. Montreal captain Jean Beliveau, trying for his 300th career goal, had to settle for three assists. In an effort to

shake things up in the third period, Leaf coach Punch Imlach benched winger Dick Duff in favour of rookie Norm Armstrong, and he shifted Ron Stewart from the wing to defence in place of Larry Hillman. These moves had little effect, but putting Keon between George Armstrong and Frank Mahovlich did result in one goal. The game featured strong skating by both clubs and was at times very physical. The win enabled the Habs to move into second place in the NHL standings and just one point out of first.

JANUARY 23, 1963
Toronto 5 Montreal 1 @ Maple Leaf Gardens

Red Kelly scored just 49 seconds into the game between the Leafs and Canadiens, leading Toronto to a 5-1 romp on home ice before 14,309 fans. The Leaf centre got around a stumbling J.C. Tremblay and then made a neat shift around the other Montreal defenceman, Lou Fontinato, before whipping a backhand drive past goalie Jacques Plante. It was Kelly's second goal in the last 17 contests. Toronto defenceman

A CLOSER LOOK

Carl Brewer may have epitomized the Maple Leaf style of "clutch and grab" quite literally. He cut out the palms of his gloves, allowing him to slow down opponents by grabbing onto their sweaters. It was a tactic not often noticed by the officials. The holes were bigger than his fist and helped him to control the opposition players in front of the Toronto net. One night after a fight, referee Vern Buffey noticed the palmless gloves strewn on the ice with all the other sticks and gloves. Buffey's findings and complaints about Brewer's methods were taken into complete account by the league, which eventually ruled that all gloves must be intact (rule 22 c).

Kent Douglas
— a closer look

Toronto defenceman Kent Douglas (#19) crashes Montreal blueliner Lou Fontinato (#19) into the boards. As a 27-year-old rookie in the NHL, Douglas became the first defenceman to win the Calder Trophy as the league's top rookie. He was highly sought after when he had a great season in the AHL while playing for Eddie Shore in Springfield; the Leafs gave up five players for his rights. He scored seven goals and added 15 assists while racking up 105 penalty minutes in his award-winning season of 1962–63. In 283 games as a Leaf, Douglas scored 20 goals and totalled 85 points with 408 penalty minutes. Fontinato's career came to a sudden end when he crashed into the boards during a game against the New York Rangers on March 9, 1963, at the Forum.

"Show me one guy that came into the league [in 1962–63] and played with the same maturity as Douglas. He's a rookie but he's one of our best defencemen, maybe the best. In many games he's the best we have. In some games he's the best in the league."

Punch Imlach (Maple Leaf game program, February 23, 1963)

TRIVIA

As a 13-year-old, Kent Douglas was stricken with spinal meningitis and was told by doctors that he would never be able to participate in sports and may not walk at all. He is also one of the few players to have survived working for Eddie Shore and still made it to the NHL. Douglas listened carefully to the crusty Hall of Fame defenceman and began using a very heavy stick that gave him a powerful shot from the point. Other NHL players tutored by Shore included Ted Harris, Floyd Smith, Bob McCord and Parker MacDonald.

Eddie Shore was asking $50,000 for the rights to Kent Douglas and settled for five players from the Maple Leafs: Bill White, Wally Boyer, Dick Mattiussi, Jim Wilcox and Roger Cote. It is also interesting to note that Douglas was once Leaf property (in 1953–54) but was let go when he got into too many fights that got him suspended at times.

Kent Douglas scored the second goal when he carried the puck right up to the Canadiens net and put it in. The line of Bob Pulford (two goals), Eddie Shack and Bronco Horvath then went to work for Toronto scoring or setting up the last three markers. The Leafs had claimed winger Horvath on waivers from the New York Rangers and the 32-year-old veteran chipped in with three assists. (He once tied for the NHL lead in goals scored while with Boston in 1959–60, when he had 39.) Allan Stanley scored the other Leaf goal while Dickie Moore counted the only Habs marker when he beat Don Simmons at 11:42 of the third period.

JANUARY 31, 1963
Toronto 6 Montreal 3 @ The Forum

Led by Red Kelly's three goals (including one on a penalty shot), the Maple Leafs beat the Canadiens 6-3 at the Forum in front of a season-high 15,334 spectators. The game was actually tied going into the third period, but a four-goal explosion sealed the win for the Leafs. One of the third-period goals came on Kelly's penalty shot after he was pulled down from behind by Canadiens defenceman Jean Guy Talbot. Very coolly, Kelly came down the ice and drilled a shot into the bottom corner of the net past Jacques Plante. Kelly, a Liberal Member of Parliament in Ottawa, ignored his political duties to play in the contest that saw him raise his goal total to 14 on the year. The Canadiens had built up a 2-0 lead on goals by Gilles Tremblay and Dickie Moore but Kelly's first two markers evened the score. George Armstrong gave the

Toronto's Red Kelly (#4) battles for a loose puck against Montreal defenceman Jacques Laperriere (#2) and J.C. Tremblay (#3). Kelly had a hat trick (his second of three in his career with Toronto) against the Canadiens on January 31 in leading the Leafs to a 6-3 victory. Kelly enjoyed a fine season in 1962–63 when he scored 20 goals and added 40 assists while also serving as a Member of Parliament in Ottawa.

Henri Richard (#16) tries to put the puck past netminder Johnny Bower. Richard scored a goal with the Canadiens goalie on the bench during a February 9 contest at the Gardens. During the 1962–63 season, Richard led the entire NHL with 50 assists. He added 23 goals and his 73 points tied for fourth in league scoring (with Frank Mahovlich of Toronto). Bower played in 42 games (with a record of 20-15-7) for the Leafs in 1962–63 and sported a 2.62 goals-against average with one shutout.

Leafs the lead while Dick Duff and Frank Mahovlich chipped in the other scores in the third. Bobby Rousseau got the other Montreal goal past Don Simmons. Bernie Geoffrion tried to do his best to brawl with Carl Brewer in the third period, but the linesmen broke it up. The Canadiens winger tried to continue the battle in the shared penalty box and the Montreal fans pelted Brewer with debris. Finally, referee Eddie

Powers gave Geoffrion a game misconduct when he persisted in trying to get Brewer to fight him. After the game, Montreal coach Toe Blake aired a number of complaints about Powers to a local newspaper and even accused the referee of having a bet on the game. The league office reviewed Blake's comments and he was fined $200. That was not good enough for Powers, who submitted his resignation, citing a lack of support from NHL president Clarence Campbell.

FEBRUARY 9, 1963
Toronto 3 Montreal 3 @ Maple Leaf Gardens

A late goal by Henri Richard allowed the Canadiens to escape with a 3-3 tie on February 9. Montreal pulled goalie Jacques Plante and Richard evened the score at 19:02 of the third period of the Saturday evening contest played before 14,401 fans. The game-tying goal came after a face-off in the Leafs end as a result of an icing call. The Habs stormed Toronto goaltender Johnny Bower and Richard finally put a rebound over the fallen Leafs netminder. Richard had served a 10-minute misconduct early in the game (at 1:28 of the first period) when he bumped into linesman Ron Wicks and raised his stick. The Leafs had built up a 2-0 lead on goals by Dave Keon and Ron Stewart, but Dickie Moore and Bill Hicke replied for the Canadiens. Keon's goal was the prettiest of the night when he took a George Armstrong pass and swept around Montreal defenceman Jean Guy Talbot along the boards. He then slipped a shot past Plante to score his 21st of the year. Red Kelly gave the Leafs the lead with his 15th at 14:50 of the third, and that set the stage for Richard's heroics.

FEBRUARY 20, 1963
Toronto 2 Montreal 1 @ Maple Leaf Gardens

Backed by the stellar goaltending of Johnny Bower and a two-goal performance by Bob Pulford, the Maple Leafs edged the Canadiens 2-1. The win pushed the Leafs into second place in the NHL standings and pushed Montreal to third spot. All the goals in the game were scored in the second period. The contest featured some hard hitting and great goaltending by Bower (37 shots) and Jacques Plante (30 shots) in the Montreal net. Pulford broke the scoreless tie by putting home a rebound, but Dickie Moore of the Canadiens tied the score on a power-play. Pulford scored his second of the night just two minutes later to give the Leafs the lead after charging down the left wing and having his shot go in off Plante's right pad. Toronto defenceman Carl Brewer went after Canadiens captain Jean Beliveau and knocked him hard into the glass. The blow appeared to daze Beliveau and he was not as effective in this game. Brewer drove many of the Montreal players to distraction with his physical play.

MARCH 14, 1963
Montreal 3 Toronto 3 @ The Forum

Leaf winger John MacMillan scored his first goal of the season as the Leafs and Canadiens battled to a 3-3 tie on March 14. MacMillan and defenceman Kent Douglas scored the first two goals of the game for the Leafs early in the first period. Douglas got the opener on a screened shot from the point on a power-play, and MacMillan knocked home Bob Nevin's rebound for his tally. Henri Richard got one back for the Canadiens late in the opening stanza and Jean Beliveau tied it in the second. Ralph Backstrom gave the Montreal squad a 3-2 lead early in the third frame but Dave Keon quickly tied it for the Leafs just 34 seconds later. The game featured rough, aggressive play, and Eddie Shack of the Leafs got into an altercation with Beliveau that carried on into the penalty box. The Canadiens captain took a roundhouse right at Shack that failed to connect, but the Leaf poked Beliveau in the chest while in the box and earned a 10-minute misconduct for his efforts.

MARCH 20, 1963
Toronto 3 Montreal 3 @ Maple Leaf Gardens

For the first time in 15 years Toronto clinched first place in the NHL when Dave Keon's goal with eight seconds remaining gave the Maple Leafs a 3-3 tie with the Canadiens. With goalie Don Simmons on the bench, the Leafs got the puck to Keon who came out from behind the Montreal net to put a shot past Jacques Plante. Dick Duff and Red Kelly did yeoman work in digging the puck out of the corner for Keon to have an opportunity. The goal by the tireless Leaf centre sent the crowd of 14,372 into a tizzy and they showered the ice with all sorts of debris. The Leafs actually had a 2-0 lead in the game but the Canadiens fought back to take a 3-2 lead. Toronto needed only one point in their last three games but were happy to do it on this night because many of their aging veterans were feeling fatigued. The first-place finish was worth $27,000 to the Leafs as a team.

Toronto forward John MacMillan (#8) comes back to help goalie Johnny Bower (#1) and defenceman Kent Douglas (#19) to stop an opposition attack. MacMillan scored his only goal of the season in 1962–63 against the Montreal Canadiens on March 14, 1963, in a 3-3 tie at the Forum. A speedy winger who was used as a penalty killer and utility forward, MacMillan first joined the Leafs in 1960–61 when he played in 31 games and scored three goals and eight points. The following year saw him get only one goal for the Leafs, and in 1962–63 MacMillan had just two points in six games. He was, however, a member of two Stanley Cup teams (1962, 1963) with Toronto before he was claimed on waivers by Detroit in December 1963. MacMillan was one of the few U.S. college-trained players in the NHL in the Sixties. He took an athletic scholarship to Denver College and graduated with a Bachelor of Science degree.

"I got a real good whack at it. I think it went through [Plante's] legs. It was low about a foot off the ice. We were trying for one shot."

Dave Keon (*The Globe and Mail*, March 21, 1963)

playoffs

SERIES A – TORONTO VS. MONTREAL
MARCH 26, 1963
Toronto 3 Montreal 1 @ Maple Leaf Gardens

The Maple Leafs took the first two games of the semi-final playoff series with a pair of wins at the Gardens. In the first contest, the Leafs played a tight defensive game to win 3-1. Goals by Bob Pulford, Dick Duff and George Armstrong gave Toronto a commanding 3-0 lead before Jean Beliveau got one back for the Canadiens in the third period. The key point in the game was the Leafs' ability to withstand two-man disadvantages on two occasions, once in the first and again in the second. Pulford opened the scoring in the second period when his shot deflected off the stick of Montreal defenceman J.C. Tremblay and past goalie Jacques Plante, who had no chance on the play. Johnny Bower played well in the Leafs net behind some excellent work by his defencemen and also earned an assist on Pulford's goal. Both coaches agreed that the Canadiens lacked their usual zip.

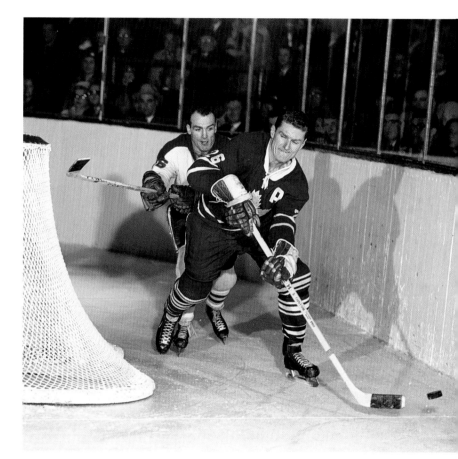

Toronto defenceman Allan Stanley (#26) stays ahead of Montreal forward Henri Richard who is chasing him behind the net. For scoring one goal and adding one assist in the Leafs second victory over the Canadiens, Stanley was named the first star of the game by the Rangers' Andy Bathgate, who was working as an analyst for Hockey Night in Canada. *Of his goal Stanley said, "Plante didn't have much of a chance on that one. It hit one of the Canadiens and deflected over his shoulder." (The Montreal Gazette, March 29, 1963)*

"There was a time when the Canadiens could rely on a couple of big guns to win for them. But we can't expect to win like that anymore. We need a good game from everybody."

Toe Blake (*The Montreal Gazette*, March 27, 1963)

Toronto goalie Johnny Bower (#1) makes a save against Montreal's Jean Beliveau (#4) with defenceman Tim Horton (#7) trying to take out the Canadiens centre at the Forum. Bower recorded two shutouts in the 1963 playoffs versus the Canadiens and even earned one assist. Horton recorded six goals and nineteen assists during the 1962–63 season and added four points in 10 post-season games. Beliveau had 18 goals and 67 points in the '62–63 season and was the best Hab in the playoffs, with two goals and three points.

MARCH 28, 1963
Toronto 3 Montreal 2 @ Maple Leaf Gardens

A second-period goal by Dave Keon proved to be the winner in another tight game won by the Leafs 3-2 on March 29. The Canadiens scored first in the second game of the series when Jean Beliveau stole the puck from Toronto defenceman Bobby Baun and then whistled a shot from 35 feet out past Bower. The Leafs tied the score just 47 seconds later when captain George Armstrong's shot took a bounce off Jacques Plante and went into the net. Allan Stanley gave the Leafs the lead in the second period when he let go a rising shot from the blueline that deflected over Plante's shoulder. Canadiens rookie defenceman Terry Harper tied the score as Henri Richard set him up smartly. On his winning tally, Keon actually lost control of the puck after he had broken around Harper. However, Plante was fooled into thinking that the Leaf player was going to cut across the ice with the puck, and even though Keon did not get much wood on it, the disk slid under his stick and into the net with the goalie too far out of position to recover. There was no scoring in the third period as the Leafs hung on for the win.

MARCH 30, 1963
Toronto 2 Montreal 0 @ The Forum

Johnny Bower recorded his first-ever playoff shutout and the Maple Leafs took a commanding 3-0 lead in the series with a 2-0 blanking of the Canadiens at the Forum in front of 14,773 frustrated fans. Bower made 32 saves in total and got help from a second-period goal by Eddie Shack (his first playoff goal and point in 16 post-season games) and a third-period tally by Bob Pulford. The Leafs held off the Habs during a two-man disadvantage in the first period when Shack was called for a five-minute major (cutting Ralph Backstrom with his stick), and then Brewer was called for holding. Conn Smythe, Maple Leaf team president, was so upset at the second penalty given to his team that he began to protest vehemently by waving his raincoat at rinkside. Fans sitting close by began to complain that they could not see the game and police had to move in to calm Smythe down. The Leafs checked hard all game long and never gave the Canadiens a chance to get going. In a surprise move, the Leafs came home after the Saturday night game and practised in Toronto at noon on Sunday.

APRIL 2, 1963
Montreal 3 Toronto 1 @ The Forum

The Canadiens fought off elimination by beating the Leafs 3-1 in the fourth game of the series. Gilles Tremblay scored twice for Montreal (including the game winner), while Henri Richard added another. Ron Stewart scored the opening goal of the game for the Leafs at 6:12 of the first period, but goalie Jacques Plante shut them out the rest of the way, including a breakaway save on Dave Keon with the score 2-1. The Habs were back to their skating game and outshot the Leafs 37-22 on the night. Rookie Terry Harper was a force all night long on the Canadiens blueline and dished out some good hits, including bouncing Frank Mahovlich into the boards. The Leafs winger came back hard at Harper and earned a penalty for cross-checking in the third period. While Mahovlich was off, Tremblay scored the Habs' third goal of the night. Bill Sutherland, a 28-

year-old rookie winger, made his NHL debut for Montreal; he would also play in the next contest against Toronto, his only two career games for the Habs.

APRIL 4, 1963
Toronto 5 Montreal 0 @ Maple Leaf Gardens

Dave Keon scored twice and Johnny Bower earned his second shutout of the series as the Maple Leafs eliminated the Canadiens with a 5-0 win. Keon's game winner came at 4:56 of the first frame and was followed by goals from Dick Duff and Ron Stewart before the period was finished. Keon added one more goal in the second and Kent Douglas scored one in the third to wrap it up for the Leafs. Bower made 35 stops to earn his shutout while Plante faced 27 Toronto shots. Toronto coach Punch Imlach matched Dave Keon against Henri Richard, and Bob Pulford went up against Canadiens captain Jean Beliveau. The strategy worked, as the two Montreal stars could not get untracked. The Canadiens were only able to win four of the nineteen contests played between the two teams during 1962–63. Montreal coach Toe Blake went into the Leaf dressing room to congratulate the winners and shook hands with Imlach and every Leaf player.

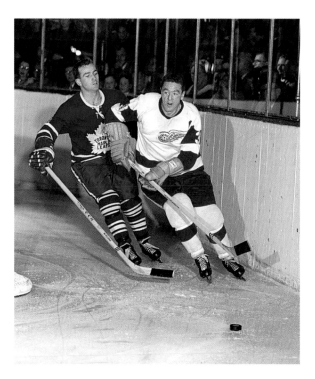

Dick Duff of the Maple Leafs checks Detroit's Marcel Pronovost. Duff set an NHL record—fastest two goals from the start of a playoff game—which still stands today. Duff scored two goals after just 1:08 of play in the first contest of the 1963 finals. Duff scored his first goal just 49 seconds after the game started by beating Terry Sawchuk in the Detroit net. Duff only had 16 goals in 69 games during the season but had four in ten playoff games.

"This is the first time in three tries my team has been able to beat the Canadiens. Why shouldn't I be happy?"

Punch Imlach (*The Montreal Gazette*, April 5, 1963)

stanley cup playoffs

TORONTO VS. DETROIT

The Leafs won their second straight Stanley Cup with a 4-1 series win over the Detroit Red Wings. The series opened in Toronto after the Red Wings upset the Chicago Blackhawks and

the Leafs took a two-game lead with a pair of 4-2 wins. Dick Duff and Bob Nevin each scored twice in the opener to get the Leafs off on the right foot. Eddie Litzenberger had one goal and two assists to pace the Leafs in the second game. Ron Stewart added two goals in the second contest. The Red Wings won the third game on home ice with a 3-2 triumph but Toronto came back to win the fourth game 4-2 as Red Kelly had two goals. On April 18, 1963, the Leafs won the Cup at home on a Saturday night with a tight 3-1 win. Eddie Shack scored the winner with about six minutes to play as he deflected a Kent Douglas shot past Detroit goalie Terry Sawchuk.

Bob Nevin — a closer look

"Although I scored 21 goals for the Leafs in my first NHL season (1960–61), they had been using me strictly as a defensive player … penalty killing and things like that. It made me a more complete hockey player but I was glad to get more of a chance to help out offensively, too."

Bob Nevin on being traded to the New York Rangers (*Hockey Illustrated*, March 1966)

All eyes search for the puck as the Maple Leaf winger Bob Nevin (#11) takes his position in front of the Detroit goal area with the Red Wing defenceman Bill Gadsby (#4) and goalie Terry Sawchuk (#1) ready to stop any scoring attempt. Nevin scored two goals in the first game of the 1963 finals as the Leafs beat the Red Wings 4-2 at the Gardens. Nevin's production dropped off in 1962–63 with only 12 goals and 21 assists in 58 games played. He scored a total of three goals in the playoffs (no assists in 10 games) and would be dealt before the 1963–64 season was over.

Toronto captain George Armstrong holds the 1963 Stanley Cup after the Leafs defeated the Detroit Red Wings in five games. After receiving the Cup from NHL president Clarence Campbell, Armstrong told Ward Cornell of Hockey Night in Canada, *"We had to go all out to beat them. It was a hard win." Armstrong was the last captain of the Leafs appointed by long-time Toronto owner and manager Conn Smythe. The Canadian war hero felt Armstrong displayed strong leadership skills and that he epitomized what a Canadian should be. It was by design that Armstrong eventually wore sweater #10 (he also wore #15 and #20 in his early years as a Leaf), a number worn by one-time Toronto great and captain Syl Apps.*

Dave Keon (#14) became the first player in NHL history to score two shorthanded goals in one playoff game on April 18, 1963, against the Detroit Red Wings. For the first goal, Keon beat Sawchuk (pictured in the Detroit net) after he swept around Alex Delvecchio of the Red Wings and put a shot in off the post. He then got one into an empty net with the Leafs nursing a 2-1 lead very late in the third period by whacking in a long drive from just inside the Toronto blueline. The 3-1 win gave the Leafs their second straight Stanley Cup.

Dave Keon — a closer look

After the final game was over and the Leafs had been presented with the Stanley Cup, Ward Cornell and Frank Selke, Jr., of *Hockey Night in Canada* came onto the ice to conduct interviews with microphones open to the crowd still in the Gardens. The fans screamed, "We want Keon," but the Leaf hero was nowhere to be seen, so interviews were conducted with Johnny Bower, and Allan Stanley, and also with Gordie Howe of Detroit. All were able to address the crowd but a large roar went up when Keon made an appearance just as the television show was signing off. *Hockey Night in Canada* stopped rolling the credits and Cornell got in a few words with Keon, who said, "I'm glad we won tonight and didn't have to go back to Detroit." Cornell then interviewed coach Punch Imlach before signing off for good.

"The best hockey player in the business."

Punch Imlach on Dave Keon (Hockey Night in Canada television broadcast, April 18, 1963)

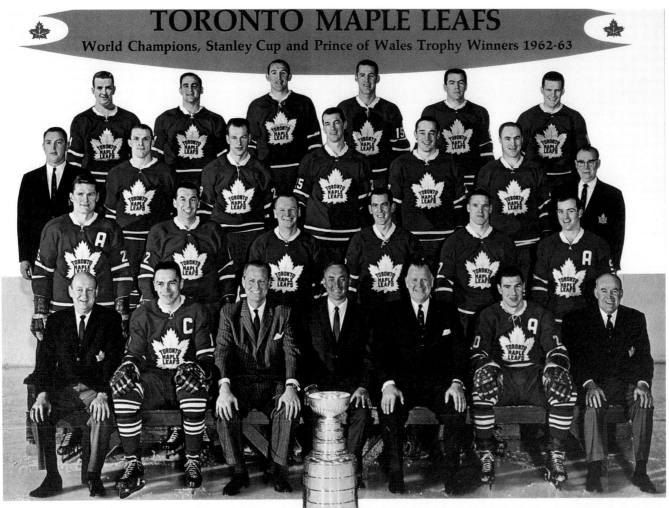

TORONTO MAPLE LEAFS
World Champions, Stanley Cup and Prince of Wales Trophy Winners 1962-63

Front row, left to right — George "Punch" Imlach (Manager and Coach), George Armstrong (Captain), John Bassett (Chairman of the Board of Directors), C. Stafford Smythe (President), Harold E. Ballard (Executive Vice-President), Bob Pulford, Frank "King" Clancy (Assistant Manager-Coach).

Second row, left to right — Allan Stanley, Ron Stewart, Johnny Bower, Don Simmons, Tim Horton, Dick Duff.

Third row, left to right — Bob Haggert (Trainer), Carl Brewer, Eddie Shack, Eddie Litzenberger, Frank Mahovlich, Leonard "Red" Kelly, Tommy Nayler (Assistant Trainer).

Back row, left to right — Dave Keon, Bobby Baun, Bob Nevin, Bill Harris, John MacMillan, Kent Douglas.

Dave Keon of the Leafs is in close against goaltender Charlie Hodge of the Canadiens. Hodge had a great year in 1963–64 (winning the Vezina Trophy) but Keon got the best of him in the last contest of a terrific seven game semi-final between the two teams that year.

The Leafs–Canadiens Rivalry
1963–64

season summary

The biggest change to the lineup of the Montreal Canadiens for the 1963–64 season took place well before training camps opened. Tired of Jacques Plante's act in net, the Canadiens boldly dealt the award-winning netminder to New York as part of a blockbuster deal in June 1963. Along with Plante, the Habs sent Phil Goyette and Don Marshall to the Rangers in exchange for Lorne "Gump" Worsley, Dave Balon, Len Ronson and Leon Rochefort. Unfortunately, Worsley got hurt and played in only eight games (and then was sent to the AHL), leaving the number-one job to little Charlie Hodge, a career minor leaguer. Hodge however proved he belonged by winning the Vezina Trophy with a stingy 2.26 goals-against average. Other award winners for the Canadiens included Jean Beliveau (Hart Trophy) and Jacques Laperriere (Calder Trophy). Muscular John Ferguson was the most significant addition up front, while Jimmy Roberts saw action in 15 contests. Defenceman Ted Harris saw brief duty (four games) with the big team in Montreal, as did Yvan Cournoyer, Andre Boudrias, Claude Larose, John Hanna, Terry Gray and Bryan Watson. Defenceman Tom Johnson was lost to Boston in the intra-league draft and Dickie Moore decided to retire.

The Maple Leafs stayed with the same lineup to start the season that had won the Stanley Cup the previous spring although they did add forward Jim Pappin to the mix. Larry Hillman and Arnie Brown were a couple of new faces who saw action on defence, and back-up goalie Don Simmons got into 20 contests. Al Arbour, Eddie Litzenberger and Gerry Ehman spent more time in the minors but were called upon to fill in, especially in the playoffs. The biggest change in the Leaf lineup took place late in the season when coach Punch Imlach felt a major shake-up was required during a somewhat lacklustre season for the team. He traded five players to the New York Rangers (Bob Nevin, Dick Duff, Rod Seiling, Bill Collins and Arnie Brown) in return for Andy Bathgate (the NHL's assist leader) and Don McKenney. The Toronto club gave up youth and a good deal of their future but felt they needed veteran leadership and goal scoring if they were to repeat as champs. It all worked out for Imlach, in the short term at least.

Once again, the Canadiens finished first (36-21-13) in the standings, edging out Chicago by one point for the regular-season title. Toronto finished third with 78 points (33-25-12) and had a great deal of trouble scoring goals, especially against Montreal who shut them out four times (taking the season series 7-5-2). The Canadiens got balanced, scoring with Beliveau (28), Balon (24), Bobby Rousseau (25), Gilles Tremblay (22) and Bernie Geoffrion (21). Toronto only got 20 or more goals from Frank Mahovlich (26), Dave Keon (24), and George Armstrong (20). The Leafs as usual relied on a stout defence (led by first-team all-star Tim Horton) and were playoff-ready.

It wasn't easy, but the Leafs did manage to take their third straight Cup by winning two series that went to the limit. In a classic battle versus the Canadiens, the Leafs won the seventh game on the road, led by the inspired work of Keon. The Canadiens were very disappointed once again but their rebuilding was just about complete. Toronto went on to face Detroit in the finals and once again won the last two games to take the Cup and denied many Red Wing veterans a chance to get their names on the coveted trophy.

OCTOBER 16, 1963
Toronto 4 Montreal 2 @ The Forum

Goalie Gump Worsley played his first game as a Canadien against the Maple Leafs, but a third-period rally spoiled the rotund netminder's stellar performance. Bob Nevin, Tim Horton and Ron Stewart scored the third-period markers to give Toronto a 4-2 win. Dave Keon had given Toronto a 1-0 lead in the first. Bill Hicke and Gilles Tremblay scored for the Habs in the game, which was quite nasty at times—Jean Beliveau rammed Toronto's Red Kelly into the boards in the opening period, cutting the Leaf for five stitches over the left eye and forcing him out of the game with a minor concussion. Beliveau was given a five-minute major on the play. Worsley was especially sharp in the first period when he made several sparkling saves, but the Leafs' Johnny Bower was equal to the task in the Toronto net when the Canadiens enjoyed a two-man advantage twice during the game. Horton played a terrific game on defence for the Leafs and scored the winning goal on a Leaf power-play when his screened shot from the point eluded Worsley. Nevin, adding one assist to his goal, and Bob Pulford (two assists) also played strong games for Toronto.

OCTOBER 30, 1963
Toronto 6 Montreal 3 @ Maple Leaf Gardens

In a penalty-filled contest at the Gardens, the Leafs downed the Canadiens 6-3. Eddie Litzenberger (two goals in 1:26), Dave Keon, Eddie Shack, Gerry Ehman and Bob Pulford all counted markers for Toronto while Montreal responded with goals from Gilles Tremblay, J.C. Tremblay and Henri Richard. The main event of the evening was a brawl between Pulford (who took 17 penalty minutes on the night) and Montreal rookie Terry Harper in the second period. The two players started shoving behind the Toronto net and then engaged in spearing each other on the way to their respective benches.

Toronto's Eddie Litzenberger (#25) circles the net against Montreal defenceman J.C. Tremblay (#3). Litzenberger was picked up by the Leafs on waivers from Detroit in December 1961 as a utility forward. A lanky six-foot-three and 195 pounds, he had an excellent slap shot and could play any forward position. He helped Toronto to Cup wins in 1962 and 1963, but spent most of the 1963–64 season with Rochester of the AHL. He played in 19 games for the Leafs and scored two goals (both against Montreal in the same game) and made one appearance in the playoffs to earn his fourth straight Stanley Cup ring (he was captain of the Blackhawks when they won it in 1961). He never played in the NHL again and finished with 17 goals and 40 points in 114 games as a Maple Leaf. In 20 post-season games he had one goal and five points. Tremblay had five goals and 21 points in 1963–64.

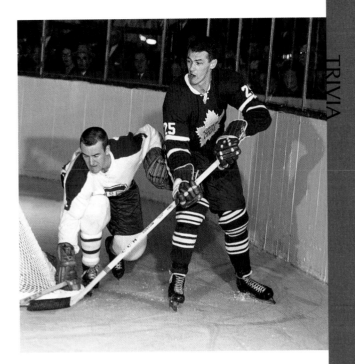

After dropping the gloves and going at it, the two continued to fight in the shared penalty box. Watching the extra action was league president Clarence Campbell, who was seated about 10 feet from the "sin bin." It took an hour and 20 minutes to play the second period, which also saw a goaltending change. Gump Worsley started in goal for the Canadiens but was injured with the Leafs up 2-0 and was replaced by Jean Guy Morissette, a senior hockey player for the Moncton Hawks a year ago, who gave up a goal (and four in total) on the first shot he

faced from Keon. Al Arbour was called up for this contest and he was paired with Tim Horton on the Leafs defence. Although he wore glasses, Arbour blocked a shot (a Beliveau shot that was heading for the top corner of the net) that helped set up a goal by Litzenberger. The game also saw a face-off between Red Berenson of the Canadiens and Red Kelly of the Leafs, who were both wearing helmets!

"He hit me in the penalty box while I was sitting down. I was surprised. But that's where I got my best licks in. I didn't do much on the ice. You can't play against these guys unless you carry your stick over your head because that's where they carry theirs."

Terry Harper (*The Toronto Star*, October 31, 1963)

"He hit me with his stick. I don't know if it was intentional but you know how it is, you lose your temper."

Bob Pulford (*The Toronto Star*, October 31, 1963)

Toronto defenceman Al Arbour (#3) has to contend with the determined checking of Montreal's Henri Richard (#16). The Leafs claimed Arbour from Chicago during the intra-league draft in June 1961. Used primarily as a fifth defenceman, Arbour played in 52 games for Toronto in 1961–62 and had one goal and five assists. He also got into eight games in the '62 playoffs when the Leafs won the Cup against Chicago (he had been with the Blackhawks the previous year when they won the championship). From then on Arbour played most of the time in Rochester of the AHL, winning an award as the top defenceman, and on occasion for the Leafs (Kent Douglas and Larry Hillman took most of his playing time away). In 1963–64 he played in six games for Toronto and recorded one assist. Arbour was in the lineup the night Toronto won the Cup against Detroit in the 1964 playoffs, his only appearance in the post season. He was the only player in the NHL to wear glasses and it did not stop him from attempting to block shots! The 1963–64 season was not a good one for Richard, who only scored 14 times and recorded 53 points.

Canadiens and Maple Leafs battled to a 2-2 draw on November 13. Montreal had not beaten Toronto in the past nine meetings between the clubs and only once in the past 13 meetings if playoffs are included. The point put the Leafs eight points back of league-leading Chicago and two behind the Canadiens. The Leafs needed a third-period goal from Dick Duff with less than seven minutes to play to earn the tie. Toronto took only 16 shots at Montreal goalie Charlie Hodge, although they took a 1-0 lead in the game on a goal by Bob Baun in the second period. Montreal scored both their goals while shorthanded and only 1:09 apart on efforts by Red Berenson and J.C. Tremblay (while Dave Balon served a five-minute major penalty). The game attracted only 12,845 fans to the Forum, 833 short of capacity. There was concern that televising mid-week games was hurting attendance.

NOVEMBER 13, 1963
Montreal 2 Toronto 2 @ The Forum

In a rather listless effort by both teams, the

NOVEMBER 20, 1963
Montreal 3 Toronto 1 @ Maple Leaf Gardens

The Canadiens scored a goal in each period and

got great goaltending from Charlie Hodge early in the game to defeat the Maple Leafs 3-1. Toronto out-shot the Habs 13-3 in the first but Montreal got the only goal of the period by Bill Hicke. The Canadiens then took control of the game on goals by Terry Harper and Dave Balon. Dave Keon got the lone Leaf goal in the second period to make it 2-1 after taking a perfect pass

from Tim Horton and whipping a hard shot home. The Leafs were generally confused and disorganized, especially after Balon restored Montreal's two-goal lead in the third. Balon picked up a Ralph Backstrom pass, came in on a screened Johnny Bower and deposited a high drive into the Leaf net. Toronto winger Dick Duff was one of the few feisty Leafs as he tangled with Bryan Watson and Claude Larose. The Leafs were roundly booed as the bell sounded to end the game.

Montreal's Dave Balon (#20) tries to put a shot past Toronto goalie Johnny Bower (#1) with Bob Baun (#21) attempting to check him. In 1963–64, Balon enjoyed a fine season with 24 goals and 42 points as the Canadiens rescued him from the New York Rangers in a June 1963 trade. Although he was not a great skater, Balon was a valued support player for the team in the four seasons he was in Montreal. Balon stayed with the Canadiens until 1967 when the Minnesota North Stars claimed him in the expansion draft. In 266 games as a Hab, Balon scored 56 goals and 56 assists in the regular season and had nine points in 35 playoff games. He was on two Cup winners with Montreal (1965 and 1966).

"We're falling apart and something has to be done about it. There are no untouchables on this team and I'll move any player from first to last. I'm not going to panic at this stage but I'll be making some moves."

Punch Imlach (*The Toronto Star*, November 21, 1963)

"You wonder about all the guys before you get there and then find out they're as good as the pals you left behind."

Dave Balon on being traded to Montreal (Maple Leaf game program, March 7, 1964)

Don Simmons — a closer look

"We lacked drive, didn't want to win enough. We missed John Ferguson — he's our policeman — and Henri Richard out there. And Simmons was good when he had to be."

Toe Blake (*The Toronto Star*, December 5, 1963)

"You could have played goal out there. Give credit where it belongs — to our defencemen. They did the big job, I had a soft evening."

Don Simmons (*The Toronto Star*, December 5, 1963)

Goalie Don Simmons (#24) makes a save against Henri Richard of the Canadiens in front of the net. Simmons became a Leaf because Punch Imlach knew what the left-handed-catching netminder could do from his days in the Boston organization where the goalie had taken the Bruins to the finals on two occasions. Imlach made it clear he was to give starter Johnny Bower a rest from time to time and Simmons would fill in during any injuries. Simmons was in net the night the Leafs won the Cup in 1962. He played in 28 games in 1962–63 and made 20 appearances in 1963–64, his last season as a Leaf. He earned three shutouts in 1963–64 (including one against Montreal), but is best remembered that season for allowing all the goals in Boston's 11-0 win over Toronto on January 18, 1964. His final record with the Leafs shows 28 wins, 21 losses and seven ties, with a 2-1 record in the playoffs.

DECEMBER 4, 1963
Toronto 3 Montreal 0 @ Maple Leaf Gardens

Toronto goaltender Don Simmons earned his 19th career shutout as the Maple Leafs blanked the Canadiens 3-0. It was not an especially difficult game for Simmons but he did have to make good saves against Bobby Rousseau, Dave Balon, Jean Guy Talbot and Ralph Backstrom. The 13,740 fans in attendance saw the Leafs get goals from Bob Baun, Dick Duff and Allan Stanley. Frank Mahovlich had two assists for the Leafs and was very aggressive throughout the game. Duff's goal was the best of the evening when he burst through the Montreal defence. Although his initial drive was stopped by Charlie Hodge, he put the rebound past the Canadiens netminder to make the score 2-0. Baun not only got the first goal of the game but also led the Leafs in hits with 11, while defensive partner Carl Brewer had seven.

DECEMBER 18, 1963
Montreal 7 Toronto 3 @ The Forum

The line of Jean Beliveau, Bernie Geoffrion and Gilles Tremblay paced the Montreal Canadiens to a 7-3 win over the Maple Leafs on home ice. Beliveau scored twice and Geoffrion and Tremblay (who added three assists) counted singles as the line combined for 10 scoring points in total. Henri Richard got two goals as well, while J.C. Tremblay added another for the winners. Montreal outshot the visitors 41-19 on the game as they blitzed the Leafs right from the outset. Jim Pappin, George Armstrong and Frank Mahovlich did manage to beat Charlie Hodge in the Montreal net. The Leafs were missing defenceman Carl Brewer and only used rearguard Kent Douglas on the power-play. On two occasions Toronto came within a goal of tying the contest but the Flying Frenchmen were far too strong in this game. Beliveau's markers gave him 14 on the season to go along with 28 assists in 29 games played. He was tied with Stan

When the 1963–64 season ended, Jean Beliveau was fourth all-time in game-winning goals in the regular season with 58. The others ahead of him were Gordie Howe (97), Maurice Richard (83) and Bernie Geoffrion (73).

TRIVIA

Mikita of Chicago for the NHL lead in points with 42. The crowd of 13,074 was the largest gathering since mid-week games had been televised but it was still about 600 short of capacity.

JANUARY 8, 1964
Toronto 6 Montreal 1 @ Maple Leaf Gardens

Frank Mahovlich was the outstanding player of the game as the Maple Leafs handed the Canadiens just their second loss in ten games with a 6-1 drubbing. Mahovlich scored the winner (his 17th of the season) when he took the puck from Montreal defenceman J.C. Tremblay near the face-off circle, chased down the loose

Jean Beliveau gets crunched into the boards by Toronto's Tim Horton (#7) with Red Kelly (#4) looking to take the puck away. Beliveau won the Hart Trophy as the NHL's best player for the second time in his career in 1963–64 when he had 78 points (28 goals and 58 assists) in 68 games. He was named to the second all-star team (the first team spot went to Stan Mikita of Chicago) and the Canadiens badly missed their captain when he missed some games against Toronto in the playoffs. Horton was determined to be a first-team all-star in 1963–64 and was the only non-Blackhawk to be named to the squad with nine goals and twenty-nine points. He was also runner-up to Chicago's Pierre Pilote for the Norris Trophy. Kelly scored just 11 goals in the season and took a couple of notable hits from Beliveau during the season.

Toronto's Frank Mahovlich (#27) raises his stick after beating Charlie Hodge (#1) in the Canadiens net. Mahovlich saw his goal production drop to 26 in 1963–64 and his point total dip to 55 in 70 games played. The Big M would have problems with his coach the rest of his days in Toronto and the fans were quite critical at times. However, his goal total of 143 was second only to Bobby Hull's 151 when the last four years were considered (1960–61 to the end of 1963–64).

puck and avoided another check. He then beat Charlie Hodge in the Montreal net with an effortless flip from about ten feet in front giving him nine goals in his last ten games. The Big M also added three assists in the game, which saw the Leafs also get goals from Red Kelly, Jim Pappin, Dave Keon (his 12th of the year), Bob Pulford (his first in 16 games) and Carl Brewer. Johnny Bower made 27 saves in the Toronto net and was only beaten by Henri Richard. The 14,036 fans in attendance saw an entertaining game for the most part, but when the Leafs made it 4-1, the pace slacked considerably. The

win moved the Leafs into a second-place tie with the Habs, just three points behind Chicago, who led the league with 49 points.

JANUARY 22, 1964
Montreal 3 Toronto 0 @ Maple Leaf Gardens

Charlie Hodge made 32 saves as the Canadiens shut out the Maple Leafs 3-0 before 14,028 fans at the Gardens. Hodge got the first star of the game and a large ovation from the crowd, who were angry at the Leafs for their second straight shutout loss at home. The win moved the Habs into a first-place tie with Chicago while the Leafs remained three points back of the leaders. The Canadiens had their skating game going and got first-period goals from Gilles Tremblay and Henri Richard. A third-period tally by Dave Balon ended the scoring when he lifted a backhander over Leafs goalie Don Simmons. The Canadiens effectively checked the Leafs at every turn and Hodge brought his goals-against average down to

2.28. It was the seventh time this season that the Leafs had been shut out—almost half their losses (15) to date.

JANUARY 29, 1964
Montreal 2 Toronto 1 @ The Forum

A lucky goal by Bobby Rousseau late in the third period gave the Canadiens a 2-1 win over the Leafs on January 29. A bouncing puck struck Rousseau's chest and went past Toronto goaltender Johnny Bower after the Canadiens winger had tried to rap home a Gilles Tremblay rebound. The Leafs opened the scoring in the second period when Jim Pappin scored his ninth goal of the season, but Dave Balon tied it with his 19th of the year just before the period ended. Bower and Hodge each faced 31 shots, and once again the diminutive Canadiens goaltender was named the first star of the game. Jean Beliveau once again ran at the Leafs' Red Kelly much as he had in an earlier meeting.

Toronto also got a look at the latest Montreal hot prospect in Yvan Cournoyer, who acquitted himself very well. The win gave Montreal sole possession of first place in the league standings and was viewed by 13,923 fans—the largest crowd of the season at the Forum.

FEBRUARY 5, 1964
Montreal 2 Toronto 0 @ Maple Leaf Gardens

Bobby Rousseau had the winner at the mid-way mark of the first period as the Canadiens once

Montreal goaltender Charlie Hodge stops a Toronto attack led by Tim Horton (#7) and Bob Pulford. With Jacques Plante traded and Gump Worsley injured, Hodge became the Habs number-one goalie in 1963–64 and he played in a career-high 62 games. He led the NHL with eight shutouts, including a remarkable four against the Maple Leafs (adding another in the playoffs versus Toronto). Hodge earned the Vezina Trophy with his 2.26 goals-against average.

During the Sixties, only one player scored five goals in one game. Bobby Rousseau accomplished the feat when he scored five times against Detroit's Roger Crozier on February 1, 1964, in a 9-3 Canadiens win at the Forum. The Montreal winger scored one in the first, two in the second and a couple in the third (the last two coming 59 seconds apart). In the Seventies, five players scored five goals in one game, while in the Eighties 15 players were able to pot five in a single contest.

Montreal's Bobby Rousseau (#15) skates in front of the Leaf net occupied by Johnny Bower with Bob Baun giving chase. Rousseau made quite an impression as a rookie in the 1961–62 season when he scored 21 times and totalled 45 points to win the Calder Trophy as the league's top rookie. He followed that with 19 markers the next season and in 1963–64 he scored 25 goals and totalled 56 points. On the small side, Rousseau was gifted with speed and agility. He relied on his accurate shot when he got himself into scoring position. Rousseau had two game-winning goals against Toronto in 1963–64.

Early in the 1963–64 season, Bobby Rousseau purchased the pocket-sized issue (at a cost of 60 cents) of Norman Vincent Peale's book, *The Power of Positive Thinking,* while the Canadiens were on an exhibition road trip visiting Fort Wayne, Indiana. Rousseau tended to worry—he had ulcers while playing for Hull–Ottawa in the EPHL—and was looking for an edge to keep him in the NHL (two of his brothers had not made it with the Canadiens). Two months after he purchased the book he scored five goals in one game. Toronto coach Punch Imlach was also a believer in Peale's message and he gave a copy of the book to each of his players.

again shut out the Leafs with a 2-0 win on Gardens ice. The speedy Montreal winger scored his 19th goal of the year when he re-directed Ted Harris's shot from the blueline past Johnny Bower from about five feet in front of the net. (Harris was called up from the minors to replace the injured Jean Guy Talbot.) Montreal put the game away when Gilles Tremblay scored his 19th of the season when he converted a two-on-one break with Henri Richard late in the third. Leaf coach Punch Imlach, at the end of his rope trying to get more goals from his injury-plagued team, benched wingers Dick Duff and Bob Nevin

at various points in the game. Kelly was also dropped back to defence in an effort to gain more attack. The shutout was the second for Canadiens goaltender Charlie Hodge against the Leafs so far this season.

FEBRUARY 12, 1964
Montreal 4 Toronto 0 @ The Forum

Bernie Geoffrion scored his 364th and 365th career goals as the Canadiens whipped the Leafs 4-0 on February 12. The two markers scored by

In his last season with the Canadiens, Bernie Geoffrion (#5) still managed to score 21 goals and 39 points in just 55 games during the 1963–64 season. The long-time star was slowing down but he could still score some important goals and had a hand in defeating the Leafs twice in February 1964. Geoffrion left the NHL after the 1963–64 season (to coach the Quebec Aces in the AHL) but returned two years later (1966–67) with the New York Rangers. The Maple Leafs were also interested in acquiring Geoffrion's playing rights, but the Rangers had first claim.

the Montreal winger placed him in a third-place tie with Ted Lindsay for the most all-time goals

(Gordie Howe and Maurice Richard held down the first two spots). Even though the Leafs had little going in the way of attack, the game remained scoreless until Geoffrion poked home a loose puck Toronto goalie Johnny Bower thought he had covered. It was Geoffrion's seventh game-winner of the season and he added his second goal on the power-play in the third when a screened shot eluded Bower. Gilles Tremblay and Dave Balon rounded out the scoring for Montreal who shut out the Leafs for the third time this season. Charlie Hodge earned the shutout in goal by making 31 saves while Bower faced 40 Hab shots. In desperation, Leaf coach Punch Imlach sent

During the early sixties, Maple Leaf road games were shown in movie theatres. In the first year of this experiment, 33 games played to a 92 percent capacity at one location. The idea then spread to nine theatres in the Southern Ontario region (six in the Toronto area) for the 1963–64 season. About 27,000 fans paid between $2.00 and $2.50 to watch the games. The theatres could hold from 800 to 1,500 people and the Leafs got a percentage of the gate.

During the 1963–64 season, CHUM radio in Toronto (1050 AM) came up with the "Chum Witch," a promotional gimmick that had Phyllis Shea (a night club entertainer originally from Calgary) dressed up as a witch and putting "hexes" on the Leafs' opposition while acting as a charm for the Toronto club. She made her first appearance on February 15, 1964, at the Gardens and the Leafs beat Chicago 4-1. The team was slumping in the month of February and her win gave the promotion a tremendous boost. The witch (she wore the traditional garb) became quite popular with fans, players and the very superstitious coach. Her record was 11-2-1 at games where the witch made an appearance and she made an important "contribution" in the playoffs when the Leafs won the Cup.

A CLOSER LOOK

out five defencemen on a Leaf power-play but to no avail. The Habs had only lost one of their last nine games, while Toronto had won only two of their last fourteen games.

FEBRUARY 26, 1964
Montreal 1 Toronto 0 @ The Forum

Bernie Geoffrion was the hero once again as he got the only goal of the game (his 17th of the season) in the Canadiens' 1-0 win over the Maple Leafs. The 33-year-old winger almost missed the game with a throat infection but decided to play that afternoon. Geoffrion's goal came in the middle stanza when the Leafs failed to clear the puck from in front of goalie Johnny Bower. Charlie Hodge earned his sixth shutout of the season (and his fourth against Toronto) by stopping 29 Leaf shots on goal. Toronto captain George Armstrong twice had Hodge at his mercy but rang both shots off the post. Hodge has not allowed a Leaf goal in 217 minutes and 55 seconds and only one in 300 minutes of play between the two teams. Imlach tried more shuffling of his lines to get some goal scoring against the very stingy Canadiens, but little worked except for some fireworks and a near goal from Eddie Shack.

MARCH 11, 1964
Toronto 1 Montreal 0 @ Maple Leaf Gardens

The Leafs finally broke off a five-game losing streak against the Canadiens and winger Frank Mahovlich got the only goal in a 1-0 Toronto victory. The Big M's marker (his 23rd on the year) came in the opening frame and was the first Toronto goal against Montreal goaltender Charlie Hodge in 226 minutes and 41 seconds. Mahovlich's goal came as he deflected a Tim Horton shot from the point while a delayed penalty was being called on Montreal's Terry Harper, who had bashed the Leafs' Andy Bathgate into the boards. In spite of the goal, Hodge was still the first star of the evening, stopping 25 shots (many of them difficult) and received a standing ovation from the 14,041 spectators on hand (Mahovlich was booed by some fans as the third star of the game). Johnny Bower got the shutout for Toronto by making 26 saves and survived a cut lip from the stick of Canadiens forward Gilles Tremblay. Ron Ellis played in the contest for the Leafs, as the 19-year-old junior star was placed on a line with Red Kelly and Mahovlich. The win was very important to Toronto, which moved four points up on fifth-place Detroit.

"I'm going to make up for the last couple of years. I have my confidence back and the club has confidence in me, too. Sure, I heard the rumours about being traded but it didn't happen so I must be wanted here. I'll score 30 goals."

Bernie Geoffrion, prior to the start of the 1963–64 season (*Hockey World*, October 1966)

Gordon "Red" Berenson

"The Canadiens tried to get me to turn pro four years ago. I didn't think I could make it in pro hockey and I figured a college education would be more beneficial at the time. I was offered scholarships to Denver and North Dakota universities [before switching to the University of Michigan]."

Red Berenson (*Hockey Illustrated*, December 1962)

Toronto's Andy Bathgate (#9) tracks down Gordon "Red" Berenson (#24 in the blue helmet) for possession of the puck. The Maple Leafs acquired Bathgate (along with Don McKenney) late in the 1963–64 season from the New York Rangers. He contributed 18 points in 15 games (three goals, fifteen assists) and scored some important goals (five in total) in the playoffs, including the Stanley Cup winner in game seven of the finals. It would be the only Cup win for the Hall of Fame player, who had a distinguished career as a Ranger. Bathgate would only play in 70 career games for the Leafs but would notch 63 points (19 goals, 44 assists). Berenson played in 69 games for the Habs in 1963–64 and scored seven goals and sixteen points. In 136 career games with Montreal, Berenson scored 14 times and totalled 37 points.

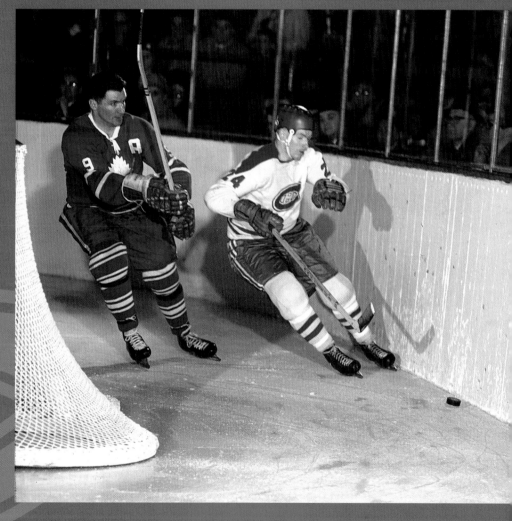

A CLOSER LOOK

Red Berenson attended the University of Michigan on a hockey scholarship and he watched the Montreal Canadiens play the Detroit Red Wings at the Olympia one night in 1958. He saw Maurice Richard score a goal right off the face-off and instantly became a fan of the Rocket and of the classy Canadiens. In 1962, one night after taking his team to the final round of the NCAA tournament, Berenson was playing for Montreal. He recorded one goal and two assists in four games to complete the 1961–62 season.

MARCH 18, 1964
Montreal 2 Toronto 2 @ The Forum

The final meeting of the season between the Leafs and Canadiens was a sometimes nasty affair that ended in a 2-2 tie. Montreal forward Bill Hicke opened the scoring in the game when he put a 20-footer past Johnny Bower after taking a set-up from rookie Andre Boudrias, who was up for one game with the Canadiens after recording 98 assists with his junior club. The Habs went up 2-0 on a goal from Claude Provost but Toronto came back with tallies by Don McKenney and George Armstrong to even the score. Eddie Shack was at his trouble-making best for the Maple Leafs when he tangled with John Ferguson and eventually got into a fight with Terry Harper. The tie meant that the Leafs were unbeaten in four games and were moving closer to clinching third place, while Montreal was still one point ahead of Chicago with two games to play in the regular schedule.

playoffs

SERIES A – MONTREAL VS. TORONTO
MARCH 26, 1964
Montreal 2 Toronto 0 @ The Forum

In a game that featured an NHL playoff-record 31 penalties, the Canadiens edged the Leafs 2-0 to take the first game of the series. Montreal got goals from Ralph Backstrom and Bernie Geoffrion to earn the win while Charlie Hodge

Frank Mahovlich (#27) tangles with Montreal defenceman Terry Harper (#19). Mahovlich was outstanding in the second game of the semi-final series against the Canadiens, a 2-1 Toronto victory. Assigned to play centre, Mahovlich was all over the ice and was very physical throughout the game.

got the shutout. Most of the penalties occurred in the first period when referee Frank Udvari was consistently thumbing players to the penalty box. In fact, there was mass confusion at the timekeeper's gate when Geoffrion opened the scoring in the first period and Udvari disallowed the goal initially because a Leaf player was not allowed back on the ice at the proper time. But he reversed his decision and the score stood. Montreal was short two men in the third period but the Leafs were unable to penetrate the Montreal defence. The previous record for most penalties in a playoff game was 29, set in 1952 in a game between Toronto and Detroit.

MARCH 28, 1964
Toronto 2 Montreal 1 @ The Forum

Led by the stellar work of Frank Mahovlich, the Leafs bounced back to take the second game of the series by a slim 2-1 score. In one of his greatest performances as a Maple Leaf to date, Mahovlich seemed to find new life when he was assigned to play at centre. The Toronto star set up the first goal of the game by Red Kelly and then scored the eventual game winner himself. Both Leaf goals came in the first period and the

"The second game [of the 1964 semi-finals against Montreal] was one of the best I ever played in the playoffs. I scored a goal and assisted on another. We won the game 2-1."

Frank Mahovlich (*Hockey Illustrated*, December 1964)

"[That was] his best game in the past three years."

Punch Imlach on Frank Mahovlich (*The Montreal Gazette*, March 30, 1964)

Canadiens were only able to reply with a Jean Beliveau goal in the second stanza. The game also featured some heavy hitting, including Montreal defenceman Jacques Laperriere running at Mahovlich. Both players crashed to the ice on impact and Mahovlich was able to brace himself at the last moment. Bob Baun of Toronto nailed Claude Provost with a devastating bodycheck, while Allan Stanley caught Dave Balon with his head down. Gilles Tremblay suffered a broken leg in the game and would be lost to the Canadiens for the rest of the playoffs. Mahovlich, Kelly and Montreal netminder Charlie Hodge were named as the three stars.

MARCH 31, 1964
Montreal 3 Toronto 2 @ Maple Leaf Gardens

In a shocking turn of events, the Canadiens scored two goals late (the last at 19:23) in the third period to pull out a 3-2 win on March 31. Henri Richard could hardly believe his luck when Toronto defenceman Allan Stanley put the puck right on his stick in the final minute of play. At first the Montreal centreman was going to shoot right away, but when he saw goalie Johnny Bower back up in his net, Richard went for the deke and made no mistake for his 17th career post-season tally. J.C. Tremblay scored the tying goal for the Habs in the 17th minute of the third period after teammate Bill Hicke took the puck away from Red Kelly of the Leafs, who was attempting a clearing pass. Tremblay let a screened shot go that Bower never saw and the

entire Montreal bench emptied to congratulate him. Toronto got two goals from Bob Pulford, who was celebrating his 28th birthday, while Claude Provost had the other Montreal goal. Dave Balon of Montreal had a strong game and knocked Leaf defender Bob Baun into a wobbly state with a hit in the first minute of play.

APRIL 2, 1964
Toronto 5 Montreal 3 @ Maple Leaf Gardens

Frank Mahovlich was once again the star for the Leafs with two goals and three assists as Toronto evened the series with a 5-3 win on home ice. The first of the Big M's goals came on a rebound from a Red Kelly drive and the second was an easy rap-in of a Don McKenney pass. Toronto also capitalized on four Montreal penalties and got goals from George Armstrong, Red Kelly and Andy Bathgate in the contest. Montreal stayed close most of the way with goals from J.C. Tremblay (his patented 70-foot blooper that bounced 10 feet in front of the Leaf net before going in), Jean Beliveau and Jacques Laperriere (a shorthanded effort). However, the Leafs were very determined not to blow a lead in this game and coasted home with a two-goal cushion. The game featured a couple of notable fights, one in the first and one in the third. The first-period brawl featured a tussle between Henri Richard and Eddie Shack. The Leaf winger ended up giving the Habs centre a head butt that opened up a cut over Richard's right eye. While this fight was going on, Toronto's Ron Stewart was getting

"But we are not giving it back to them. We will take it and the Stanley Cup too if we have to win all the games this way."

Toe Blake (*The Montreal Gazette*, April 1, 1964)

"They didn't win the game, we gave it to them. But what can you say? My best two players in the first two periods, Kelly and Stanley, each made goofs in the final minutes and it cost us the game."

Punch Imlach (*The Montreal Gazette*, April 1, 1964)

the best of Dave Balon in another battle. The brawl was actually ignited by defenceman Carl Brewer, who had run Richard into the boards but received no penalty. In the third period, Stewart got into another scrap with Montreal enforcer John Ferguson with just five seconds to play. Beliveau hurt his knee when Shack put him into the boards with a hit. His status for future games was doubtful.

"It's their funeral if they want to tangle with 200 pounders when we outweigh them by 40 pounds."

Punch Imlach (*The Montreal Gazette*, April 3, 1964)

APRIL 4, 1964
Montreal 4 Toronto 2 @ The Forum

Montreal goaltender Charlie Hodge got the better of his Toronto counterpart Johnny Bower as the Habs took a 3-2 lead in the series with a 4-2 win on Saturday night. Bower had the opportunity to stop the first three Montreal goals but was beaten by a trio of Canadiens in the second period (the last goal was into an empty net in the third). Bobby Rousseau scored the winning goal after being set up by teammate Jim Roberts. The Habs were forced to shuffle their lineup with the injury suffered by captain Jean Beliveau (Gilles Tremblay was also out) and coach Toe Blake was credited with doing a masterful job. Claude Larose was called up as an emergency replacement and Ralph Backstrom was given first-line status in place of Beliveau. Toronto coach Punch Imlach was very displeased with the effort shown by his Maple Leafs. He was contemplating calling up Gerry Ehman and Eddie Litzenberger from the minors.

APRIL 7, 1964
Toronto 3 Montreal 0 @ Maple Leaf Gardens

Facing elimination, the Stanley Cup champs got

a great game from goaltender Johnny Bower and pulled out a 3-0 victory to even the series on April 7 before 14,417 fans. Bower bounced back from a poor game to make three great stops in the first period alone to keep the game scoreless. He made 25 saves on the night to record his third shutout in 123 post-season games. The Leafs responded by scoring twice in the second and once in the third to force a seventh game in Montreal. Don McKenney got the winner after some great work by Dave Keon, and Allan Stanley set him up for a couple of swipes at the puck. Bob Baun and Andy Bathgate scored the others. Baun's goal came as he escaped from the penalty box and took a pass that sent him in on a solo breakaway. He didn't get much of a shot away but it slid under Charlie Hodge to give the Leafs a 2-0 lead. The little Canadiens goalie made 29 stops during the game.

"I told them after the game, if they have the guts or determination or whatever you call it of a championship club, now is the time to prove it or forever hold their peace. I warned them it's going to be a long summer [if they don't]."

Punch Imlach (*The Montreal Gazette*, April 6, 1964)

APRIL 9, 1964
Toronto 3 Montreal 1 @ The Forum

Dave Keon scored all three goals and Johnny Bower was sensational in net as the Leafs edged the Canadiens 3-1 to advance to the Stanley Cup finals for the third straight year. Keon's first goal came at 8:22 of the first period after some good digging by George Armstrong and Don McKenney in the Canadiens end. The puck came back to Bob Baun at the point, who let a shot go that was stopped by Charlie Hodge, but

Keon rapped home the loose puck. With Toronto's Andy Bathgate off for hooking, Tim Horton broke up a Montreal rush at the blueline

Toronto's Don McKenney tries to find a spot in front of the Canadiens net but is closely watched by defenceman Terry Harper (#19). McKenney scored the winning goal in the sixth game of the series, won 3-0 by the Leafs. The smooth-skating McKenney had 12 points in 12 playoff games as he provided the scoring Punch Imlach was looking for when he acquired the veteran in a late-season deal with New York (McKenney suffered an injury in the finals and missed the last two games). As a Maple Leaf, McKenney played in 67 regular-season games and recorded 45 points (15 goals, 30 assists).

and Armstrong hit a hard-skating Keon with a pass. The slick centreman skated away from defenceman Jean Guy Talbot and beat Hodge with a nifty shot to the far side at 11:15 of the first. The game remained that way until the third period when Ralph Backstrom put the Habs on the board at 7:27 when he finally found a way to

> *"It would have been a miscarriage of justice if the Canadiens had beaten us."*
>
> Punch Imlach (*The Montreal Gazette*, April 10, 1964)

> *"I guess it just wasn't in the books for us to win. We had all those chances in the third period and just couldn't score."*
>
> Toe Blake (*The Montreal Gazette*, April 10, 1964)

get the puck past Johnny Bower in the Leaf net. Montreal did their utmost to tie the game, but Bower locked the door and Keon put one into the empty net to seal the win for Toronto before 14,541 disappointed fans. Bower was named the first star of the game while Hodge, who also played an outstanding game, was the second star. Keon got the third star of the game.

> *"That's the best hockey club I've ever beaten — I know we have a much better all-round team but they forced us to the limit and never quit."*
>
> George Armstrong (*The Montreal Gazette*, April 10, 1964)

Toronto's Dave Keon (#14) is about to put the puck past Montreal goalie Charlie Hodge at the Forum with defenceman J.C. Tremblay (#3) giving chase to the fast Leaf forward.

stanley cup finals

TORONTO VS. DETROIT

The Detroit Red Wings surprised the Chicago Blackhawks in seven games to set up a rematch with the Leafs for the Stanley Cup. A late goal (at 19:58 of the third) by Bob Pulford helped the Leafs pull out a 3-2 win in the opener, but Detroit tied the series on Larry Jeffrey's overtime winner in the second contest that gave the Red Wings a 4-3 win. Alex Delvecchio's goal late in the third game, (with just 17 seconds to go), gave Detroit the series lead, but the Leafs bounced back to take the next game 4-2 with a terrific effort from Andy Bathgate (who got the winner) and Dave Keon who scored twice. Goalie Terry Sawchuk was the difference back in Toronto for the fifth contest, won 2-1 by the Red Wings. Sawchuk stopped 32 Toronto shots and got goals by Gordie Howe and Eddie Joyal to get the win. The Leafs evened the series on Bob Baun's historic overtime tally, scored with a broken bone in his foot, and the 4-3 win forced the teams back to Toronto for a seventh game. It was tight for two periods, as only Bathgate was able to score (at 3:04 of the first), but the Leafs broke it open with three third-period markers (Keon, Red Kelly and George Armstrong) to take the Cup with a 4-0 victory.

Dave Keon picked a great time to score his first professional hat trick in the seventh game of the semi-finals against Montreal. He had not played very well in the series to that point, but perhaps his mind was occupied with the health of his father, who had just undergone surgery and was still lying in a hospital bed. Keon decided to dedicate the seventh game to his father and he came up with perhaps the most memorable performance of his career.

A CLOSER LOOK

Toronto's Allan Stanley (#26) battles Detroit's Norm Ullman (#7) for a loose puck. Both players scored in the second game of the 1964 finals won in overtime by Detroit 4-3. The goals by the two veterans had the score deadlocked at 1-1, but the Red Wings took a 3-1 lead into the third period. Toronto tied it on goals by Ron Stewart and Gerry Ehman but Larry Jeffrey scored at 7:52 of overtime to even the series at one game each. Stanley also recorded three assists in the series against Detroit, while Ullman had the same number of helpers for the Red Wings.

> *"This has to be one of my happiest moments, to come here [to Toronto] and eventually beat Detroit."*
>
> Red Kelly (Maple Leaf game program, February 16, 1966)

> *"Sure I perspire with [the helmet] but it is air conditioned and besides my doctor advised me to wear it. I don't put on my helmet or take it off for any superstitious reason."*
>
> Red Kelly (Maple Leaf game program, February 16, 1966)

TORONTO MAPLE LEAFS

WORLD CHAMPIONS
1963-64

STANLEY CUP WINNERS
1963-64

FRONT ROW, left to right: George "Punch" Imlach (Manager and Coach), George Armstrong (Captain), John Bassett (Chairman of the Board), C. Stafford Smythe (President), Harold Ballard (Executive Vice-President), Bob Pulford, Frank "King" Clancy (Assistant Manager-Coach).

SECOND ROW, left to right: Johnny Bower, Ron Stewart, Allan Stanley, Frank Mahovlich, Andy Bathgate, Tim Horton, Don Simmons.
THIRD ROW, left to right: Bob Haggert (Trainer), Dave Keon, Carl Brewer, Red Kelly, Bill Harris, Bob Baun, Tom Nayler (Assistant Trainer).
BACK ROW, left to right: Eddie Shack, Jim Pappin, Don McKenney, Larry Hillman.

Montreal's Claude Provost (#14) ended Toronto's hopes of a fourth straight Stanley Cup by scoring an overtime winner against Johnny Bower (#1) in the sixth game of the 1965 playoffs.

The Leafs–Canadiens Rivalry
1964–65

season summary

Although the Maple Leafs had won a third straight Stanley Cup, they had some new faces on the team to start the next season. The most significant addition was right winger Ron Ellis, who graduated from the junior champion Toronto Marlboros to join the big club. He tied Frank Mahovlich for most goals (23) and displayed a remarkable maturity as a rookie. Peter Stemkowski, another member of the Memorial Cup-champion Marlies, made 36 appearances for the Leafs and scored five goals. Don Simmons was dropped as the back-up goalie and Terry Sawchuk was brought in to work with Johnny Bower, who was still going strong. Together they combined to win the Vezina Trophy, but the Leafs had trouble scoring goals. Gerry Ehman and Eddie Litzenberger were deleted, while Jim Pappin, Billy Harris and Don McKenney spent time in the minors. Duane Rupp, Brit Selby (still a junior) and Larry Hillman also had a quick look with the big club. Poor play along with an injury to Andy Bathgate and an illness to Mahovlich also plagued the Leafs during the season. Toronto talked Dickie Moore out of retirement but he could only play in 38 regular-season games and scored just two goals. The Toronto club slipped back to fourth place with a 30-26-14 record and finished two points behind Chicago.

For a cost of $1.00 hockey fans in Toronto and Montreal could buy calendars that highlighted the regular-season hockey schedule and events at Maple Leaf Gardens and the Forum respectively. The calendars were a great promotional item for the arenas and the teams. The Leaf calendar featured all the major championship-winning teams and they could be spotted predominantly in barber shops. In 1964–65 the print run for the Gardens calendar was 100,000 and for the Forum it was 200,000. The hockey calendar was the brainchild of hockey executive Frank Selke back in the 1930s.

In Montreal there were few changes to start the season, but long-time star Bernie Geoffrion decided to retire. Charlie Hodge (52 games) and Gump Worsley (18 games) split the goaltending chores, while a tough defender named Ted Harris joined the Montreal blueline, as did Noel Picard (for 16 games). Yvan Cournoyer played in 55 games as a rookie, scoring seven goals, while Jim Roberts and Claude Larose were now regulars. Gilles Tremblay missed most of the season with a broken leg, suffered in a game against the Leafs. The Canadiens did not win the regular-season title in '64–65, as the Red Wings edged them out by four points (87 to 83), but they still posted a healthy 36 wins to go along with 11 ties. However, the Canadiens were not especially concerned about the Prince of Wales Trophy; they wanted to see if they could take back the Cup, which had eluded them for five years. The loyal Hab supporters were wondering if they could get by the champion Leafs in the playoffs. A 7-4-3 record against Toronto in the season was a source of inspiration, as was the fact that the Leafs were aging and perhaps overworked by their coach.

For the third straight year the two teams met in the playoffs and this time the Canadiens finished off a stubborn Leaf team in six games. It looked like it might be easy for the Habs when they won the first two games of the series, but the Toronto club had the pride of a champion and did not go down without a fight. It took an overtime goal in the sixth game at the Gardens to end the Leaf reign and put the Stanley Cup within sight (although the Habs lost all-star defenceman Jacques Laperriere with a broken ankle in the last game against Toronto). It took all seven games and home ice advantage to do it, but eventually the Canadiens prevailed, led by their great captain, Jean Beliveau. Five years without a Cup win in Montreal seemed like an eternity, but the rebuilding Habs had now won the first of what has come to be known as their "Quiet Dynasty."

OCTOBER 28, 1964
Montreal 5 Toronto 2 @ Maple Leaf Gardens

Claude Larose scored two goals, including the winner, as the Canadiens won the first meeting of the season against the Maple Leafs with a convincing 5-2 win. The Habs used three power-play markers to subdue the Leafs and also got goals from Ralph Backstrom, Claude Provost and Bobby Rousseau. Don McKenney opened the scoring for the Leafs and Ron Ellis tied the game at 2-2, but then Larose got hot and popped in two consecutive goals past Johnny Bower. The Canadiens winger scored the winner when he was left alone in front of the Toronto net and Larose converted a Rousseau pass into a goal. Backstrom was the best player on the night and was given a great ovation from the 14,006 fans in attendance when he was announced as the first star. The forward line of Larose, Rousseau and Gilles Tremblay was the most effective trio in the game and Tremblay recorded three assists for the Habs. The Leafs generally performed sluggishly after playing a rough contest in Chicago the previous evening (a 3-2 win). Montreal outshot the Leafs 39-31.

NOVEMBER 5, 1964
Montreal 2 Toronto 2 @ The Forum

A late second-period goal by defenceman Jean Guy Talbot lifted the Canadiens into a 2-2 tie with the Maple Leafs in the first meeting of the season at the Forum. The tying goal came on a three-man break after a great save by Canadiens goalie Charlie Hodge. Henri Richard, playing in his first game of the season, scored his first of the year to make it 1-0 on a Montreal power-play. The Pocket Rocket took a pass from Jean Beliveau 10 feet in front of Toronto goalie Terry Sawchuk and made no mistake to score his 199th career goal. He then had to leave the contest with a recurrence of his groin injury. Carl Brewer managed to get off a 30-foot shot that

Toronto's Carl Brewer (#2) keeps close tabs on Henri Richard (#16) of Montreal. For the second time in his career, Brewer led the NHL in penalty minutes with 177 in 1964–65. In addition to his rambunctious style, Brewer also earned a selection to the second all-star team with a four-goal, twenty-seven-point season. It would be Brewer's last full season in a Leaf uniform in the Sixties, as his dislike of coach Punch Imlach grew too intense for him to remain in Toronto. As well, Brewer was never content with his contractual arrangements. He had held out prior to the 1963–64 season as a broken arm was healing, and threatened to enroll at the University of Toronto to complete his education (he had thoughts about becoming a teacher) when he could not come to terms with the Leafs. He was eventually signed, but two seasons later he would walk away from the team.

caught the far corner of the net to tie the score. Rookie Ron Ellis gave Toronto a 2-1 lead with his sixth of the season (two behind NHL leader Bobby Hull of Chicago) when he used Montreal defenceman Ted Harris as a screen to put a shot into the top corner of the net. This game marked the return of Dickie Moore to Montreal as a Maple Leaf and the Toronto winger received some polite applause when he stepped on the ice to start the game with Bob Pulford and Ron Stewart as linemates.

NOVEMBER 18, 1964
Toronto 3 Montreal 1 @ Maple Leaf Gardens

The Maple Leafs outplayed the Canadiens in every aspect of the game to take a 3-1 win and claim third place. The win moved Toronto to within one point of Montreal and just two behind league-leading Detroit. Bob Pulford scored the game winner on a shorthanded effort for the Leafs by having his shot deflect off defenceman Ted Harris and flip over the shoulder of goalie Charlie Hodge. Toronto goalie Terry Sawchuk received an assist on the play (the first point for any NHL goalie so far this season) and ran his unbeaten streak to six games. The Leafs nursed a 2-1 lead into the final

minute of play when Pulford scored his second of the game when he was set up by Ron Ellis. Eddie Shack played very well for the Leafs and set up a goal by Andy Bathgate that tied the game 1-1. John Ferguson opened the scoring in the game less than two minutes from the start of the contest. Ferguson was leading a three-on-one break and drove the puck into the short side off Sawchuk's glove. Toronto's Allan Stanley played in the game despite a broken toe.

DECEMBER 3, 1964
Montreal 4 Toronto 2 @ The Forum

The Canadiens scored four straight times after a scoreless first period and cruised to a 4-2 victory. Dave Balon opened the scoring in the second stanza when he tipped home a Claude Provost pass. Jean Beliveau upped the score to 2-0 when goalie Johnny Bower was out of position after stopping an Yvan Cournoyer blast on a Montreal

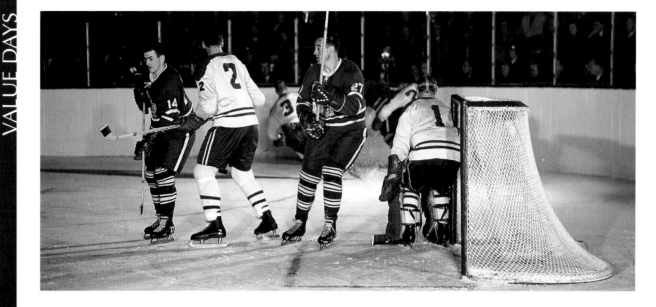

Frank Mahovlich (#27) and teammate Dave Keon (#14) are on the attack for the Leafs in the Canadiens end with Jacques Laperriere (#2) and goalie Charlie Hodge (#1) defending. Mahovlich returned to play for Toronto in December after missing nearly a month of action early in the 1964–65 season. Despite his off ice troubles, Mahovlich still managed to score 23 goals and add 51 points (both team high marks) in 59 games played. Keon had 21 goals and 50 points in 69 games in '64–65.

DECEMBER 9, 1964
Montreal 3 Toronto 2 @ Maple Leaf Gardens

In a game that featured the return of Frank Mahovlich to the Toronto lineup, the Canadiens skated away with a 3-2 victory. The Big M had been out for almost an entire month while he was being treated for stress-related problems. The Toronto crowd of 14,176 gave him a nice reception and he responded with a robust effort as he flattened Terry Harper and Claude Provost with thundering bodychecks. He nearly scored as well but was thwarted by goalie Charlie Hodge. Provost and Dave Balon made it 2-0 for the Habs before Ron Stewart (with his eighth) replied for the Leafs. Gilles Tremblay scored the eventual game winner in the second period when he stole the puck from Toronto defenceman Kent Douglas while the Leafs were on a power-play. Tremblay went in on a breakaway and put the puck under Terry Sawchuk in the Toronto goal. Don McKenney brought the Leafs closer in the third, but Hodge shut the door, as he often did when he played against Toronto. Hodge had to survive a butt-end administered by Eddie Shack, who crashed into the little goalie.

power-play. Bobby Rousseau scored in the third and then Jimmy Roberts added another on a shorthanded effort when Leafs coach Punch Imlach iced a forward line made up of defencemen Allan Stanley, Tim Horton and Bob Baun in the hopes of shaking things up. Just as Roberts scored, he was crushed into the boards by Baun who took a double minor and misconduct for his efforts. Terry Harper of the Canadiens moved in to show his displeasure with Baun and also earned a double minor and misconduct. The skirmish seemed to give the Leafs some life and Dave Keon scored his 100th career goal (his first in 16 games) on the still-active Leaf power-play. Ron Ellis scored his seventh of the year to make it 4-2. The Leafs continued to press but they could get no closer in the final seven minutes, as goalie Charlie Hodge was sharp.

"[Bobby] Hull may score more goals but no one will score them any better than Frank. He makes it look so easy."

Dave Keon on Frank Mahovlich (*Hockey Illustrated*, April 1968)

John Ferguson — a closer look

John Ferguson was recommended to the Canadiens by scout Floyd Curry and Montreal signed the left winger as a 25-year-old for a salary of $9,000 in 1963–64. His minor-league contract belonged to the Cleveland Barons of the AHL and he could just as easily have been sold to Boston or New York, who were also looking for new talent. The Canadiens did very well in signing Ferguson as he played on a line with Jean Beliveau in his rookie year and the Montreal captain won the Hart Trophy. In his second season, Ferguson played with Ralph Backstrom and the slick Canadiens centre returned to form with twenty-five goals in 1964–65 (after just eight in '63–64).

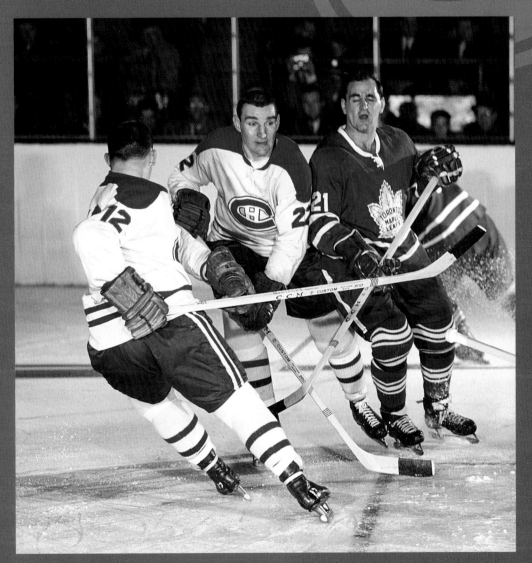

Montreal's John Ferguson (#22) tries to hold his position against Toronto's Bob Baun (#21), with Yvan Cournoyer (#12) looking away for the puck. Ferguson gave the Canadiens the toughness he was acquired for (281 penalty minutes in his first two years), but he also showed he could score with 18 goals as a rookie in 1963–64 and 17 in 1964–65. The hard-nosed left winger also totalled 89 points in his first couple of seasons in the NHL. Baun played in all 70 games in the 1964–65 season for the Leafs and did not score a goal (he did have 18 assists). In six playoff games in 1965, Baun recorded one assist.

> *"Ferguson did a very good job at left wing, more than anyone expected. He's a fine, rough, tough hockey player."*
>
> Punch Imlach on John Ferguson's rookie year
> (*Hockey Illustrated*, December 1964)

Ron Ellis, Gilles Tremblay
— a closer look

Ron Ellis was nicknamed "Chuvalo" because of his resemblance to Canadian heavyweight boxing champion George Chuvalo. One time, Toronto coach Punch Imlach asked Ellis if he minded being called by his nickname. "Not at all, Elmer," replied Ellis. (Maple Leaf program, December 9, 1967)

"He's young, strong and fast and he seems to have the ability to do everything a good hockey player should be able to do."

Toe Blake on Gilles Tremblay
(*Hockey Annual, 1964*)

Montreal's Gilles Tremblay (#21) is closely checked by Ron Ellis (#11) of Toronto. Ellis had a very impressive season as a rookie for the Leafs in 1964–65 when he scored 23 times and totalled 39 points in 62 games played. He had many good games against Montreal throughout the year and was involved in the play that ended Tremblay's season when the Canadiens winger broke his leg. Tremblay's season was reduced to just 26 games in which he scored nine goals and totalled sixteen points.

DECEMBER 17, 1964
Montreal 2 Toronto 2 @ The Forum

The Canadiens were forced to score two third-period goals to pull out a 2-2 tie, but their real loss was an injury to winger Gilles Tremblay. Toronto's Ron Ellis (a dominant Leaf on the night) nailed Tremblay with a solid shoulder hit and it sent the Habs player feet first into the end boards. The result was a broken leg that would sideline Tremblay for the rest of the season. The injury happened with just four minutes to play and came after John Ferguson and Jacques Laperriere had scored to even the contest. Frank Mahovlich in the first and Carl Brewer at 37 seconds of the third had given the Leafs a 2-0 lead. Brewer was caught making a bad change that led to Ferguson's goal and then Laperriere used defenceman Bob Baun as a screen to beat Johnny Bower with the tying goal. The two coaches tried to match lines all night, as Toronto wanted Bob Pulford out against Henri Richard. This battle was pretty much even, as Pulford played his usual strong-checking game and Richard still had a couple of great scoring chances.

DECEMBER 30, 1964
Montreal 4 Toronto 3 @ Maple Leaf Gardens

The Maple Leafs blew a two-goal lead for the third time in the last six games as the Canadiens won a tight game 4-3. The Leafs had won just four of their last fifteen games and had slipped back to fourth place in the league standings while Montreal vaulted over the Detroit Red Wings into first. Red Kelly and Dave Keon had given the Leafs a 2-0 lead with first-period goals. However, Montreal came back with four consecutive goals (two in the second by Claude Larose and Bobby Rousseau and a couple more in the third by John Ferguson and Jean Guy Talbot) to take a two-goal lead on a somewhat shaky Terry Sawchuk in the Leaf net. Ron Ellis rounded out the scoring with just 16 seconds to play with his team-leading 13th goal of the year. Both teams were missing key

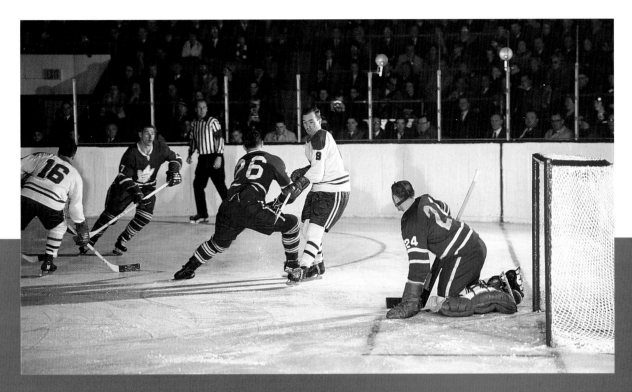

"If Duff plays anything like he used to play for Toronto, I don't see why he shouldn't help us. He was a good two-way player for the Leafs."

Toe Blake (Maple Leaf program, December 30, 1964)

Dick Duff (#8) made his first appearance at the Gardens with the Canadiens late in December 1964 and earned one assist against Toronto goalie Terry Sawchuk (#24) when teammate Bobby Rousseau scored. Montreal acquired the left winger from the New York Rangers in exchange for Bill Hicke after Duff had trouble adjusting to Broadway. In a more familiar hockey environment, Duff's career was revived in Montreal and he helped the Canadiens to four Stanley Cups (1965, 1966, 1968, 1969). In 305 career games with the Habs, Duff recorded 172 points (87 goals, 85 assists) in the regular season. He added an impressive 43 points in 60 playoff games for Montreal.

players (Jean Beliveau for Montreal and Andy Bathgate for Toronto) and the game marked the first time Dick Duff returned to Maple Leaf Gardens as a Canadien (earning an assist on Rousseau's goal). There were 14,682 fans in attendance but many of the grey seats were empty.

JANUARY 14, 1965
Toronto 5 Montreal 3 @ The Forum

Two goals from the stick of centreman Bob Pulford led the way as the Leafs finally won a game at the Forum with a 5-3 victory. Toronto rookie Peter Stemkowski scored his first NHL goal in the game and added two assists for the visitors, who extended their unbeaten streak to seven games (five wins, two ties). The win also moved the Leafs just one point behind the second-place Canadiens and three behind league-leading Chicago. Toronto took the lead in the contest on four occasions and also got tallies from Jim Pappin and Allan Stanley. Montreal goaltender Charlie Hodge had a rare bad night against the Leafs, allowing two goals in the second period on just five shots. The crowd of 14,866 fans quickly got on Hodge and began cheering his most routine saves. Toronto goalie Johnny Bower on the other hand was at his best, facing 43 shots in the game, 17 in the first period alone. John Ferguson and Claude Provost (with two) did manage to beat Bower in the second period but he stopped all 15 Montreal drives in the third. The Leafs were very physical in the contest and Pappin tangled with Claude Larose, while Pulford and Ferguson raised their sticks and roughed each other up in the third period. Ron Stewart also had an encounter with Larose before the game was over.

JANUARY 20, 1965
Montreal 2 Toronto 1 @ Maple Leaf Gardens

Former Leafs winger Dick Duff was credited with the winning goal for the Canadiens in the second period in a 2-1 win at the Gardens. Bobby Rousseau's pass banked off Duff's skate and into the net past goalie Johnny Bower at 7:50 of the middle frame. Three minutes earlier, the Canadiens had opened the scoring when Claude Larose converted a loose puck during a goalmouth scramble into a goal. Jim Pappin got that one back quickly for the Leafs when a Bob Baun blueline shot bounced in off the Toronto winger. The game featured some fast-paced action and the crowd of 14,357 wit-

nessed great goaltending by Gump Worsley (the first star of the game) and Bower. Baun and Tim Horton had some good hits during the game, which was not marred by any brawling. The Leafs dressing room was closed for several minutes after the game was over while in the Montreal quarters, injured captain Jean Beliveau was congratulating all of his teammates on their victory.

FEBRUARY 4, 1965
Toronto 5 Montreal 2 @ The Forum

The Maple Leafs set the tone early for this game by starting five defencemen and scoring a goal at the 10-second mark as they ran over the Canadiens 5-2. Tim Horton scored the opening goal on Gump Worsley in the Montreal net with an assist to fellow blueliner Bob Baun. But the Canadiens quickly tied it up at the one-minute

---

Toronto defenceman Allan Stanley (#26) manages to get the puck past Montreal netminder Charlie Hodge (#1) while being chased by blueliner J.C. Tremblay (#3). Stanley scored only two goals in 1964–65 and added 15 assists in 64 contests while playing in his 1,000th career game. Tremblay scored three times in 68 games and totalled 20 points in 1964–65. The numbers for both defenders were typical for this era.

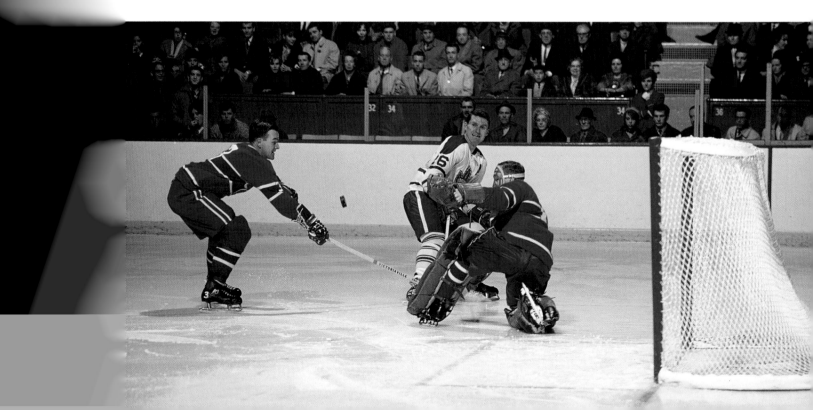

mark on a goal by Claude Larose (his first of two). However, that was only a minor setback for the Leafs, who scored the next four goals in the game when Andy Bathgate, George Armstrong, Dave Keon and Red Kelly all scored before the Canadiens got one back late in the third. Ten Toronto players earned points on the night and goalie Terry Sawchuk got his second assist of the season (and the fifth of his career). Toronto defenceman Carl Brewer led the physical assault by the Leafs on the Montreal forwards as he decked Dave Balon and John Ferguson with hard bodychecks. The 15,485 fans (the largest crowd of the year) on hand to see the contest were upset that their team was being manhandled by the Leafs. Only Ferguson and Larose (who now had 16 goals on the year, six against the Leafs) were willing to mix it up with the rambunctious Leafs.

FEBRUARY 10, 1965
Toronto 6 Montreal 2 @ Maple Leaf Gardens

In a brawl-filled contest, the Leafs got two goals from rookie Ron Ellis on the way to a 6-2 defeat of the visiting Canadiens. Toronto was ahead 3-0 when a second-period brawl broke out at the 5:54 mark. Toronto's Frank Mahovlich boarded Terry Harper, with the Leafs having an extra man on the ice (Bob Pulford) as the Habs were about to be called for a delayed penalty. Mahovlich battled Harper and Ted Harris, who got nailed with a great punch by the Big M, while Montreal enforcer John Ferguson was busy taking on Kent Douglas and then Peter Stemkowski. The big Leafs centre managed to pull Ferguson's sweater off and Douglas tossed it into the stands (it was returned by a Leafs fan who would have nothing to do with a Canadiens jersey). Ellis joined the battle on the ice by coming off the bench, as did Montreal's Claude Larose (although neither was

By the end of the evening of February 10 each team had been penalized 33 minutes by referee Bill Friday and fines for the brawling would total $475 for both clubs combined (any player coming off the bench was subject to a $25 fine as was anyone who received a misconduct). Seven Toronto players were fined, while thirteen Canadiens found themselves lighter in the pocket book.

VALUE DAYS

penalized). When Montreal coach Toe Blake noticed the Leafs had the extra man on, he signalled goalie Charlie Hodge to the bench and sent Jim Roberts over the boards. Both coaches then began designating players to go out, and by the time it was over, only Hodge was left on the Montreal bench while only four Leafs were not sent into the brawl (Carl Brewer, Red Kelly, Dave Keon and Andy Bathgate). After the 18-minute delay was over, Keon scored to make it 4-0. Ralph Backstrom and Ferguson got a couple of goals for the Canadiens in the third, but Kelly and Douglas scored for the Leafs to round out the scoring.

"You see the way I restrained my troops? Never lost my head at all when the fight started. I controlled most of my people."

Punch Imlach (*The Globe and Mail*, February 11, 1965)

MARCH 4, 1965
Montreal 2 Toronto 2 @ The Forum

Claude Provost scored his 25th goal of the season in the third period to salvage a 2-2 tie for the Canadiens against the visiting Maple Leafs. With

Bob Pulford — a closer look

Toronto's Bob Pulford (#20) is checked in front of the Canadiens net by Montreal's Ted Harris (#10). Pulford scored 19 times in 1964–65 and added 20 assists for the Leafs and had many good games against the Canadiens. Harris played 68 games with Montreal in 1964–65 and scored one goal and 14 assists while adding 107 penalty minutes as a rookie. The previous six seasons were spent in the minors, the last with Cleveland in the AHL where he was named the top defenceman, winning the Eddie Shore Award. Harris recorded 20 or more assists in the minors on four occasions, but in the NHL he decided to play a tough, defensive style that allowed him to keep up with the faster pace of game.

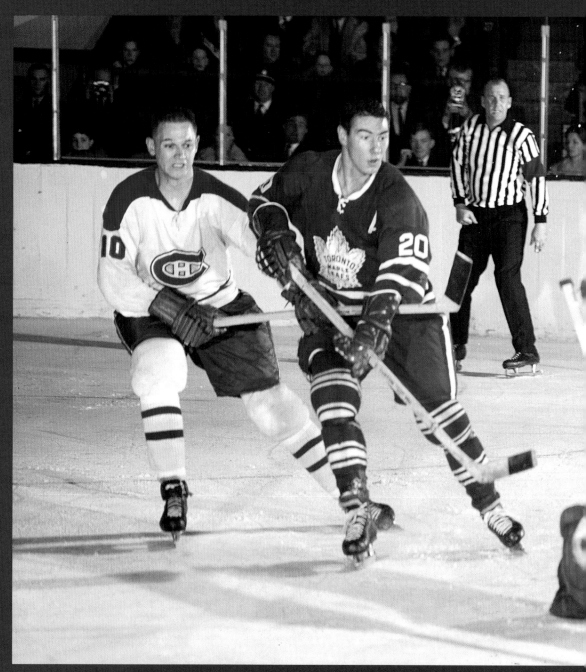

"His name always comes up in trades. But there are very few players I'd give him up for. Bob's my most honest hockey player … a hard worker and very valuable. He's always good in the playoffs where the real brilliance shows."

Punch Imlach (*Hockey Illustrated*, January 1965)

Toronto's Kent Douglas off for hooking, Provost knocked in a loose puck past goalie Terry Sawchuk by hanging around the Leaf net. The Leaf netminder stopped 31 of 33 shots, with Jean Beliveau getting the other Montreal goal in the second period. The Leafs got goals from Frank Mahovlich (their best player on the night while being double shifted) and Don McKenney, as they earned their first point in five games, good for fourth place, five points behind Detroit. Montreal's point brought them to within two of first-place Chicago. Gump Worsley was especially sharp for the Canadiens in goal despite playing for the first time in eight games.

Toronto's Red Kelly (#4) is foiled by Charlie Hodge of the Canadiens. Kelly scored 18 goals and 46 points in 1964–65 while playing in all 70 games and acting as a Member of Parliament. He was sometimes unavailable for practice and he was often fatigued, but he still managed to score his 250th career goal during the season. Hodge allowed 135 goals against in 52 appearances in 1964–65.

MARCH 18, 1965
Montreal 4 Toronto 1 @ The Forum

Jean Beliveau scored twice while wingers Dick Duff and John Ferguson added singles as the Canadiens beat the Leafs 4-1. The injury-plagued Beliveau got his 14th and 15th goals of the season in the third period to clinch the win for the Habs, who were nursing a 2-1 lead at the time. Ferguson's goal was the game winner, his 17th on the year and sixth versus the Maple Leafs. The Canadiens tough guy stole the puck from Toronto's Eddie Shack and beat Terry Sawchuk with a quick shot from about 15 feet out. Montreal had 42 shots on goal compared to the 27 taken by Toronto, but the Leafs may have been tired from practising for three hours twice during the week. Sawchuk became very frustrated and took a minor for slashing Gary Peters of the Canadiens and then took a 10-minute misconduct when he protested too loudly to referee Vern Buffey. Don McKenney scored the only Leaf goal of the game in the second period.

"I don't care. It'll hurt now but help in the playoffs."

Punch Imlach on practising his Leafs for three hours (*The Globe and Mail*, March 19, 1965)

MARCH 24, 1965
Toronto 3 Montreal 2 @ Maple Leaf Gardens

Toronto goaltender Johnny Bower stopped Montreal rookie Yvan Cournoyer on a penalty shot in the third period as the Leafs hung on to win 3-2. Carl Brewer grabbed the puck in the Leaf crease, which led to the penalty shot being called. The Leafs were already shorthanded at the time and a goal could have given the Canadiens all the momentum, but Bower stopped Cournoyer (an odd choice to take the shot considering he only had seven goals) with an easy pad save. The Canadiens actually led the game 2-1 going into the third (on tallies by Bobby Rousseau and Ralph Backstrom) but goals by Frank Mahovlich and Ron Ellis gave the Leafs the winning margin. Montreal had outplayed the Leafs for most of the first 40 minutes (only Leaf defenceman Kent Douglas was able to beat Charlie Hodge) but Bower's work inspired his teammates, who finally responded with a couple of goals. Mahovlich had the nicest goal of the night when he burst down his wrong wing after taking a Peter Stemkowski pass and beat Hodge as he swerved across the ice. The 14,331 fans gave Mahovlich an ovation and then watched Ellis bank a shot into the net off the skate of J.C. Tremblay at 8:11 of the final period.

playoffs

SERIES A – MONTREAL VS. TORONTO

APRIL 1, 1965
Montreal 3 Toronto 2 @ The Forum

In a game that resembled a war, the Canadiens outlasted the Maple Leafs 3-2 to win the first game of their semi-final playoff series. The Leafs seemed more intent on bashing the Canadiens than on playing with the puck and Dickie Moore took a penalty with just four seconds gone in the game. Tim Horton followed that with a five-minute major when he high sticked and cut Jim

Roberts of the Habs. With the Leaf defenceman in the box, Henri Richard scored the opening goal by rapping in a J.C. Tremblay rebound. Then another Leaf rearguard, Kent Douglas, clubbed Dave Balon with his stick and was given a major and match penalty. The Habs were given a minor penalty to nullify their power-play but still managed a goal by Ralph Backstrom to give them a 2-0 lead at the end of the first period. Just before the opening frame ended, Toronto winger Frank Mahovlich nailed Montreal defenceman Terry Harper with such force in the Montreal end that he slumped to the ice with a cut face. Harper suffered a concussion and needed six stitches to close the cut (he was expected to play in the next game). The second period featured a brawl that saw Mahovlich, Peter Stemkowski and Bob Baun all get penalized for the Leafs while Ted Harris, John Ferguson and Roberts sat in the box for Montreal. The Leafs evened the scoring with a pair of goals in the third (by Dickie Moore and Carl Brewer) but a beautiful goal by Bobby Rousseau gave the Canadiens the win. Rousseau took a neat pass from Jean Beliveau and split the Leaf defence before putting a shot past Johnny Bower. In all, 75 penalty minutes were called in the contest by referee Vern Buffey and the total would have been higher had Roberts been given a major as called by the referee. Somehow, the major was not recorded and Roberts did not serve it, much to the displeasure of Leaf coach Punch Imlach.

Toronto's Frank Mahovlich (#27) looks to nail Terry Harper (#19) of Montreal as he battles Dave Keon (#14) for a loose puck behind the net. Mahovlich knocked Harper out of the first game of the playoffs with a thundering hit. Mahovlich did not get a goal in the 1965 playoffs but did set up three Toronto markers, including an overtime winner by Keon in the third game. Harper did not miss a game but had no points in 13 playoff contests for the Canadiens and Keon had four points in six post-season games.

APRIL 3, 1965
Montreal 3 Toronto 1 @ The Forum

The Canadiens took advantage of a tired group of Leafs to take the second game of the series 3-1 and give them a two-games-to-none lead. Claude Provost, Jean Beliveau (with the game winner) and Henri Richard got the Montreal goals, while Ron Ellis got the lone Leaf marker. The Habs got their first goal while the Leafs were down two men when Provost put the puck into a yawning cage. The Leafs had a two-man advantage of their own for a full two minutes but could not score, with Montreal goalie

Charlie Hodge robbing Red Kelly and Andy Bathgate. Ellis tied it for the Leafs in the second period, but the Canadiens took over the contest. Beliveau scored with less than a minute left in the second period when the Montreal captain took an Yvan Cournoyer pass and lifted the puck over Leafs netminder Terry Sawchuk. Richard's fluke goal in the third killed any hopes of a Toronto comeback. Johnny Bower was scheduled to be the Leaf starter in net but he accidently rubbed wintergreen in his eyes and was unable to play. Al Arbour played for the Leafs in place of the suspended Kent Douglas. J.C. Tremblay and Bobby Rousseau played strong defensive games for the Habs.

> *"We expect to win four games, any four. But there's no doubt about it, the Leafs are not playing like they did last year."*
>
> Toe Blake (*The Montreal Gazette*, April 5, 1965)

APRIL 6, 1965
Toronto 3 Montreal 2 @ Maple Leaf Gardens

Dave Keon scored at 4:17 of overtime to give the Leafs a 3-2 win, their first of the playoff series. Frank Mahovlich swept the puck away from Montreal defenceman J.C. Tremblay and the loose disk was picked up by the swift-skating Keon who put a low drive past goalie Gump Worsley, sending the 14,502 fans in attendance home happy. The Leafs had to battle back twice in the game to send it into overtime. Montreal opened the scoring on Jean Beliveau's screened shot in the first period, but the Leafs tied it on a goal by Eddie Shack in the second. Henri Richard scored to make it 2-1 early in the third. However, Andy Bathgate redeemed himself in the eyes of the hometown fans (they had been booing him all game long for missing great opportunities to get goals) by scoring on the power-play with a low 35-foot blast to make it all even again. The crowd had booed Imlach's decision to bring in Bathgate with the man advantage just a few seconds before he scored. John Ferguson and Kent Douglas renewed hostilities between the two clubs with the only fight of the evening after both had crashed into Leafs goalie Johnny Bower.

APRIL 8, 1965
Toronto 4 Montreal 2 @ Maple Leaf Gardens

Toronto netminder Johnny Bower was simply superb and Red Kelly scored twice as the Maple Leafs evened the series with a 4-2 win on home ice. Except for the stellar work of Bower, the Leafs were actually quite lethargic in their play until the third period when they decided to support their overworked goaltender and stage a rally. Montreal was up 2-0 before the first period

> *"It was robbery what Bower did. We should have been up 6-0 after two periods."*
>
> Jean Beliveau (*The Globe and Mail*, April 9, 1965)

> *"When he's playing like that he gives some guys a lift but it makes you feel all the more ashamed of your contribution to the game than anything."*
>
> George Armstrong on Johnny Bower (*The Montreal Gazette*, April 9, 1965)

was six minutes old on goals by Bobby Rousseau and Henri Richard. However, Bower locked the gate and eventually the Leafs found some scoring of their own. Kelly got the Leafs on the board in the second and Ron Ellis split the Canadiens defensive tandem of J.C. Tremblay and Jacques Laperriere, then faked Gump Worsley out of position before sliding it home to tie the score early in the third. George Armstrong shot the winner on a play that was started by former Canadien Dickie Moore. Moore passed it to Keon who relayed it to Armstrong who rifled a back-hander past Worsley. Kelly's second of the night went into the empty net. But without Bower working his magic, it would have been a long night for the Leafs. The 41-year-old codger made brilliant stops on Claude Larose, Ralph Backstrom and Bobby Rousseau to give the Toronto side a chance to come back in the contest. Bower also had to withstand assaults from Dave Balon and John Ferguson (both were penalized) who were determined to run him.

> *"I told the boys after the first period that the Canadiens may have gone all out and shot their bolt. It looked like I was right."*
>
> Punch Imlach (*The Montreal Gazette*, April 9, 1965)

APRIL 10, 1965
Montreal 3 Toronto 1 @ The Forum

A third-period shot by Bobby Rousseau broke a 1-1 tie and sent the Canadiens to a 3-1 victory over the Leafs, who now faced elimination in the series. Rousseau, who played an outstanding game, cleverly used Toronto defenceman Kent Douglas as a screen to fire a 55-foot blast past Johnny Bower and give the Canadiens a 2-1 lead. An empty-net marker by Beliveau sealed the win for the Habs, who did not play as well at home as they had in Toronto. After a scoreless first period, Toronto's Bob Pulford opened the scoring at 3:45 of the second period on a lucky bounce after the Leaf centre just threw the puck out in front from the corner and it hit goalie Gump Worsley before going in the net. Worsley kept the score to only 1-0 by making some great saves, especially on drives from Peter Stemkowski, Frank Mahovlich, Red Kelly and Andy Bathgate. Montreal tied the game on Yvan Cournoyer's first-ever playoff goal with the Leafs two men short when he lifted Claude Provost's pass over Johnny Bower in the Leaf net. Toronto enjoyed a two-man advantage twice in the game but could not score with the opportunities. The Leafs started five defencemen for the opening face-off, including Allan Stanley, who did not see the ice again until late in the game.

> *"The Canadiens aren't good enough to win in Toronto. You can put that in because I want them to know it so they'll be at their very best."*
>
> Punch Imlach (*The Globe and Mail*, April 12, 1965)

> *"I don't think we played as well tonight as we did in the two games at Toronto but our defence was solid (especially Ted Harris and Jacques Laperriere) and we got strong goaltending."*
>
> Toe Blake (*The Montreal Gazette*, April 12, 1965)

APRIL 13, 1965
Montreal 4 Toronto 3 @ Maple Leaf Gardens

An overtime goal by Montreal's Claude Provost ended Toronto's three-year grip on the Stanley Cup as the Canadiens edged the Maple Leafs 4-3 to take the playoff series in six games. The extra-session winner came at 16:33 when Provost took a backhanded swipe at a loose puck and it went past a partially screened Johnny Bower in the Leaf net. The goal capped a furious rally by the Canadiens in the second and third periods as the Habs fought back from

Toronto's Allan Stanley tries to block Claude Provost from getting to a loose puck. Provost ended the Leafs' three-year Stanley Cup reign with a dramatic overtime winning goal in the sixth game of the semi-finals at the Gardens. Provost had eight points (two goals) in thirteen playoff games in 1965 and did a masterful job of checking Bobby Hull of the Blackhawks in the finals, holding the "Golden Jet" to just two power-play goals.

a 3-1 deficit. Defenceman Jacques Laperriere started the comeback with a goal, a blistering shot from the point on the power-play, in the middle stanza and then Bobby Rousseau (also with the extra man) tied it in the final frame. The Leafs had stormed out to a 2-0 lead on goals by Dave Keon and Red Kelly (both were short-handed efforts) in the first period, only to have John Ferguson reply for Montreal. The Leafs got that one back on a goal by Ron Ellis (the teams set a playoff record with three goals in 1:32) but could not beat Gump Worsley in the Montreal net again. The Leafs played their best game of the playoffs but the Habs were just as determined to end the series. The Toronto side had the better of the play in the extra time but Worsley was there to thwart them at every turn and then Provost crushed the hopes of the 14,702 fans on hand at the Gardens. Montreal lost Laperriere for the rest of the playoffs with a broken ankle suffered when he slid into the

Bob Pulford of the Leafs and Jacques Laperriere of the Canadiens battle for the puck. During the 1964–65 season, the lanky Montreal rearguard had 27 points (five goals, 22 assists) and made the NHL's first all-star team. Laperriere scored a very important goal for the Habs in the sixth game of the semi-finals in 1965 against the Leafs and then broke his leg before the contest was over. He was unable to play in the finals against Chicago.

boards on what appeared to be a routine play. The win sent the Canadiens to the Stanley Cup final for the first time since 1960.

"We went down like champs. And I'd have to say this was our best all-round game in the playoffs."

Punch Imlach (*The Globe and Mail*, April 14, 1965)

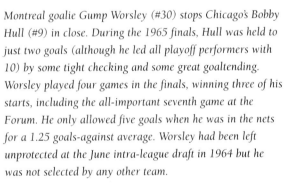

Montreal goalie Gump Worsley (#30) stops Chicago's Bobby Hull (#9) in close. During the 1965 finals, Hull was held to just two goals (although he led all playoff performers with 10) by some tight checking and some great goaltending. Worsley played four games in the finals, winning three of his starts, including the all-important seventh game at the Forum. He only allowed five goals when he was in the nets for a 1.25 goals-against average. Worsley had been left unprotected at the June intra-league draft in 1964 but he was not selected by any other team.

stanley cup finals

MONTREAL VS. CHICAGO

The Chicago Blackhawks upset the Detroit Red Wings in the other semi-final to meet the Canadiens in the finals. The Montreal side took the opener at the Forum with a 3-2 win on goals by Henri Richard, John Ferguson and Yvan Cournoyer with the winner. Gump Worsley got the shutout in the second game as the Habs won it 2-0 on markers by Dick Duff and Jean Beliveau. The Blackhawks got all-stars Pierre Pilote and Ken Wharram (who scored the game winner on Worsley) back into their lineup for the third game and won it 3-1 on home ice. Charlie Hodge was back in the Montreal nets for the fourth game but the Canadiens were blitzed 5-1 as Bobby Hull got his only two goals of the series. Back at the Forum, the Canadiens went on a

Chicago's defenceman Pierre Pilote (#3) is chased by Henri Richard of the Canadiens with Elmer Vasko and goalie Glenn Hall watching. Richard scored three goals in the 1965 finals against Chicago and in typical fashion scored a key goal in the 4-0 seventh game victory that gave the Canadiens their first Stanley Cup since 1960. Only Richard, Jean Beliveau, Claude Provost, Jean Guy Talbot and Ralph Backstrom were holdovers from the '60 Cup win.

"With four of the six NHL clubs based in the U.S. I think it is reasonable to expect that the next president [of the league] to be an American. The four U.S. teams likely would want it that way. They should have the votes to win their point."

David Molson, president of the Montreal Canadiens (*Hockey News*, April 10, 1965)

rampage, winning 6-0. Ferguson beat up Eric Nesterenko to set the tone early in the game with Beliveau scoring twice and Hodge recording the shutout. The Chicago team was not finished yet, however, as they bounced back to win 2-1 on goals by Elmer Vasko and Doug Mohns. For the first time ever, the Stanley Cup playoffs stretched into May, but the seventh game was very one-sided as the Canadiens got a goal from Beliveau after just 14 seconds of play and went on to win 4-0. All the goals came in the first period and Worsley was sharp in the opening stanza to choke off the Blackhawks. The rest of the contest was an easy romp for the Habs.

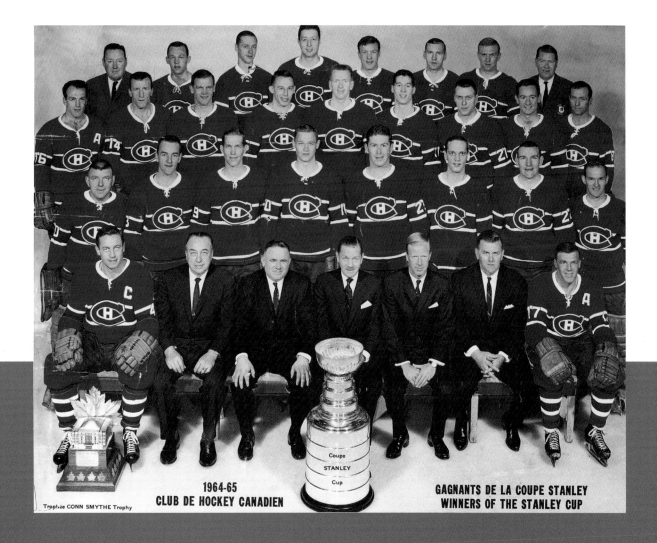

Trophée CONN SMYTHE Trophy

**1964-65
CLUB DE HOCKEY CANADIEN**

**GAGNANTS DE LA COUPE STANLEY
WINNERS OF THE STANLEY CUP**

*The Leafs' Orland Kurtenbach (#25) staged a memorable fight with Canadien
Terry Harper (#19) at Maple Leaf Gardens during the 1965–66 season.*

The Leafs–Canadiens Rivalry
1965–66

season summary

Considering that the Montreal Canadiens had just won the Stanley Cup after a few years devoted to rebuilding their team, it was no surprise that the club stood pat with the same lineup. The only addition to the team was defenceman Noel Price who came from the Detroit organization. Goalie Gump Worsley was back to play on a full-time basis and he teamed with Charlie Hodge to win the Vezina Trophy (allowing 14 fewer goals than the Toronto and Chicago goaltending tandems). Jacques Laperriere was named the NHL's best defenceman (six goals, 25 assists) and was named to the first all-star team. Jean Beliveau, Bobby Rousseau and Worsley were named to the second all-star squad. The Canadiens won forty-one games while losing twenty-one, and eight ended in a tie, good enough for ninety points and a comfortable eight points ahead of the second-place Blackhawks. Winger Leon Rochefort was a strong addition for the playoffs.

As dethroned champions, the Toronto Maple Leafs made plenty of off-season moves. A major trade with Detroit in May 1965 saw Toronto acquire Marcel Pronovost, Larry Jeffrey, Eddie Joyal, Autry Erickson and Lowell MacDonald, with Andy Bathgate, Gary Jarret and long-time Leaf Billy Harris going the other way. Orland Kurtenbach was picked up from Boston in a trade involving Ron Stewart, while Bruce Gamble came on board to help Johnny Bower and Terry Sawchuk in goal. The Leafs' biggest loss

Toe Blake (*Who's Who in Hockey* magazine, 1965 edition)

"If our young players, who played so well last year [1964–65], can improve as much as this season, we'll be in good shape. A little improvement from some of our veterans would also enable us to have a good year."

Montreal's John Ferguson (#22) tries to get position on Toronto's Brit Selby (#11). Ferguson's goal output dropped to 11 and he had just 25 points in 1965–66 but he still managed to record 153 minutes in penalties and was always prominent in games against the Leafs. Selby wore number 11 because Ron Ellis had enjoyed a great rookie season wearing that number and coach Punch Imlach asked Ellis to give it to Selby. The idea worked as the left winger won the Calder Trophy with a 14-goal, 27-point season.

was the very unexpected departure of defenceman Carl Brewer. The all-star defender walked away from the Leafs during training camp and he would be badly missed. The other huge surprise for the Leafs was the great season produced by Eddie Shack who had been demoted before the year began but was quickly recalled when the team was doing badly. He responded with 26 goals (second best on the team) and 43 points in 63 games. New Leafs for the '65–66 season included Brit Selby (the Calder Trophy winner with 14 goals), Wally Boyer and Mike Walton (for six games). Al Smith and Gary Smith also saw action in the nets for the Leafs. Veteran

defenceman Larry Hillman also made a return to the Leaf lineup. The Leafs managed a third-place finish with a 34-25-11 record.

During the season, the Leafs won seven of the fourteen contests (7-5-2) played between the two clubs and shut out the Habs twice right in the Forum. The games were very physical and there were plenty of memorable fights as the rivalry intensified during the year. A 2-0 whitewash of Montreal late in the season had the Leafs feeling rather giddy about their chances in the playoffs. However, when post-season play began, the Habs took Toronto in four straight games. Only one game proved to be close (a 4-3 Montreal win in the opener) and a wild brawl in the fourth game did little to preserve the Leafs' dignity. The Leaf defence certainly missed all-star defenceman Allan Stanley, who was injured, but it's unlikely the veteran would have made much difference.

The Habs surprisingly lost the first two games of the finals on home ice to Detroit, but the Red Wings were premature in calling themselves champions. The Canadiens put that to an end in a real hurry. Although the finals concluded in controversial fashion, the Canadiens were full value for their win as they took the next four games in a row. Roger Crozier was outstanding in the Detroit net and was given the Conn Smythe Trophy but many felt defenceman J.C. Tremblay deserved the honour, especially the blueliner himself!

NOVEMBER 4, 1965
Montreal 5 Toronto 1 @ The Forum

The Canadiens easily won the first meeting of the 1965–66 season against the Leafs with a 5-1 victory before 15,229 fans. Henri Richard led the way for the Habs with two goals (and one assist) while singles went to Ralph Backstrom, Bobby Rousseau and Gilles Tremblay. The Leafs, who dressed only 16 players (two short of the limit), got their only goal from the stick of defenceman Tim Horton. The Toronto club was hurting for depth. Coach Punch Imlach was displeased with Peter Stemkowski and Eddie Shack and had them both sent to the minors. The game got to be so bad that the Forum crowd began chanting, "We want Shack," a cry usually heard in Maple Leaf Gardens. Montreal clearly dominated the contest throughout and had 41 shots on Leaf goalie Terry Sawchuk, compared to just 25 for Toronto on Canadiens netminder Charlie Hodge.

NOVEMBER 10, 1965
Toronto 3 Montreal 3 @ Maple Leaf Gardens

The Maple Leafs got two goals in the third period to earn a 3-3 tie with the visiting Canadiens. Ron Ellis and Orland Kurtenbach scored the final frame markers after the recently returned Eddie Shack got the Toronto club fired up. Shack managed to get John Ferguson into a scrap and he generally ran all over the ice causing havoc, taking five penalties in the process. Shack revived the Leafs out of their apparent slumber and Ellis started the comeback with a short-handed effort. A few minutes later, Kurtenbach followed up an Ellis drive to put home the

rebound and tie the score. Montreal had opened the scoring with goals from Ralph Backstrom and Ferguson. Dave Keon got the Leafs into the game with his second of the year, but Dick Duff quickly got that back for Montreal just 18 seconds later. The Leafs had just come off a 9-0 loss to the Chicago Blackhawks, their third loss in a row, and it might have been four but for the antics of "the Entertainer." Coach Punch Imlach wanted to keep Shack in the minors but his team needed some life and he was forced to bring the winger back up to the big club from Rochester. Leaf rookie Brit Selby played in his sixth game, meaning that he would now have to stay with the big team for the rest of the season.

NOVEMBER 18, 1965
Toronto 3 Montreal 1 @ The Forum

Leafs coach Punch Imlach put together a new line and each member of the trio scored in the third period as the visitors beat the Canadiens 3-1 before 13,376 fans who braved a snowstorm to attend. Imlach threw Larry Jeffrey, Bob Pulford and Eddie Shack onto the ice as a unit and they played with an aggressiveness that got results. Shack got the ball rolling when he whacked home a Pulford pass for his third goal of the season (in

Brit Selby first played for the Maple Leafs in the 1964–65 season when he was called up from the junior Marlies for three games, replacing the injured Ron Ellis. He played his first game on January 2, 1965, against Detroit and was told before the game that he would be counted on to check Gordie Howe throughout the game. The 19-year-old kept Howe off the scoresheet and then scored a goal the next night in New York. Selby added another goal, a game winner against Chicago before his three-game trial was over. A brilliant junior career featured 94 goals in 138 games, but his stay in Toronto was relatively short in spite of a Calder Trophy win and the hopes of the Leaf organization. In a couple of stints with the Leafs (between 1965 and 1971) he posted 29 goals and 59 points in 169 games.

A CLOSER LOOK

Punch Imlach
— a closer look

George "Punch" Imlach spent 12 years with the Quebec Aces of the QSHL as a player, coach, general manager and part owner. He made the league finals nine times in those years and in 1957–58 he became general manager of the Springfield Indians of the AHL in the Boston organization. He eventually took over as coach of the team and got them into the playoffs for the first time in years. He was made the manager of the entire Bruin farm system but the Leafs made him an offer that included being the assistant general manager at the NHL level. By November 29, 1958, Imlach was behind the Leaf bench after firing Billy Reay, and he stayed there until April 6, 1969. In 760 games during that time, Imlach won 365 contests, lost 270 and tied another 125. He added 44 wins in the playoffs (in 89 games) and won four Stanley Cups.

"I'll have my usual contract problems, that's par for the course every Fall, but I'll be fair with my players even though I'm in the driver's seat. I intend to continue as both general manager and coach. I feel it eliminates conflict and there's no quibbling over decisions. I make up my mind and right or wrong, it's my responsibility."

Punch Imlach (*Hockey Pictorial*, October 1965)

"Punch Imlach handles the team very well and is very good with us individually. I have every faith in him."

Carl Brewer (*Hockey Pictorial*, October 1962)

"I think his coaching methods, which a lot of writers and players criticize as being too tough have added at least six years to my NHL career."

Johnny Bower (*Hockey Illustrated*, February 1966)

"He treats a team as a unit rather than as individuals."

Bert Olmstead (*Hockey Annual*, 1967)

just five games) at 6:09 of the third. Jeffrey (who replaced Red Kelly) scored the next goal as he swiped at a loose puck after Pulford did much of the work by getting around defenceman Jacques Laperriere. Pulford then worked hard to put one into the empty net as the Canadiens pulled goalie Gump Worsley. Montreal had a 1-0 lead going into the third on a goal by Ralph Backstrom. Shack was named as the first star of the game and received quite an ovation from the Montreal crowd when he put on a stick-handling display in the first period. The Leafs' unpredictable left winger seemed to be a different player since his time on the farm with the Rochester Americans.

NOVEMBER 24, 1965
Montreal 2 Toronto 1 @ Maple Leaf Gardens

Henri Richard scored an early third-period goal

Toronto coach Punch Imlach has a discussion with winger Eddie Shack. The Leafs sent Shack down to the minors to start the 1965–66 season but quickly came to realize they missed his infectious style of play as the losses started to mount. Motivated like never before, Shack produced the best year of his career with the Leafs when he scored 26 times and totalled 43 points in 63 games. He was especially effective against the Canadiens and had three points in four playoff games versus the Habs.

Frank Mahovlich circles the net at the Forum while he is chased by Claude Provost of the Canadiens. Mahovlich once again led the Leafs in goal scoring (for the sixth straight season) with 32 markers in 1965–66 and was tied with Bob Pulford for the team lead in points (for the fifth time in six years) with 56.

that stood up as the winner in the Canadiens 2-1 win over the Maple Leafs. Richard, who usually makes his presence known when an important goal is required, put in a Claude Provost rebound to give the Montreal squad first place in the league standings. Richard was the outstanding player on the night and he displayed superb puck control every time he was out on the ice. Dave Keon scored the opener for the Leafs but they could not get anything else past Gump Worsley in the Montreal net, despite 33 shots on goal. The Canadiens could not cash in on a two-man advantage but Yvan Cournoyer tied it for the Habs on a power-play later in the second period. That left the somewhat dull contest to be settled by Richard in the final frame. John

Ferguson tried to get Eddie Shack into a fight all night but the Leaf refused to accept the offer, much to the delight of 14,460 fans on hand. Toronto also used rookie Mike Walton in the game (replacing the injured Red Kelly) and he recorded one assist.

DECEMBER 16, 1965
Toronto 3 Montreal 2 @ The Forum

Toronto left winger Frank Mahovlich had one of his best games of the season as the Leafs edged the Canadiens 3-2 before 13,761 fans. The Big M scored the winner (for the second consecutive match) late in the second period by blasting a shot past goalie Gump Worsley and Toronto hung on to win the game. The Maple Leafs built up a 3-1 lead on goals by Bob Pulford, Brit Selby and the Mahovlich marker, but had to withstand a furious assault by the Montreal attack that produced one power-play goal by Yvan Cournoyer (all of his nine goals had come with the extra man) in the third. Bobby Rousseau got the other goal for Montreal in the first when he beat goalie Johnny Bower. The Leafs used two rookies in the game, Darryl Sly, who helped on defence and with some penalty killing, and Wally Boyer, who set up Selby for his goal.

DECEMBER 29, 1965
Toronto 3 Montreal 2 @ Maple Leaf Gardens

Three straight third-period goals carried the Maple Leafs past the Canadiens 3-2 before 14,996 fans at the Gardens (the largest crowd of the season). Toronto trailed the contest 2-0 going into the third period after Dick Duff and Jean Beliveau had beaten Leaf goalie Terry Sawchuk, despite outshooting the Habs 18-8 in the opening frame. After a goal-

"I've drawn a curtain around myself this season. I hope I can keep it there."

Frank Mahovlich on his attempts to concentrate on hockey and avoid any
more trouble with coach Punch Imlach (*The Globe and Mail*, December 17, 1965)

less second, Bob Pulford and Frank Mahovlich tied the game for Toronto before captain George Armstrong scored a shorthanded marker for the winner. Armstrong picked up a loose puck, calmly walked in on Charlie Hodge and picked the corner of the net with a shot. Toronto played a solid defensive game and blueliner Tim Horton was likely the best player on either team. Hodge played very well for the Habs, who were now in second place, one point behind Chicago. Toronto moved to within four points of the league-leading Blackhawks and were unbeaten in nine games.

> ## "Heck, I had to change my suit — nine games is a long time."
>
> Punch Imlach on his superstitions
> (*The Globe and Mail*, December 30, 1965)

Toronto captain George Armstrong (#10) is about to put the puck into the net with Charlie Hodge out of the play. Armstrong scored 16 times in 1965–66 to go along with 35 assists in 70 games. In the latter years of his career, Armstrong would only sign one-year contracts because he did not want the feeling that a longer-term deal would eventually mean retirement when it was over. He would play in 1,187 games as a Leaf and record 296 goals and 713 points. Armstrong added 26 goals and 34 assists in 110 playoff games.

Montreal captain Jean Beliveau (#4) moves in close to the Toronto net occupied by Terry Sawchuk (#30). Beliveau had another outstanding season in 1965–66 when he scored 28 times and led the NHL with 48 assists. His 77-point total placed him fourth in league scoring and earned him a spot on the second all-star team. Sawchuk's workload was reduced to 27 games (winning 10) in '65–66 and he allowed 80 goals for a 3.16 goals-against average, with one shutout.

JANUARY 13, 1966
Toronto 6 Montreal 0 @ The Forum

Eddie Shack scored for the Maple Leafs at the 21-second mark of the first period as Toronto went on to whip Montreal 6-0. Shack stole the puck from defenceman Jean Guy Talbot and then pulled goalie Gump Worsley out of position to score his 15th goal of the season. Leaf defencemen Larry Hillman and Marcel Pronovost each scored their first goals of the season in the second period to make it 3-0. In the third, the Leafs poured it on and got tallies from Wally Boyer, Red Kelly and Frank Mahovlich (who added two assists) to round out the scoring. They also managed to keep the shutout intact for goaltender Johnny Bower (the first star of the game), who had to block 40 Montreal shots. It was the worst defeat absorbed

by the Canadiens in two years. The Montreal fans began cheering for the Leafs and the chant "Go Leafs Go" could be heard in the Forum. It was speculated that it would not be a good idea to get next to Montreal coach Toe Blake after this game.

FEBRUARY 3, 1966
Montreal 5 Toronto 4 @ The Forum

Canadiens captain Jean Beliveau scored his second goal of the game in the third period as the Habs came back to squeak out a 5-4 victory over the Leafs on home ice. Toronto entered the third period up 4-3, but Henri Richard tied the score when he was sent in alone by a Bobby Rousseau pass. Beliveau then scored the winner at 14:13 when he batted in a Gilles Tremblay setup. The play on the winning goal was actually started by defenceman Noel Price who was in the Montreal lineup replacing the injured Jean Guy Talbot. Beliveau took a late penalty but the Canadiens managed to kill it off and preserve the victory. It looked like the Leafs were going to pull another upset at the Forum after Eddie Shack (with his 18th of the year), Frank Mahovlich (his 19th), Ron Ellis and Dave Keon had all scored for Toronto. However, Rousseau, Beliveau and Claude Provost kept the Canadiens close with goals of their own before they scored twice in the final stanza. The Leafs went with Terry Sawchuk in goal but would have preferred to use Johnny Bower (he was out with a groin injury) after Sawchuk's poor play in an 8-4 loss to the New York Rangers in his last start. But the Leafs goalie played very well in facing 40 shots but Toronto was without the services of defenceman Marcel Pronovost, and Bob Baun was just back from an injury. Leaf rookie Brit Selby was cut on his forehead after taking a punch from Montreal's John Ferguson in the first period. Selby had been ridden into the boards by Terry Harper and came out swinging at the Canadiens defenceman. That's when Ferguson stepped into the action and earned the

only major given out on the play. For the rest of the night Toronto defenceman Tim Horton played it rough against Ferguson, who was wise to steer clear of the tough Leaf defender.

FEBRUARY 16, 1966
Toronto 3 Montreal 1 @ Maple Leaf Gardens

The Maple Leafs beat the Canadiens for the fifth time in the 1965–66 season with a 3-1 win at the Gardens before 14,996 fans. Ron Ellis scored twice for the Leafs, including the winner about half-way through the third period when he slapped a drive past goalie Gump Worsley from about 20 feet out. The goal came on a three-on-one break with Wally Boyer setting up Ellis for the shot. Ellis had tied the game in the first period after Jean Beliveau had scored to give the Habs a 1-0 lead earlier in the period. Worsley held the Canadiens in the game with good saves even though the Habs actually had more shots on goal than Toronto (32-31). Bob Pulford finished the scoring at 19:59 when he put one into the empty net. It was the second consecutive game involving Toronto that saw a goal scored with one tick remaining on the clock; Detroit's Paul Henderson had scored on Terry Sawchuk the previous Saturday at the Gardens to give the Red Wings a 3-3 tie with the Leafs.

MARCH 2, 1966
Toronto 3 Montreal 3 @ Maple Leaf Gardens

George Armstrong scored a power-play goal in the third period for the Maple Leafs as Toronto and Montreal skated to a brawl-filled 3-3 tie at the Gardens. The Leafs had to battle back three times in the contest to pull out a draw, but they clearly won one of the fights. Ralph Backstrom opened the scoring for Montreal in the first period, only to have Red Kelly get it back for the Leafs. Jean Beliveau scored his 380th career goal to give the Habs the lead; but then, Frank Mahovlich notched his 25th of the year for Toronto. The two teams

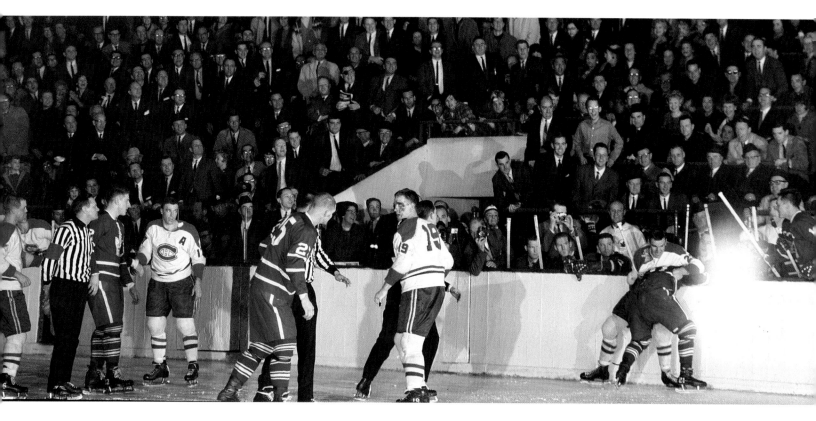

exchanged goals in the third when Gilles Tremblay scored his 22nd and then Armstrong connected to once again even the score. Early in the second period, a full-scale brawl broke out when Bob Baun and John Ferguson were trying to get at each other. While they were jousting, Terry Harper decided he would take on Leafs centre Orland Kurtenbach and it would prove to be a bad move. When the battle was over, Harper was sporting cuts over both eyes that required 16 stitches to close. Both eyes were blackened as Harper took a severe beating from a very good fighter. Meanwhile, Baun had wrestled Ferguson to the ice. All four players were given majors. The game was a chippy affair and even goalie Gump Worsley got upset after he took a stick to the head from Toronto's Peter Stemkowski in the third period. His penalty for slashing gave the Leafs' Armstrong

Toronto's Orland Kurtenbach (#25) got the better of Montreal's Terry Harper (#19) during a donnybrook that took place at the Gardens on March 2, 1966. The Maple Leafs gave up Ron Stewart to Boston for the six foot, two inch centre who was considered the heavyweight champion of the NHL (the Leafs also got Pat Stapleton and Andy Hebenton in the deal). Although he played well at times in the 1965–66 season, Kurtenbach was essentially a part-time performer and he lasted just the one season with the Leafs. In seventy games he scored nine goals and added six assists before the New York Rangers took him in the intra-league draft.

the opportunity he needed to score with the extra man. The Leafs had 38 shots on goal against Worsley and Charlie Hodge (who played the first two periods), while Montreal had 36 on the Leafs goalie Bruce Gamble, who played very well in

"Mr. Harper's always pushing and shoving and coming in late. So I decided we better have what we might call a little altercation."

Orland Kurtenbach (*The Globe and Mail*, March 3, 1966)

Toronto goalie Bruce Gamble is assisted by Dave Keon (#14) in clearing the puck against the Montreal Canadiens. A portly type, Gamble was out of hockey in 1964–65, but the Leafs rescued him from the clutches of Eddie Shore with Springfield of the AHL and he was sent to Tulsa of the CPHL for most of the 1965–66 season. When injuries struck regulars Terry Sawchuk and Johnny Bower, Gamble was called up and recorded a remarkable four shutouts in just ten appearances, including one against the Canadiens at the Forum. Gamble also got a bottle of champagne from Toronto radio station CKEY when he stopped Bobby Hull of Chicago from scoring his 51st of the season against the Leafs that year. Keon scored 24 goals in 1965–66 to go along with 30 assists in 69 games.

place of Terry Sawchuk. Gamble was given the third star of the game.

MARCH 3, 1966
Toronto 4 Montreal 0 @ The Forum

Toronto netminder Bruce Gamble earned his second career shutout and forward Dave Keon was simply outstanding as the Leafs blanked the Canadiens 4-0 before 15,457 fans. Gamble stopped 34 Montreal shots and the Leafs scored two in the first and two in the third for the victory. The win moved the Leafs into a third-place tie with Detroit. Red Kelly opened the scoring early in the first and Peter Stemkowski got the other in a penalty-filled period. John Ferguson took three penalties on his own as the Habs looked for a little revenge for what happened to them in the previous game in Toronto. In the second period, Terry Harper showed tremendous courage by going after Orland Kurtenbach who had whipped him in a one-sided fight the night before (they were both given high sticking minors). Bob Pulford made it 3-0 in the third and then Keon mesmerized the Montreal team with some fancy moves before sending a cross-ice pass to a wide-open Mahovlich, who put in the fourth Leaf goal past Gump Worsley. Brent Imlach played at centre for the Leafs and the son of the coach played well but did not have a scoring chance. The younger Imlach was replacing a flu-ridden Brit Selby and he returned home to Toronto right after the game to write a high school exam. He played between Kurtenbach and Tim Horton on a fourth line. Trouble threatened to break out at various points in the game but referee Bill Friday kept a tight rein on the proceedings, although the Leafs' defenceman Larry Hillman did get a spearing penalty in the third.

MARCH 16, 1966
Montreal 7 Toronto 2 @ Maple Leaf Gardens

It took just nine seconds for the Canadiens to begin a 7-2 rout of the Maple Leafs. Bobby Rousseau opened the scoring for the Habs with his 26th of the year and it seemed to rattle goalie

Boston scout Harold "Baldy" Cotton spotted Bruce Gamble at an outdoor rink and was impressed by the goalie despite the freezing temperatures. Cotton encouraged the 12-year-old Gamble and even sent him a chemical to put on his skate boot to give him some warmth when he played out in the cold. Gamble wanted to play in net so he followed the scout's advice and eventually started his NHL career with the New York Rangers in the 1958–59 season. He also played with the Bruins before he was picked up by the Leafs.

A CLOSER LOOK

Bruce Gamble, who had only given up eleven goals in seven appearances. He gave two more third-period tallies to the Canadiens (Gilles Tremblay, Claude Larose) before the Leafs got one back from the stick of Ron Ellis. In the second, Jean Beliveau scored twice (he now had 26 on the year) and Ralph Backstrom added another, while Dave Keon got the only Toronto marker. The two teams combined to score three goals in just 43 seconds. Gamble was replaced in the third and Johnny Bower gave up one goal to Dave Balon to close out the scoring. Beliveau, with his two goals and three assists, moved to within two points of 1,000 for his career. The game was very physical and fights broke out between Montreal's Ted Harris and Toronto's Orland Kurtenbach. Just before the end of the game, Leaf defenceman Kent Douglas took on John Ferguson. The Canadiens enforcer was cut for six stitches and claimed he suffered the wound from a Douglas high stick. The seven goals allowed by the Leafs gave the Canadiens the lead in the Vezina Trophy race (157 to 165).

MARCH 24, 1966
Toronto 2 Montreal 0 @ The Forum

Johnny Bower made 34 saves and the Leafs won in the Forum for the fifth time in seven tries with a 2-0 victory over the Canadiens before 15,478 fans. The Habs stormed out of the gate and fired 13 shots at Bower but the veteran was up to the task and turned away all the point-blank chances. The game remained scoreless until 16:04 of the third when Toronto's Dave Keon scored a controversial goal. Keon took a Tim Horton pass right at his skates as he crossed the blueline and although it appeared offside to some, the play was allowed to continue. Keon had a half-step on Montreal defenceman J.C. Tremblay and he put a beautiful move on Gump Worsley to score the winning goal. Canadiens captain Jean Beliveau argued strongly with referee Frank Udvari and the crowd showered the ice with rubber boots and debris. The crowd went

"Did you notice that the crowd didn't yell for an offside call until Beliveau started to complain? That should be proof that Keon was onside on the play."

Allan Stanley (*The Globe and Mail*, March 25, 1966)

Toronto's Bob Pulford (#20) is about to put the puck past goaltender Gump Worsley (#30) during a scramble in front of the Canadiens net. Worsley was back and healthy for the first time since the Canadiens had acquired him in 1963. He played in 51 games, winning 29 times and recording two shutouts with a goals-against average of 2.36. Along with Charlie Hodge (who played in 26 games and had a 2.58 goals-against average), the two netminders combined to win the Vezina Trophy, the first for Worsley. Pulford enjoyed a fine season for the Leafs with 28 goals (the most during his time with Toronto) and totalled 56 points, also a career high.

wild again when Leaf defenceman Larry Hillman was not called for hauling down Henri Richard, and just seconds later Frank Mahovlich was sent in on a breakaway after being sprung into the clear with a George Armstrong pass. The Big M got behind Bobby Rousseau (who was playing the point for the Habs) and then applied his patented swooping move on Worsley to score at 19:00. Al Arbour replaced Kent Douglas on the Leaf blueline and played very well, blocking seven shots alone in the first two periods.

MARCH 30, 1966
Montreal 3 Toronto 1 @ Maple Leaf Gardens

The Canadiens overcame a 1-0 deficit in the third period by scoring three times in the final frame and skated away with a 3-1 victory. Bob Pulford opened the scoring in the first period on a hotly disputed goal at 19:33 by beating Gump Worsley in the Montreal net. The rotund Canadiens netminder felt he had the puck covered but the Leafs dug it out. Worsley was named the first star of the game and he kept the

Habs in the contest until the third period when Yvan Cournoyer tied it up on the power-play with his 16th of the year at 8:35 by deflecting J.C. Tremblay's shot from the point. Henri Richard scored the winner with a low blast that eluded Johnny Bower in the Leaf goal less than a minute later. Gilles Tremblay added another, squeezing a shot just over the goal line. The win, Montreal's third at the Gardens this season, assured the Canadiens of at least a tie in the battle for first place with Chicago. Former Leaf boss Conn Smythe was in the crowd enjoying his first game after severing all ties to the team he had once owned and managed.

Bobby Rousseau. Ferguson's goal came after some hard work by Claude Larose, who beat Baun to a loose puck and slid it over to Ralph Backstrom. Ferguson took the relay and made the score 2-2. Larose was playing his first game in two weeks but showed he had regained his stride quickly. Leaf defenceman Allan Stanley played briefly in the contest but would not play again in the series due to a knee injury.

"It was a game of mistakes; we gave the puck away 20 times and the Leafs a little more. A win like that is a bonus, believe me."

Toe Blake (*The Toronto Star*, April 9, 1966)

"The main thing is to provide your home fans with good entertainment, fast, exciting hockey … We didn't do that last season and we decided on a major face lifting. We're still rebuilding because as of now we're still not satisfied with the product our players are serving Toronto fans."

Stafford Smythe, Maple Leafs president (*Hockey Illustrated*, March 1966)

playoffs

SERIES A – MONTREAL VS. TORONTO
APRIL 7, 1966
Montreal 4 Toronto 3 @ The Forum

The Montreal Canadiens didn't play very well but still managed to pull out a 4-3 win over the Maple Leafs in the first game of the playoffs. Canadiens captain Jean Beliveau had to rescue his team with a late goal in the third period to pull out the win when he got by defenceman Bob Baun and then put a shot past Toronto goalie Terry Sawchuk. Montreal trailed 1-0 and 2-1 but rallied to take the lead 3-2 heading into the third. Bob Pulford tied it for the Leafs when he beat Gump Worsley after 11 minutes of play. Eddie Shack and Frank Mahovlich scored the other Toronto goals, while the Hab markers came from J.C. Tremblay, John Ferguson and

APRIL 9, 1966
Montreal 2 Toronto 0 @ The Forum

Montreal netminder Gump Worsley recorded his third career playoff shutout as the Canadiens beat the Leafs 2-0 to take a two-game lead in the series. Both of the Montreal goals came in the third period as Claude Provost and Bobby Rousseau finally solved Leaf goaltender Terry Sawchuk. Provost, whose main job was to shadow Frank Mahovlich of the Leafs, got the winner when he broke over the Toronto blueline and took a pass from Gilles Tremblay. His shot seemed to surprise Sawchuk, who was expecting a pass back to Tremblay. The Habs had 40 shots on goal compared to Toronto's 25 but had to absorb a concerted Leaf effort to play physical. The Leafs were coached by King

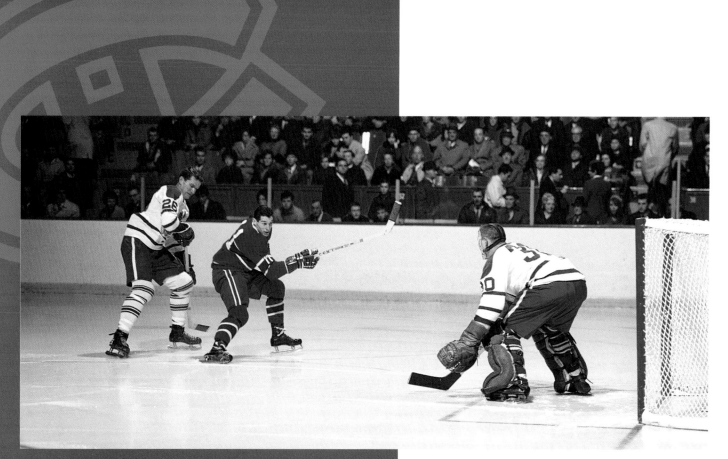

Montreal's Claude Larose (#11) fires a shot at Toronto goalie Terry Sawchuk (#30) with defenceman Allan Stanley giving chase. Larose was a major factor throughout the 1966 semi-final playoff series against Toronto. He set up an important goal in the first game (his only point in the playoffs) and then fought Eddie Shack in the second contest. Larose scored 15 goals in the season and added 18 assists in 64 games, but in the finals Leon Rochefort replaced him after a couple of games. Stanley was a second-team all-star in 1965–66 but played in only one game during the playoffs due to a serious knee injury.

Claude Larose — a closer look

Claude Larose was born in Hearst, Ontario, and played his junior hockey for the Peterborough Petes of the OHA where he was considered a hot-headed player (258 penalty minutes in his last two years). He turned professional with the Hull-Ottawa Canadiens and also spent time with Omaha of the CPHL, helping that team to a championship with eight goals in eight playoff games. He gave credit to coaches Sam Pollock and Scotty Bowman for correcting flaws in his game and he scored 21 times in his first full year with Montreal (1964–65), although he failed to score during the final third of the season. During two different stints with Montreal, Larose scored 117 goals and 240 points in 529 games. He added 27 points (11 goals) in 82 playoff contests.

Clancy in this game, filling in for an ill Punch Imlach, and he had his troops dishing out the body. The game threatened to break out at times, starting with a Bob Pulford charge at Montreal's Terry Harper from behind. Harper was helped from the ice with a bad bruise below the eye, a sore back and a hurt knee. There was no penalty on the play. Baun ran at Henri Richard, which angered the Canadiens, but the only fight of the night occurred just before the Canadiens scored their first goal. Claude Larose got the best of Eddie Shack in that one. Before the game was over, Richard was injured when Leaf defenceman Larry Hillman ran him into the boards.

APRIL 12, 1966
Montreal 5 Toronto 2 @ Maple Leaf Gardens

The Maple Leafs started the third game of the playoff series strongly with two goals in the first period (by Eddie Shack and Tim Horton), but then saw the Canadiens score the next five straight to win the contest 5-2. Ralph Backstrom and Bobby Rousseau evened the score in the second period as the Leafs began to wilt. Defenceman Terry Harper got the winner before the middle stanza was over on a long, low shot from the point. John Ferguson ended any idea of a Leaf comeback when he picked the top corner on Johnny Bower from 30 feet out after just 16 seconds of the final period. Jean Beliveau scored into the empty net for good measure with just 10 seconds to play.

Tremblay scored twice to give the Habs the lead for good. Jimmy Roberts then scored a short-handed goal, which was the back breaker for the Leafs in the third period. Former Leaf Dick Duff put the icing on the cake with another tally to further add to Toronto's misery. The first-period fight caused the opening frame to last some 65 minutes and eight playoff penalty records were established. It all started with a

> *"They should know by now that they're not going to chase us out of the rink. We haven't been manhandled the past three years and that stuff doesn't work against the Canadiens anymore."*
>
> Toe Blake (*The Montreal Gazette*, April 11, 1966)

> *"Toe Blake has a heckuva nerve inferring I sent players out to 'get' his stars. I have never done such a thing as coach and I never tried to do it as a player. Toe played it my style, tough, rough but fair when he played left wing for the Canadiens. Now that he's coaching, he's become the league's biggest crybaby."*
>
> King Clancy (*The Toronto Star*, April 12, 1966)

> *"I think [the Leafs] were just plain tired. You can't work out as much as they do and play hard the whole game."*
>
> Claude Provost (*The Montreal Gazette*, April 13, 1966)

APRIL 14, 1966
Montreal 4 Toronto 1 @ Maple Leaf Gardens

A brawl-filled first period did the Maple Leafs absolutely no good as the Canadiens won the game 4-1 and took the playoff series in four straight. Larry Hillman actually opened the scoring just after a first-period brawl to give Toronto a 1-0 lead. But in the second Gilles

delayed penalty call as Montreal's Ted Harris and John Ferguson tangled with Toronto's Peter Stemkowski. Soon all the players on the ice were involved and the best fight was staged between Harris and the Leafs' Orland Kurtenbach. Harris nailed the big Leaf with a solid punch, knocking Kurtenbach to the ice. Ferguson got the best of Stemkowski and then switched partners by taking on Eddie Shack. Montreal's Dave Balon also tangled with Shack, and as he held the Leaf player down, teammate Claude Larose punched the defenceless Toronto winger. Hillman came in to help Shack and they double-teamed Larose. Shack also took a swing at Roberts. As a result of all the penalties, the teams had to play shorthanded for 32 minutes. Punch Imlach threatened to come on the ice (he laced up his skates) when

The last game of the 1966 semi-final series between the Leafs and Canadiens set eight penalty records at the time, including most penalties in one game, 19 (by Toronto); most penalties one game both teams, 35; most penalty minutes both teams one game, 154; and most penalty minutes one team, one period, 66 (by Montreal). Due to all the penalties called, both teams had to play shorthanded for quite a period of time and this forced a rule change prior to the start of the next season. To start the 1966–67 season, the NHL instituted a rule change allowing for substitution of players who received five-minute majors.

Montreal's Jimmy Roberts (#26) crashes into the Toronto net occupied by goalie Johnny Bower (#1) with Tim Horton looking to clear the crease. Roberts got a shorthanded goal (his only tally in the post season) that killed any hopes of a Leaf comeback in the fourth game of the playoff series. As a utility forward (who sometimes played defence) Roberts became a top penalty killer and scored five goals and five assists in seventy games during the season. He was not expected to be an NHL regular by coach Toe Blake but he worked very hard and played in 611 games as a Hab during his NHL career with 63 goals and 100 assists to his credit. He added another 11 goals in 101 playoff appearances for the Canadiens. Horton had another standout year for the Leafs with six goals and twenty-two assists during 1965–66.

he disagreed with the penalty assessment by Art Skov. The Canadiens were now in the finals for the 17th time since 1927.

"A fight was the last thing I wanted tonight. I told my players stick to hockey at all costs. I was afraid costly penalties might get us disorganized. That scrap just goes to show you how much these guys listen to me. But we won the game and that counts most."

Toe Blake (*The Montreal Gazette*, April 15, 1966)

"I was going out after the referee. We had 64 minutes in penalties and Montreal had 66 when he told us we would be short-handed. I just wouldn't go for it."

Punch Imlach (*The Toronto Star*, April 15, 1966)

stanley cup finals

MONTREAL VS. DETROIT

The Detroit Red Wings pulled off a seven-game upset in the other semi-final against Chicago.

Using the momentum of that series win, the Red Wings went into the Forum and took the first two games of the finals. They won the opener 3-2 on a goal by Paul Henderson. Terry Harper and Ralph Backstrom scored for the Canadiens, but goalie Roger Crozier was out-

Montreal coach Toe Blake holds court during a practice at the Montreal Forum. Blake took over as coach of the Canadiens on June 8, 1955, and held the job until May 11, 1968 (he was actually under contract to the Canadiens in some capacity from 1936 until his death). During that time he won eight Stanley Cups (a record he shares with Scotty Bowman) and posted an 82-37 playoff record in 119 games. It took Blake only 345 regular-season games to record 200 victories. An intense coach capable of colouring the air blue with his language, he was tough on his players but rarely in public. He chose to deal with problems in private and was often a father-type figure to his players. A fair man but a very hard loser, Blake relished the thought of beating the Maple Leafs and his archrival Punch Imlach the most. Imlach (with the Quebec Aces) and Blake (with the Valleyfield Braves) first feuded in the Quebec Senior Hockey League and carried it on in the NHL. Blake won his first NHL game against Toronto on October 5, 1955, in a 2-0 victory with King Clancy coaching the Leafs.

A CLOSER LOOK

although of losing to any team in the playoffs was most what Toe Blake could stand and he always seemed to know what buttons to push at the most crucial time of the year. In the 1966 finals against Detroit, the master motivator was at work again when Blake cut a newspaper photo out and put it on the bulletin board for the Canadiens to see. The picture showed some Red Wing players smoking cigars as though they had already won the Stanley Cup. The Habs were down 2-0 in the series at the time but Blake made all the right moves and his motivated team won the next four games to win the Cup.

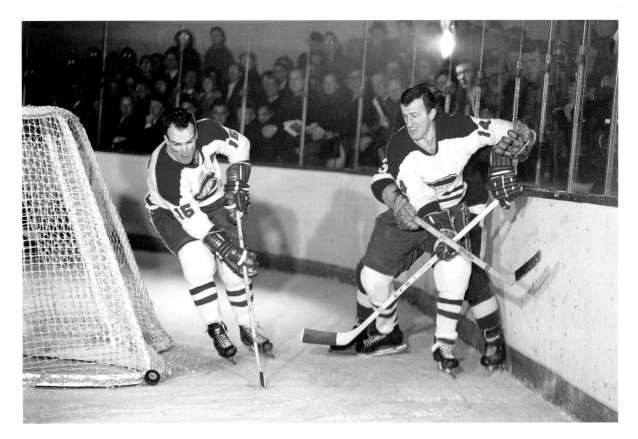

Henri Richard (#16) and teammate Claude Provost (#14) battle for a loose puck behind the Detroit Red Wings goal at the Olympia. Richard scored a controversial winning goal to close the 1966 Stanley Cup finals with an overtime victory. The Red Wings were adamant that Richard had knocked the puck into the net with his body as he slid toward and into the Detroit net, and replays from behind the net verify this version, but the goal still stood. Richard would score another Cup winner in 1971 against Chicago.

standing for Detroit. The Wings were in great shape after winning the second game 5-2 with three straight tallies in the third period when the score was 2-2. J.C. Tremblay and Yvan Cournoyer were the Canadien goal-getters. The Montreal team was very motivated for the next two contests in Detroit and took both games by scores of 4-2 and 2-1 to even the series. Gilles Tremblay had two in the first contest at the Olympia while Backstrom scored the winner in the next game. Five different Montreal players

scored in the fifth game that turned out to be an easy 5-2 win. The sixth game back in Detroit was an "original six" classic and it took overtime to settle the issue. In a well-played contest, Jean Beliveau opened the scoring and Leon Rochefort had another for Montreal, but Norm Ullman got one for Detroit. Floyd Smith tied it for the Wings in the third, but Henri Richard got the controversial winner after 2:20 of overtime. Detroit claimed Richard knocked the puck in with his hand or body as he slid into the goal area, but the referee let the score stand and the Canadiens had another Stanley Cup.

"The coach called it when he sent me out there in overtime. He said, 'I have a feeling you are going to get the winner for us.'"

Henri Richard on Toe Blake
(*Hockey Illustrated*, November 1966)

"I never win anything. They never pick me as an all-star; they don't consider me when it comes to trophies. It doesn't seem to matter how hard I try. [Detroit goalie Roger Crozier] got the car (valued at $5,000) and the $1,000 [for winning the Conn Smythe]. With me, it will remain the same until I retire."

J.C. Tremblay (*Toronto Telegram*, May 6, 1966)

STANLEY CUP & PRINCE OF WALES TROPHY WINNERS 1965-66

FRONT ROW, left to right: Lorne Worsley, Hector "Toe" Blake (Coach), Hon. Hartland de M. Molson (Chairman of the Board), Jean Beliveau (Captain), J. David Molson (President), Sam Pollock, (General Manager), Charlie Hodge. SECOND ROW, left to right: Jean-Guy Talbot, J.-C. Tremblay, Terry Harper, Ted Harris, Jacques Laperriere, John Ferguson, Gilles Tremblay. THIRD ROW, left to right: Henri Richard, Ralph Backstrom, Claude Provost, Claude Larose, Bob Rousseau, Dick Duff. FOURTH ROW, left to right: Andy Galley (Head Train Yvon Cournoyer, Dave Balon, Leon Rochefort, Noel Price, Jim Roberts, Larry Aubut (Assistant Trainer).

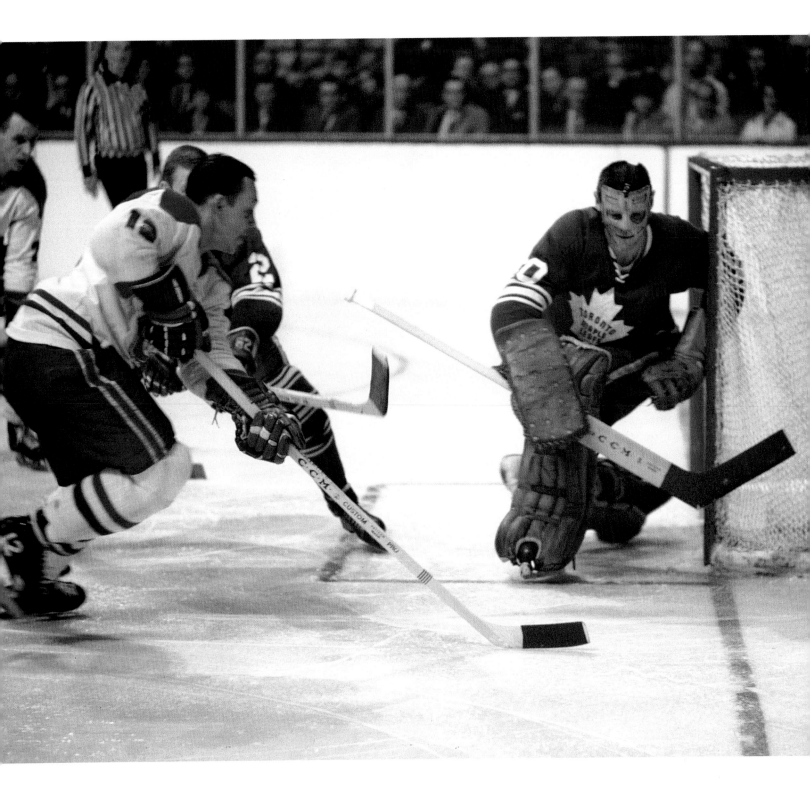

Toronto goaltender Terry Sawchuk (#30) keeps a close eye on Montreal's Yvan Cournoyer (#12) during the last game of the 1967 Stanley Cup finals. Sawchuk was outstanding all night long and the Leafs won their fourth Cup in the Sixties.

The Leafs–Canadiens Rivalry
1966–67

season summary

As defending Stanley Cup champions, the Montreal Canadiens made very few changes going into the 1966–67 season. Rogie Vachon came up to take the bulk of the goaltending duties by the end of the season and Red Berenson was dealt to the Rangers. Noel Price saw more action on defence (24 games) as did rookie Carol Vadnais (11 games) with forward Leon Rochefort seeing a little more duty during the season (27 games). The team struggled in the early going but survived to finish in second place, edging out Toronto and New York as runner-up to the Chicago Blackhawks, who ran away from the pack. The Canadiens posted a 32-25-13 record, growing stronger as the year went along. Bobby Rousseau, Henri Richard and John Ferguson were all strong performers during the season while Yvan Cournoyer was outstanding as a power-play specialist primarily and posted 25 goals. Jean Beliveau suffered a serious eye injury and was restricted to 53 games and 38 points.

The Maple Leafs made more changes in an effort to get more young players in the lineup but, as usual, coach Punch Imlach would come to rely on his trusted veterans. Wally Boyer was sent to the minors and the Rangers drafted Orland Kurtenbach. Brit Selby broke his leg and spent all but six games in the minors, but

Mike Walton played 31 games for the Leafs during the season. Brian Conacher made the team from the start of the year and chipped in with 14 goals. Forward John Brenneman was claimed in the intra-league draft from New York and he

Toronto's Frank Mahovlich (#27) tries to elude Montreal defenceman J.C. Tremblay behind the net. The 1966–67 season marked the final full season for Mahovlich in a Leaf uniform in which he scored 18 goals and recorded 46 points in 63 games. The big winger would score 19 times in 50 games the next season before he was traded in March 1968, to finish his Leaf career with 296 goals and 597 points in 720 games. His playoff totals include 24 goals and 36 assists in 80 games. Tremblay would score 8 goals and 34 points in 1966–67.

played 41 games while Autry Erickson and Milan Marcetta provided depth in the playoffs. Jim McKenny and Wayne Carleton, each scoring one goal, also made brief appearances for the Leafs, who finished in third place with a 32-27-11 record, three points up on the Rangers. Five different goalies were used by the Leafs as injuries struck, but veterans Johnny Bower and Terry Sawchuk carried the club into the post season and both were outstanding. Ron Ellis, Dave Keon and Jim Pappin (who finally played most of the season in Toronto) had good years on a low-scoring club.

Although neither team was especially strong in the regular season, the Canadiens and Leafs showed that playoff experience is invaluable.

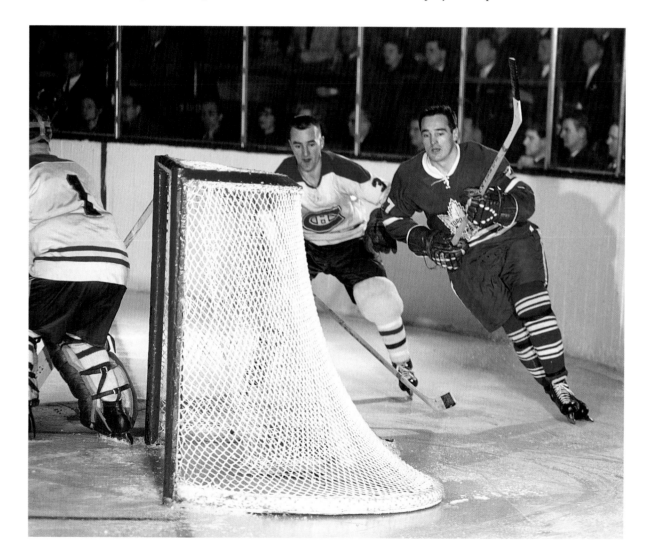

Leafs–Canadiens Rivalry   167

Toronto knocked off the mighty Blackhawks in six games while Montreal was far too strong and determined for the still green New York Rangers. This set up another meeting for the Cup between Canada's two teams. It would be extra special since 1967 was the Centennial Year and bragging rights were clearly on the line. Montreal dearly wanted the Cup to display at Expo '67, while Punch Imlach was as confident as ever that his Leafs would spoil the party. It didn't look good for Toronto after the first game (a 6-2 loss) but they rebounded to take the next two contests, including a 3-0 shutout in the Forum. Montreal routed the Leafs again in the fourth game, but Sawchuk then decided he would not let the Canadiens embarrass him again. He gave up one goal in each of the next two games as the Leafs posted 4-1 and 3-1 victories to win their 11th Stanley Cup. Dave Keon was awarded the Conn Smythe Trophy for his relentless efforts.

In the final year of the "Original Six," it seemed fitting that Toronto and Montreal would meet for the Stanley Cup. The final game of the series, played in Maple Leaf Gardens, closed hockey's greatest era with an epic battle.

NOVEMBER 2, 1966
Toronto 2 Montreal 2 @ Maple Leaf Gardens

Montreal defenceman J.C. Tremblay scored on a bloop shot early in the third period to lift the Canadiens into a 2-2 tie with the Maple Leafs. Tremblay flipped a shot from just inside the Toronto blueline that eluded goalie Terry Sawchuk. Speedy forward John Brenneman opened the scoring for the Leafs in the first period when he put in a rebound past goalie Charlie

Hodge. Brenneman started the play by rushing past a couple of Canadiens to a loose puck in the Montreal end and getting it to his waiting teammates. Frank Mahovlich made it 2-0 for the Leafs when he moved around Tremblay and Ted Harris before snapping a drive that Hodge stopped but the Leaf winger put home the rebound. It was a typical Mahovlich marker that started with long, fluid strides once he gathered in the puck at centre ice. Yvan Cournoyer got Montreal on the board in the second period on a power-play goal by lifting a shot over Sawchuk's shoulder, with Tim Horton in the penalty box. Bobby Rousseau assisted on both Montreal goals. The Canadiens outshot the Leafs 34-30.

NOVEMBER 9, 1966
Toronto 3 Montreal 2 @ The Forum

Jim Pappin's goal mid-way through the third period gave the Leafs a 3-2 win over the Canadiens before 14,203 fans. The goal was Pappin's first of the season as he ripped a shot past Charlie Hodge from just inside the Montreal blueline with the Habs two men short. Yvan Cournoyer opened the scoring in the game on a power-play in the first period, but the Leafs tied it when Brian Conacher (Toronto's best player on the night) got his fifth of the season by putting a high drive past Hodge. George Armstrong gave the Leafs the lead in the second, but Dave Balon tied it for the Canadiens in the third when he put home a Bobby Rousseau rebound. The Leafs were outshot 34-25 and were held in the contest by the brilliant work of goalie Terry Sawchuk. The victory moved the Leafs into second place past the Canadiens and

"I don't think we have ever had as much publicity about being the club to beat — even with those great teams of the 1950s. Maybe it had an effect on the players."

Toe Blake (*The Globe and Mail*, November 10, 1966)

the contest marked the seventh straight game without a loss. Toronto moved to within one point of first-place Chicago. It was the second consecutive loss for the Canadiens.

NOVEMBER 19, 1966
Toronto 5 Montreal 1 @ Maple Leaf Gardens

The largest crowd to see a hockey game in Toronto since 1946 witnessed the Maple Leafs whip the Canadiens 5-1. The Saturday night gathering of 15,986 fans saw the Leafs' so-called "Quiet Line" of Red Kelly, Ron Ellis and Larry Jeffrey combine to score four goals in the contest. The line was put together at the Leafs training camp and earned their nickname with their quiet demeanour off the ice. Jeffrey opened the scoring in the second when he broke in with Ellis and put home a rebound past goalie Gump Worsley as he was tripped into the Montreal net. Jim Pappin gave the Leafs a 2-0 lead but Dave Balon rifled a shot past Terry Sawchuk to get the Habs into the game briefly. But then Ellis scored two straight by scoring on the power-play and shorthanded to pull the Leafs away. Kelly, with two assists on the night, closed out the scoring when he stole the puck from defenceman Jean Guy Talbot and moved in alone on Worsley, whom he beat with a low shot into the corner of the net. The goal was the 271st of Kelly's career and moved him past Aurel Joliet and Howie Morenz on the all-time list.

"I don't think Red got enough credit for his play last year [1965–66]. Pulford and Shack had great years. Pulford got 28 [goals] and Shack got 26. And who did they play with? Kelly."

Punch Imlach (*The Globe and Mail*, November 21, 1966)

NOVEMBER 30, 1966
Toronto 3 Montreal 2 @ Maple Leaf Gardens

Brian Conacher scored the game-winning goal in the third period as the Leafs defeated the Canadiens 3-2 before 15,665 fans. Conacher unleashed a rising 20-foot blast that sailed past goalie Gump Worsley. The young Leaf winger stole the puck from Leon Rochefort in the Montreal end and then outmaneuvered defenceman Jean Guy Talbot before he beat Worsley.

Montreal's John Ferguson (#22) is about to run Peter Stemkowski (#12) into the boards. Ferguson would lead the NHL in penalty minutes in 1966–67 with 177, but he also found time to score 20 goals and 42 points in 67 games. Stemkowski got into 68 games with the Leafs in 1966–67 and he responded with 13 goals and 35 points with 75 penalty minutes. The big Leaf centre would be dealt the following season and his career Maple Leaf numbers show 29 goals and 93 points in 221 regular-season games.

Defenceman Tim Horton (the first star of the game) and John Brenneman scored the other Toronto goals before the game was five minutes old, while Claude Provost and Henri Richard scored for the Canadiens. Provost's goal was verified only by the goal judge and hotly disputed by the Leafs. Montreal policeman John Ferguson was out looking for trouble all night long and ended up battling three Leafs in the first period. Ferguson put an arm lock on Red Kelly, which brought Larry Jeffrey into the fray for the Leafs, followed by Bob Baun. Montreal coach Toe Blake was upset with Jim Pappin when his errant stick cut Gilles Tremblay on the left ear. Blake reminded observers that Pappin had cut Jim Roberts for 25 stitches in the head with his stick during a November 9 contest between the two clubs. The win gave the Leafs 21 points, keeping them in a second-place tie with New York, just one point behind Chicago.

DECEMBER 7, 1966
Montreal 6 Toronto 3 @ The Forum

The Canadiens finally beat the Maple Leafs for the first time this season as they clearly outplayed the visitors to post a 6-3 victory. Looking more like Stanley Cup champions, the Canadiens got goals from Claude Larose (with two), Yvan Cournoyer, Bobby Rousseau, Jean Beliveau and Henri Richard with his 250th career marker. It was rumoured that Larose was headed for the minors, but he scored two in the previous game against New York and added a pair versus the Leafs, who got a poor game from goalie Terry Sawchuk. Larose's second goal of the game proved to be the game winner when his 30-foot drive went into the far corner of the net past Sawchuk. The Leafs stayed close for a little more than half the contest on power-play goals by Jim Pappin, Tim Horton and George Armstrong. Toronto forward Eddie Shack was cut for 15 stitches in the third period when he was hit by Montreal defenceman Ted Harris. Shack hit the ice with blood pouring out from his forehead

while Harris was given a five-minute major for elbowing. The Canadiens were very aggressive throughout the contest and took two elbowing penalties in addition to the Harris penalty and calls for cross-checking and boarding.

DECEMBER 21, 1966
Montreal 6 Toronto 2 @ The Forum

The Canadiens won a brawl-filled contest with the Maple Leafs with a 6-2 victory on home ice before 13,829 fans. The Leafs opened the scoring on a goal by Larry Jeffrey in the first minute of play, but the Habs then scored four straight times to take the lead. Yvan Cournoyer led the way with three goals, all on power-plays, tying a team mark established by Jean Beliveau, who scored three times on one penalty during the 1953–54 season. Ralph Backstrom had a pair, while Jim Roberts (his first point of the season) got the other Montreal marker. The hat trick by Cournoyer gave him six goals on the year against the Leafs. John Ferguson started the brawling by trying to engage Eddie Shack in a fight but ended up fighting Kent Douglas, and he later fought with Jeffery. Shack later fought with Backstrom and Bob Pulford tangled with Claude Larose. Toronto's Bob Baun battled with Montreal blueliner Jacques Laperriere but ended up taking on Claude Larose. Peter Stemkowski and Terry Harper staged a fight in the second period. The game also featured a rush to centre ice by Leaf goalie Gary Smith (who replaced a shaky Bruce Gamble) and the wandering net-minder was bumped by J.C. Tremblay before he was forced to get rid of the puck. Tremblay fired the puck back into the Leaf end and defenceman Marcel Pronovost was forced to make a save.

JANUARY 11, 1967
Toronto 2 Montreal 1 @ The Forum

Ron Ellis let go a hard drive that appeared to be headed wide of the net but Montreal goalie Charlie Hodge tried to catch the puck and it dropped into the net for the winning goal in the Leafs 2-1 victory over the Canadiens. Ellis let go his 30-foot shot with less than four minutes to play and was only one of 20 shots the Leafs had taken all night long. Leaf forward Larry Jeffrey bumped into Hodge and it appeared the jolt knocked the puck loose from the goalie's catching glove. Yvan Cournoyer opened the scoring for the Canadiens in the first period, who picked the far corner of the net on the Leafs goalie Bruce Gamble (who made 27 saves). Bob Pulford, the Leafs' best player on the night, tied the score in the second period after winning a face-off and going to the net for a rebound after taking a pass from teammate Allan Stanley. Pulford also assisted on the winning goal and was double shifted because of an injury to Dave Keon. The rather dull contest was also played without Jean Beliveau of the Canadiens, who had suffered a serious eye injury.

JANUARY 25, 1967
Montreal 3 Toronto 1 @ Maple Leaf Gardens

The Canadiens handed the Maple Leafs their fifth straight loss before 15,848 fans with a 3-1 victory. Yvan Cournoyer scored his 15th goal of the season to open the scoring in the second period, but Dave Keon tied it for the Leafs just

a minute later with assists to linemates Frank Mahovlich and George Armstrong. But Montreal took the lead for good when Bobby Rousseau set up Gilles Tremblay for the winning goal past goalie Bruce Gamble on a power-play. Claude Larose, with his first goal in 16 games, got an insurance marker in the third period for the Habs when a point shot from the blueline went in. In addition to losing the game, the Leafs lost Mahovlich with a charley horse after getting belted by Montreal defenceman Ted Harris. Mahovlich crashed into the boards and had to be helped off. Jean Beliveau was back in the Montreal lineup following an eye injury and his presence helped the Habs win in Toronto for the first time this season. Gamble made several great saves in the game and Mike Walton made an exciting full-length rush to give the Leaf fans their only bright moments.

FEBRUARY 1, 1967
Montreal 7 Toronto 1 @ The Forum

Henri Richard scored a key goal early in the third period that seemed to change the tide of the contest and the Canadiens went on to a 7-1 romp over the Maple Leafs. The loss was the eighth straight for Toronto. Richard's goal came with the score 2-1 in favour of the Habs and the Leafs had just missed a great opportunity when Red Kelly hit the post. The puck went to Montreal defenceman Terry Harper who got it to Gilles Tremblay and he drilled a shot that Leaf goalie Johnny Bower stopped but could not control on the rebound. Richard bunted the puck out of mid-air and into the net. The Canadiens popped in two more goals before the period ended to give them a 5-1 lead and kill any Toronto hopes. The Leafs scored the first goal of the game when defenceman Bob Baun (who was on the ice for five Montreal goals) scored his first of the season just 1:53 into the contest when he beat Charlie Hodge. Yvan Cournoyer then scored his 17th and 18th goals of the season to give Montreal the lead. Ralph

Backstrom, Dick Duff, Jean Beliveau and Tremblay scored the other goals. Bobby Rousseau had three assists for the Canadiens. The Maple Leafs had three players up from Rochester for this game, the best of whom was defenceman Larry Hillman who was paired with Tim Horton. The other call-ups for Toronto were forwards Jim Pappin and Dick Gamble. Montreal was now in third place with 45 points while the Leafs were in fourth with 42.

FEBRUARY 22, 1967
Toronto 5 Montreal 2 @ Maple Leaf Gardens

The Maple Leafs won their fourth in a row with a 5-2 win on home ice before 15,871 fans. The game was also the fifth behind the bench for King Clancy (normally the assistant general manager) and his record was now 4-0-1 while substituting for the ailing Punch Imlach. From his hospital bed, Imlach watched goalie Johnny Bower turn in a sparkling performance, stopping 38 of 40 shots. Eddie Shack and Dave Keon, off a goalmouth scramble, gave the Leafs a 2-0 lead in the first, but Dick Duff scored one for the Habs in the second. The Leafs got third-period markers from Ron Ellis, Jim Pappin and Brian Conacher, while only Claude Larose was able to respond for the Canadiens. Frank Mahovlich, appearing to thrive under the coaching of Clancy, had a couple of assists in the game and forced goalie Charlie Hodge to make some good stops. Clancy kept the Canadiens off balance by constantly mixing up his line combinations. John Ferguson was penalized for spearing Eddie Shack of the Leafs and it would cost him an automatic league fine of $25.

MARCH 1, 1967
Montreal 1 Toronto 1 @ The Forum

Toronto's Jim Pappin scored a goal with just 49 seconds to play as the Leafs and Canadiens battled to a 1-1 tie. With the draw, the Leafs ran

Bob Baun — a closer look

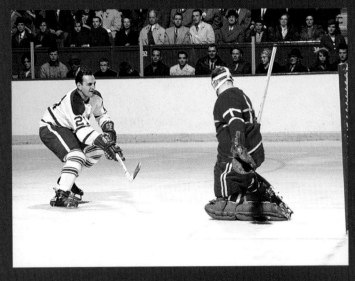

Toronto defenceman Bob Baun (#21) moves in on Montreal netminder Charlie Hodge. Baun had a somewhat diminished role with the Leafs in 1966–67, especially in the playoffs, and scored two goals and ten points in 54 games with 82 penalty minutes. The next season saw Baun claimed in the expansion draft by the Oakland Seals, but the sturdily built defender would return to Toronto in 1970–71 to bring his Maple Leaf totals to 29 goals and 169 points in 739 games with 1,155 penalty minutes. The 1966–67 season was also the final one for Hodge in Montreal and he posted three shutouts to bring his Canadien career total to 21 in 236 games played.

VALUE DAYS

By 1966–67, Bob Baun's relationship with Leafs coach Punch Imlach had deteriorated (largely because of contract disputes) to the point where Toronto left him unprotected in the expansion draft (although Imlach would claim he did everything he could not to lose Baun). The defenceman was taken by the Oakland Seals, who named him as their first captain, and he signed a three-year deal for $31,000, $32,000 and $33,000 a year. After the Seals dealt him to Detroit for the 1968–69 season, the business-minded and smooth-talking Baun got the Red Wings to give him a renegotiated contract to a reported $70,000 a year, or more than double his agreement with the Seals. He made this fact known to Detroit teammate Gordie Howe who was, to say the least, quite upset to find this out.

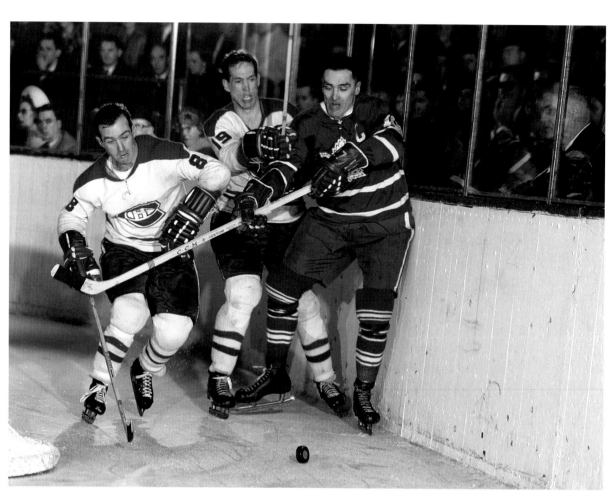

"*The first time I put on a Canadiens uniform I thought to myself this team has a heritage left behind by players such as Maurice Richard and Butch Bouchard. Everyone from the coach on down has an intense desire to win.*"

Canadiens Dick Duff (#8) and Terry Harper (#19) go for a loose puck with George Armstrong (#10) of the Leafs. Injuries limited Dick Duff to just 51 games in 1966–67 and he scored only 12 goals and 23 points. He was also playing poorly the following year when a severe talking-to by coach Toe Blake got the fiery winger turned around. Duff responded with 25 goals and 46 points in 66 games. Duff was on four Cup-winning teams in Montreal and scored 87 goals and 172 points in 305 games. He added 43 points (15 goals, 28 assists) in 60 playoff games.

their unbeaten streak to nine games (seven wins, two ties) and brought them to within four points of second-place New York. It looked like a first-period goal by Henri Richard would hold up, as the Leafs could not beat rookie Rogie Vachon (up from Houston of the CPHL) in the

Montreal net. But the Canadiens could not get another shot past veteran goalie Johnny Bower after Richard had deflected a drive home for his goal. The 42-year-old Bower received a great ovation from the Montreal crowd when he was pulled for the extra attacker after making five scintillating saves during the game. Bower was run over twice by John Ferguson of the Canadiens during the contest. Tim Horton and Larry Hillman came to his defence and took on the Montreal enforcer.

MARCH 8, 1967
Toronto 6 Montreal 4 @ Maple Leaf Gardens

The Maple Leafs scored five goals in the first eleven minutes of the first period and coasted to

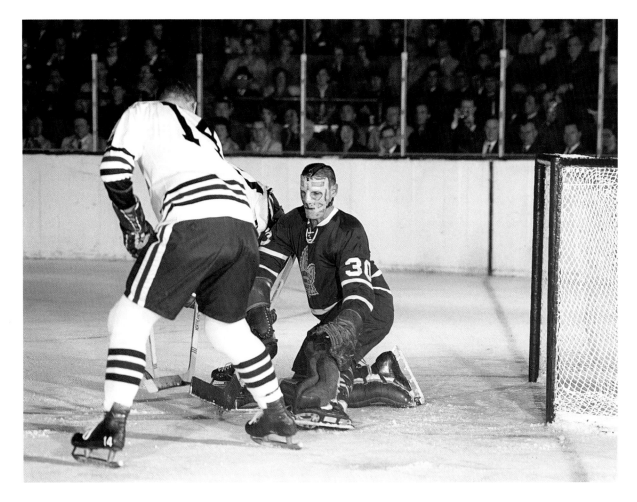

On March 4, 1967, goalie Terry Sawchuk (#30) made hock-ey history by becoming the first goaltender to record 100 career shutouts when the Leafs blanked Chicago 3-0 at the Gardens. Sawchuk is left defenceless in this photo but he still stopped 22 shots and got goals from George Armstrong, Peter Stemkowski and Jim Pappin to post the milestone. For his performance in '66–67 Sawchuk was awarded the J.P. Bickell Trophy as the best Leaf player (posting a 15-5-4 record in 28 games with two shutouts).

a 6-4 win over the Canadiens. After Montreal opened the scoring when Gilles Tremblay scored at 48 seconds of the first, the Leafs roared back with goals from Bob Pulford, Peter Stemkowski, Dave Keon, and Tim Horton. Bob Baun got the Leafs' other goal on a long shot (the third far-out drive that ended up as a Leaf tally) in the second period. It was the first rough outing for Montreal rookie goalie Rogie Vachon

"Bower and Sawchuk were the best goaltenders in the NHL last season. I think they'll be the best again this season [1965–66]. That's why I didn't drop one to gamble on a kid [Gerry Cheevers] who has yet to prove he belongs in the NHL."

Punch Imlach (Maple Leaf program, November 10, 1965)

since he joined the Canadiens. Claude Provost, J.C. Tremblay and John Ferguson scored the other Montreal goals while Henri Richard got three assists for the Habs. Jean Beliveau record-

---

Montreal's Terry Harper (#19) holds his position in front of the net with Toronto's Jim Pappin (#18) lurking in the background. Both players staged a spirited fight against each other on March 22, 1967, in a Canadiens victory at the Gardens. Harper did not score a goal in 1966–67 but recorded 16 assists to go along with 99 penalty minutes. Pappin had his first 20-goal season when he had 21 in 64 games during 1966–67. He was outstanding in the playoffs and led all scorers with 15 points. Two years later, he was dealt to Chicago and finished his Leaf career with 54 goals and 100 points in 223 games.

ed his 600th career assist on Ferguson's goal. Montreal's Carol Vadnais and Toronto's Mike Walton engaged in a fight during the first period and Ferguson and Larry Hillman of the Leafs went at it in the second. Terry Sawchuk was in goal for the Leafs and made 31 saves.

MARCH 22, 1967
Montreal 5 Toronto 3 @ Maple Leaf Gardens

The Montreal Canadiens jumped out to a 3-0 lead on the strength of two goals from defenceman J.C. Tremblay and beat the Maple Leafs 5-3. Ralph Backstrom, Henri Richard and Jean Beliveau (with his first in 21 games) got the other Montreal goals. The Leafs staged a strong comeback attempt but were held off by the solid goaltending of Rogie Vachon and Beliveau's goal killed any Leaf chances of pulling off a tie. Ron Ellis scored twice for Toronto (including his 21st of the year) and Bob Pulford notched his 200th career goal as the Leafs showed some great resiliency. The first period featured a pair of fights that were going on at the same time. John Ferguson pounded on Leaf defenceman Larry Hillman; the Toronto rearguard responded with a choke hold and tried to bang the Hab enforcer's head into the glass. While this fight was going on, Toronto forward Jim Pappin went at it with Montreal defenceman Terry Harper. The Leaf player suffered a head cut during the scrap. The win moved the Canadiens into a third-place tie with the Leafs in the standings.

"[Terry] Sawchuk said he wasn't ready so I went with [Bruce] Gamble [in goal]. He wasn't sharp. The Montreal kid [Vachon] was lucky but he came up with big saves that beat us."

Punch Imlach (*The Montreal Gazette*, March 23, 1967)

Ralph Backstrom (#6) had a rather mediocre year in 1966–67 when he scored only 14 times in 69 games to go along with 41 points. It was a year much like 1963–64 when he scored only eight goals. Once again Backstrom bounced back (just like he did in 1964–65 when he scored 25) to score 20 goals and 45 points in 1967–68 and helped the Canadiens regain their championship form. The slick centre stayed with the Habs until 1971 and recorded 215 goals and 512 points in 844 games. In 100 post-season games, he had 22 goals and 26 assists.

"*Two weeks before training camps opened, I practiced every day from midnight to 2 o'clock in the morning. That was the only time of day we could get the ice. But it didn't matter to me, I was that determined.*"

Ralph Backstrom (*Hockey Illustrated*, February 1965)

MARCH 29, 1967
Montreal 5 Toronto 3 @ The Forum

A 5-3 win on home ice over the Maple Leafs set up the Canadiens for a second-place finish in the league standings as the 1966–67 season draws to a close. The Maple Leafs were also vying for second place but that hope evaporated with the loss and were more likely to finish in third or fourth spot (a second-place finish was worth $1,250 per man in bonus money, while fourth place paid only $250 per player). The teams exchanged goals in the first period that ended in a 2-2 tie,

but Montreal scored twice in the second to take the lead and knocked a very shaky Terry Sawchuk from the Leaf net (he was replaced by Johnny Bower). Larry Hillman scored his fourth of the year to open the scoring but the Canadiens got goals from Jean Guy Talbot (shorthanded) and Gilles Tremblay to take the lead. Red Kelly tied it for the Leafs but second-period markers from Yvan Cournoyer (his 11th versus the Leafs this season) and Leon Rochefort put the Canadiens in the lead for good. Mike Walton got one back for Toronto but J.C. Tremblay got the Habs an insurance goal in the third. Montreal's John Ferguson was his usual aggressive self and picked up three penalties to break a club record (held by Lou Fontinato with 167) for most penalty minutes in one season (Ferguson now had 171 penalty minutes). Toronto defenceman Bob Baun played a tough game and got into a fight with Ralph Backstrom.

playoffs

SERIES A – TORONTO VS. CHICAGO

The Maple Leafs were considered no match for the first-place Chicago Blackhawks, who had finished 19 points ahead of Toronto during the regular season. The first game of the series was no surprise when the Blackhawks whipped the Leafs 5-2 at the Chicago Stadium. But the next game saw Terry Sawchuk play a great game in net and the Leafs got goals from Dave Keon and

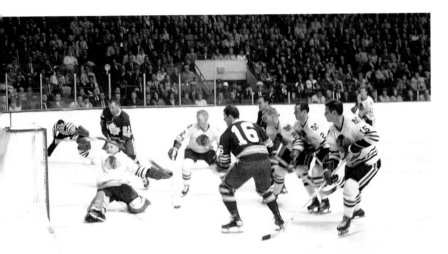

Mike Walton (#16) of the Leafs scores a goal against Denis DeJordy of the Blackhawks during the 1967 semi-final series. As a rookie with the Leafs in 1966–67, Walton scored seven goals and seventeen points in thirty-one games. In the play-offs, Walton had seven points in twelve games in Toronto's run to the Cup. In spite of his good performance coach Punch Imlach, who never got along with the long-haired Leaf, wanted to leave the winger unprotected in the 1967 expansion draft, but was overruled by Toronto team president Stafford Smythe, since Walton was talented and had married his niece.

Peter Stemkowski to win 3-1. Back at home, the Leafs took the third game by a 3-1 score with Ron Ellis, Frank Mahovlich and Jim Pappin scoring the goals. However, Chicago responded with a 4-3 win at the Gardens in the fourth contest as they got a goal after just nine seconds of play by Ken Wharram. The pivotal fifth game was played on a Saturday afternoon in Chicago and Terry Sawchuk stole the show when he came into the game in the second period to replace an unsteady Johnny Bower and with the score tied 2-2. Sawchuk did not allow another Blackhawk goal despite a barrage of shots, and Mike Walton scored the winner in a 4-2 win. A stop Sawchuk made on Bobby Hull has become legendary and the Blackhawks were a demoralized group of players. The sixth contest saw Chicago get the first goal but the Leafs got two from Brian Conacher (who played a great game)

and one from Stemkowski to eliminate the Blackhawks with a 3-1 win.

SERIES B – MONTREAL VS. NEW YORK

The New York Rangers made the playoffs for the first time since 1962 but were not expected to give the Canadiens much of a battle. For the most part the experts turned out to be right, although it was not as easy as the four-game sweep might indicate. The first game had the Rangers leading 4-1 with 11 minutes to play, but the Canadiens roared back with three goals in just under two minutes (Claude Provost at 9:12, J.C. Tremblay at 9:34 and John Ferguson at 11:03) to tie the game. Ralph Backstrom then got the winner and Jean Beliveau added another in a 6-4 Montreal win. The shell-shocked Rangers never recovered and Montreal took the next three games by scores of 3-1, 3-2 and 2-1. The final game went into overtime and John Ferguson got the winner at 6:28 of the extra session. Rogie Vachon played in net during all four games for the Habs.

stanley cup finals

APRIL 20, 1967
Montreal 6 Toronto 2 @ The Forum

The Canadiens used their speed to great advantage as they beat a weary group of Maple Leafs 6-2 in the first game of the Stanley Cup finals. The Leafs were only in the game for a brief period when Larry Hillman scored just 15 seconds after Yvan Cournoyer (with his first of two on the night) had given the Habs an early 1-0 lead at 6:25 of the first period. After that, the Canadiens simply dominated the contest with three goals coming from the stick of Henri Richard (his first-ever playoff hat trick) while Jean Beliveau added another. Jim Pappin scored the only other goal for Toronto. The Canadiens outshot the Leafs 44-26 and Terry Sawchuk was replaced by Johnny Bower in the Toronto net for the third period (giving up the last two goals to Richard). Rogie Vachon was in goal for Montreal and made a spectacular save against Leaf defenceman Tim Horton in the first period. Both of Cournoyer's goals came on the power-play, giving him an even dozen against the Leafs with the extra man for the year.

APRIL 22, 1967
Toronto 3 Montreal 0 @ The Forum

Johnny Bower was back in the net for Toronto and he was outstanding in recording his first playoff shutout since 1964 as the Maple Leafs bounced back to beat the Canadiens 3-0. Centre Peter Stemkowski scored the opening goal of the game in the first period when he beat goalie Rogie Vachon in close by converting a Bob Pulford pass during a power-play opportunity. Second-period goals by Mike Walton and Tim Horton gave Bower all he needed as he turned back 31 Montreal shots. It appeared that Bower

was run at a couple of times by the Canadiens' John Ferguson and this drew the ire of Toronto coach Punch Imlach. The Leafs were even more upset that Ted Harris speared Stemkowski just as Horton scored his goal. The Leaf penalty killers were especially strong throughout the game led by centre Dave Keon. A determined effort by the Leafs handed the Canadiens their first loss in 16 games (dating back to the regular season), breaking an 11-game winning streak as well. The contest was played on a Saturday afternoon to accommodate U.S. television demands.

A fallen Peter Stemkowski (#12) tries to get off a shot against Canadiens goalie Rogie Vachon (#29) during the finals. Stemkowski scored a big goal when he got the opener in the second game of the series, a contest the Leafs had to win. The large centre had a fantastic post season for the Leafs with 12 points (five goals) in 12 games. He worked well with linemates Bob Pulford and Jim Pappin to give the Toronto club their best unit during the playoffs (recording a combined total of 13 goals and 25 assists).

"I tried to warn them. They [the Leafs] did it to Chicago, played a bad first game and bounced right back. I tried to warn our guys but … we didn't deserve to win so we lost it. It's pretty hard to be unbeaten all season."

Toe Blake (*The Montreal Gazette*, April 24, 1967)

Brian Conacher

"I was sick and tired of him [Claude Larose] always swinging his stick from behind at you. He's been doing it to me all season long."

Brian Conacher (*The Globe and Mail,* April 26, 1967)

Brian Conacher (#22) of the Leafs fights with Claude Larose (#11) of the Canadiens during the third game of the finals. Conacher brought some size (six foot three, 197 pounds) and youth to the Leafs in 1966–67. He scored 14 goals and totalled 27 points as a rookie during the season and shone in the playoffs with three important goals and five points in twelve games. Larose scored 19 in 1966–67 and added one more in the playoffs.

The son of Lionel Conacher (Canada's Athlete of the Half Century), Brian Conacher also had to live up to the name of his uncle Charlie who was a Leaf star during the Thirties. Brian played football at the University of Western Ontario and hockey for the Canadian National Team (he was a member of the Olympic team for the 1964 games at Innsbruck, Austria) before turning professional in 1965. He played one season in the minors with Rochester of the AHL (14 goals in 69 games and another six in twelve playoff matches) before joining the Leafs for the 1966–67 season. Conacher's forte was his ability to play good defensive hockey and kill penalties. Despite a good year and an excellent playoff in 1966–67, Conacher managed 11 goals in 64 games for Toronto and would find himself back in the minors briefly for 1967–68. It was a year that saw him battle with Punch Imlach, starting with a contract dispute that got the manager to respect Conacher as a negotiator and netted the player about $20,000 per season. He was claimed by Detroit in the intra-league draft of June 1968.

APRIL 25, 1967
Toronto 3 Montreal 2 @ Maple Leaf Gardens

Bob Pulford scored in the 28th minute of overtime as the Leafs defeated the Canadiens 3-2 to take the series lead. Before 15,977 fans, the two teams staged one of the most thrilling games ever played at Maple Leaf Gardens. The winner came as a result of some good Leaf work after a face-off in the Montreal end. Linemates Peter Stemkowski and Jim Pappin, who both scored earlier in the game, got the puck to an alert Pulford, who got himself free in front of the Montreal net and simply redirected the puck home (it was his first overtime winner in 83 playoff games). The Montreal goals came from Jean Beliveau and John Ferguson as the Canadiens outshot the Leafs 62-54 during the long game. Johnny Bower was terrific in the Toronto net making many good saves in overtime and getting a lucky break when Gilles Tremblay hit the post on a two-on-one break with Ralph Backstrom. Toronto's Brian Conacher and Montreal's Claude Larose staged a spirited battle in the second period earning majors. Conacher nailed Larose with a crunching right hand that caused a seven-stitch cut to the forehead. It was a physical match throughout and the checking was close. Leaf defenceman Allan Stanley hit Henri Richard with a solid shoulder in the second overtime period forcing the Montreal centre to retire for the night.

"That was the first overtime goal I've ever scored and it wasn't too difficult. I had about three quarters of the net open and just steered the puck in after it came across from Pappin."

Bob Pulford (*The Montreal Gazette,* April 26, 1967)

"We trained all year for this. I thought the club was getting stronger as we went along."

Punch Imlach (*The Montreal Gazette,* April 26, 1967)

APRIL 27, 1967
Montreal 6 Toronto 2 @ Maple Leaf Gardens

The Canadiens took a 2-0 lead in the first period of the fourth game and a shaky Terry Sawchuk was unable to stem the tide in net as the Leafs were bombed 6-2 before the hometown crowd. Ralph Backstrom and Jean Beliveau had the first-period markers and each player scored again in the second as the Canadiens took a 5-2 lead into the final frame (the other goal came from Henri Richard and proved to be the winner). Although the Leafs tried to make a game of it, with goals from Mike Walton and Tim Horton in the second, the Habs

Toronto's Bob Pulford (#20) knocks in the winning goal in overtime to give the Leafs the series lead 2-1 in the finals. The goal came in the second overtime period of a classic battle between the two rivals that was one of the best playoff games ever played at Maple Leaf Gardens. Pulford was nearly traded to Boston during the season but an injury to Bruins defenceman Ted Green nixed the deal. As it turned out, it was one of the best deals Punch Imlach never made.

added another goal (by Jimmy Roberts) in the third to salt the game away. Sawchuk was pressed into service when Johnny Bower was injured in the pre-game warmup and was finished for the year. The Montreal team sensed Sawchuk was not ready and poured 40 shots at the veteran netminder. The Leafs had 37 shots on Rogie Vachon in the Montreal net.

APRIL 29, 1967
Toronto 4 Montreal 1 @ The Forum

Goaltender Terry Sawchuk stopped 37 of 38 shots and the Maple Leafs chased Montreal goalie Rogie Vachon from the net in their 4-1 win over the Canadiens. Sawchuk was superb during this crucial match, making an outstanding save on Ralph Backstrom in the opening minutes of the game. Leon Rochefort gave the Canadiens the opening goal but Sawchuk then shut the door and Toronto scored four straight to win the game. The Leafs tied it on a power-play marker by Jim Pappin after a boarding penalty to Claude Larose of the Habs. Brian

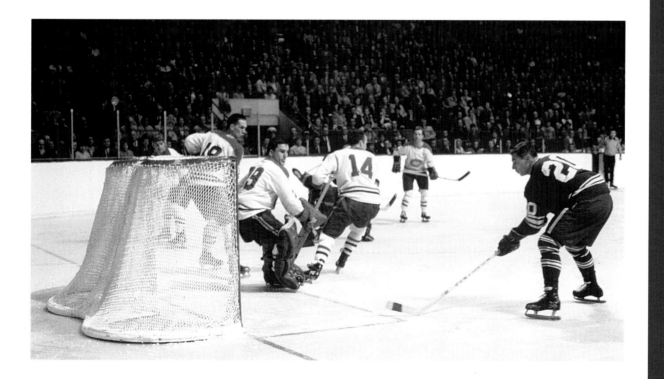

"Sawchuk played a terrific game, but I wasn't surprised. I expected it. Some of you guys might have said that goaltending was my problem in Thursday's game. You didn't hear it from me."

Punch Imlach (*The Globe and Mail*, May 1, 1967)

Henri Richard of the Canadiens is pinned against the boards by the Leafs' Tim Horton during the finals. Richard got the Montreal team off to a good start in the series against the Leafs by scoring three goals in the first game. He then potted a winning goal in the fourth game to even the series but could work no more magic afterwards. Horton was his usual, steady self for the Toronto side and had five points (two goals) in the six-game final.

Conacher scored the winner when he rapped home a Red Kelly rebound early in the second period. Defenceman Marcel Pronovost broke away to score a crushing goal that came short-handed when he drilled a low shot past a surprised Vachon. Dave Keon added another before the period was over when he pounced on a Tim Horton rebound after the Leaf centre had weaved his way through the Montreal end with the teams playing four on four. Gump Worsley (who had not played a full game since December and not seen any action after March 12) started the third period for the Canadiens. There was no

scoring in the third as the Leafs got their checking game in gear and shut the Habs down, although Sawchuk did face 12 shots. The victory marked the third consecutive Saturday afternoon win for the Leafs during the playoffs.

MAY 2, 1967
Toronto 3 Montreal 1 @ Maple Leaf Gardens

Terry Sawchuk was superb in goal once again as the Maple Leafs won the Stanley Cup with a

Toronto goaltender Terry Sawchuk (#30) stops the Canadiens attack in close with help from Marcel Pronovost (#3) who watches Claude Provost (#14) during the fifth game of the finals. Sawchuk was once again superb in the Leaf net and gave his team a chance to win the Stanley Cup on home ice. Pronovost contributed to the cause by scoring a key goal during the Saturday afternoon contest. Pronovost and defensive partner Larry Hillman did not give up a single goal at even strength during the entire 1967 playoffs for the Leafs.

tension-packed 3-1 win in the last game of the "Original Six." Sawchuk repeatedly frustrated the Canadiens with a great effort in the net, stopping 40 of 41 shots and the Leafs gave him all the support he needed to clinch the Cup. Winger Ron Ellis opened the scoring for the Leafs in the second when he combined with Red Kelly and knocked in a rebound. Just before the second period ended, Jim Pappin scored what turned out to be the winner when his shot deflected off a skate past a startled Gump Worsley in the Canadiens net. Dick Duff scored for the Canadiens on a great individual effort and the tension in the Gardens heightened as

the Canadiens did everything but tie the score. A face-off in the Toronto end with 55 seconds to play saw coach Toe Blake pull Worsley from the net for the extra attacker but the Leaf veterans did the job and protected Sawchuk perfectly. The puck went to captain George Armstrong and he calmly crossed the centre red line before he sent a long shot into the empty net. The Leafs dressed three goalies for the game, with Johnny Bower on the bench (even though he could not play) and Al Smith who watched the game from the Leaf dressing room in full gear. The loss marked the first time the Habs lost in the finals since 1955 (to Detroit) and Punch Imlach became the first general manager-coach to win four Cups.

Montreal netminder Gump Worsley looks on forlornly as the Leafs have just taken a 2-0 lead in the sixth game of the finals on a goal by Jim Pappin. While Worsley is down the Leafs are off to the left celebrating their good fortune as the puck caromed in off the skate of Montreal defenceman Terry Harper. The Leafs would go on to win the game 3-1 and take the Stanley Cup on home ice.

"It was a lousy goal. The puck hit somebody [Terry Harper] and just dropped. It was in before I could move."

Gump Worsley on Jim Pappin's winning goal (*The Montreal Gazette*, May 3, 1967)

"I wanted all our old guys to enjoy this one. This may have been their last game together."

Punch Imlach (*The Montreal Gazette*, May 3, 1967)

"I can't fault my players for a game like this. They worked hard but the puck wouldn't go in."

Toe Blake (*The Montreal Gazette*, May 3, 1967)

"We played 97 games this year but it feels like a thousand. We beat the Canadiens the only way we can win — playing tough hockey. Let them come at us, then counter punch to get a goal or two we could protect."

Dave Keon (*The Globe and Mail*, May 3, 1967)

"[Sawchuk] came up with big saves and gave them time to get ahead."

Jean Beliveau (*The Globe and Mail*, May 3, 1967)

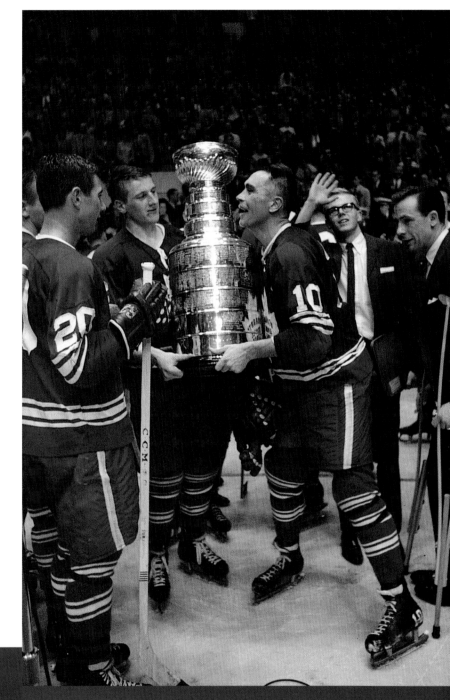

"I was on television with [Prime Minister Lester] Pearson and told him to knock off the stuff about Canada not being a nation! Stuff like this win proves we're a nation and have been for 50 years. Anybody who wants to know about a nation ought to come in this room and see how these guys wear the Maple Leaf."

Former Leafs owner Conn Smythe (*The Globe and Mail*, May 3, 1967)

Montreal defenceman J.C. Tremblay (#3) gets to the puck ahead of the Leafs forward Murray Oliver (#11). Tremblay helped lead Montreal back to the Stanley Cup in 1967–68 while Oliver joined Toronto in a trade with Boston that involved Eddie Shack.

The Leafs–Canadiens Rivalry
1967–68

The 1967–68 season witnessed the biggest change in hockey history when six new teams began play. St. Louis, Pittsburgh, Philadelphia, Minnesota, Los Angeles and Oakland were all placed in the Western Division of the new NHL while the six original teams formed the Eastern Division. While expansion gave many players a chance to experience big-league hockey, it also began a watering-down process that has yet to be curtailed. The Maple Leafs were hurt badly by expansion while the Canadiens were more prepared, as the results clearly show.

The defending champion Leafs were hit hard in the expansion draft and by retirement. Terry Sawchuk, Bob Baun, Larry Jeffrey and Kent Douglas were all gone from the team and Red Kelly deported to coach the Los Angeles Kings. Depth players such as John Brenneman, Brit Selby, Milan Marcetta and Autry Erickson were also in new cities for '67–68. Many of the returning Leafs were long in the tooth (Allan Stanley, Marcel Pronovost, George Armstrong) although Tim Horton (an all-star), Johnny Bower (his last good season) and Bob Pulford still had lots to contribute. Dave Keon had an uncharacteristic bad season (11 goals), Jim Pappin scored only 13 and the only new forward of significance was Murray Oliver (16 goals). A few of the Leafs had contract problems (Brian Conacher,

Larry Hillman) that seemed to affect their play as well. Coach Punch Imlach felt he had to shake up his team and he pulled the trigger on March 3, 1968, when he dealt superstar Frank Mahovlich (along with Peter Stemkowski, Garry Unger and the rights to the retired Carl Brewer) to Detroit in exchange for Norm Ullman, Paul Henderson and Floyd Smith. The deal was too late to rescue the season since the Leafs were such a poor road team and had a great deal of difficulty against the expansion clubs. The Leafs missed the post season for the first time since Imlach took over the team but they did have bright spots in the play of Mike Walton and Ron Ellis.

By comparison, the Canadiens made a smooth transition to the new era of hockey. They lost few players of significance (Charlie Hodge, Jean Guy Talbot, Dave Balon, Noel Price, Jean Gauthier) and the depth players selected by the new clubs did not make a significant difference since the Canadien veterans were still producing (like Jean Beliveau's 31 goals and Dick Duff's 25 markers). The Habs now gave Yvan Cournoyer a full-time role, plus they had good youngsters in Jacques Lemaire, Serge Savard, Danny Grant, Carol Vadnais and Mickey Redmond ready to make contributions in '67–68. During the season, Beliveau scored his 400th career goal and recorded his 1,000th point en route to becoming the team's all-time scoring leader (surpassing the 965 points held by Maurice Richard). The Habs breezed through the season finishing with a 42-22-10 record, good enough for first place in the East, and then lost only once in the post season in taking back the Stanley Cup.

The Leafs and Canadiens played only 10 games against each other in '67–68 (Montreal won the series 5-3-2) as the rivalry began a steady decline. Even when both clubs were battling for first place as late as January, the intensity seemed to have dissipated. The Montreal club was prepared for the new NHL while the Maple Leafs stumbled and eventually fell out of the race. As the Leafs began to decline, so did the great rivalry.

OCTOBER 19, 1967
Montreal 1 Toronto 0 @ The Forum

Yvan Cournoyer scored the only goal of the game on a power-play and goaltender Gump Worsley never recorded an easier shutout (15 saves) as the Canadiens defeated the Maple Leafs 1-0 during the first meeting of the 1967–68 season between the two clubs. The game was played before 15,205 largely bored spectators who kept hoping something would happen to liven up a rather dull affair. Cournoyer's goal came at 5:36 of the first when his high, hard drive from the point was dropped into the net by Leaf goalie Johnny Bower, who otherwise played well in facing 27 shots. The tight-checking Habs gave the Leafs little room to move and their only good chance to score was a Bob Pulford shot that beat Worsley but hit the post. Toronto pulled Bower with 79 seconds to play but could not come close to scoring. The shutout was the 29th of Worsley's career.

NOVEMBER 1, 1967
Toronto 5 Montreal 0 @ Maple Leaf Gardens

The oldest player in hockey made 40 saves as the Maple Leafs beat the Canadiens 5-0 on home ice before 15,927 fans. Johnny Bower, almost age 43 (his birthday was coming up on November 8), turned back the Habs with one great stop after another before his teammates finally came to life about half-way through the contest. Montreal fired 17 first-period shots on Bower but the Leafs scored on three of fifteen drives at the Canadiens net during the second stanza. Dave Keon, Frank Mahovlich and Bob Pulford all scored in the middle frame to give the Leafs a 3-0 lead. They got goals from George Armstrong and Mike Walton to salt away the victory in the third but Bower was again under siege with another 15 shots coming his way in the last period. Bower had to stop two breakaways during the contest (by Claude Provost and Henri Richard) and had to make another

Yvan Cournoyer

Montreal's Yvan Cournoyer (#12) looks to get away from Toronto's Tim Horton. Cournoyer finally saw full-time duty with the Habs in 1967–68 and he responded with 28 goals and 60 points in 64 games played. No longer just a power-play specialist, Cournoyer started to establish himself as a star player and would be a part of 10 Stanley Cup wins with Montreal before his Hall of Fame career was over. He would score 428 goals and 435 assists in 968 career games, all of which were played for the Canadiens.

Yvan Cournoyer had a couple of firsts against the Maple Leafs in his career. He played his first NHL game against Toronto on January 30, 1964, with his father in attendance. Cournoyer also had his first goal (and only penalty shot) versus the Leafs on March 25, 1965, against goalie Johnny Bower at Maple Leaf Gardens, a game the Leafs won 3-2. Bower stopped Cournoyer, who would always have trouble on breakaways on the Leaf goalie. In fact, Bower made a key stop on the man known as the "Roadrunner" when Cournoyer had a clear chance during the overtime session of the third game of the 1967 finals (another game won 3-2 by Toronto) by poke checking the speedy Hab.

A CLOSER LOOK

In his final year of junior hockey, Yvan Cournoyer had 63 goals and 48 assists in 53 games for the Montreal Jr. Canadiens of the OHA. His outstanding performance earned him a position on the first all-star team along with future NHL players such as Bobby Orr, Doug Jarrett, Andre Boudrias and Dennis Hull. The only first-team member not to make the NHL was goaltender Chuck Goddard.

excellent stop on Jean Beliveau. Mahovlich and Armstrong each had a goal and two assists on the night, but the Big M was greeted with a smattering of boos when he was picked as one of the three stars of the game. Tim Horton was also prominent for the Leafs in his own end.

> *"I was right in and was sure I would slide the puck under his legs as he hit the ice. But he was too quick! Who said he was losing his reflexes?"*
>
> Henri Richard on Johnny Bower (*The Toronto Star*, November 2, 1967)

NOVEMBER 29, 1967
Toronto 2 Montreal 1 @ Maple Leaf Gardens

A late third-period goal by Toronto's Jim Pappin turned out to be the winner as the Maple Leafs prevailed 2-1 over the Canadiens. Pappin's goal (his eighth of the season) went in on a shot that deflected into the Montreal net off the skate of goaltender Gump Worsley and gave the Leafs a 2-0 lead at 17:14 of the final period. The Canadiens finally got on the board at 18:20 of the third when Gilles Tremblay beat Johnny Bower in the Leaf net, negating the possibility of a second consecutive shutout by the Leaf net-minder, who faced 34 shots on the night. Mike Walton got the only other goal of the game when he opened the scoring for the Leafs early in the first period on a setup by Frank Mahovlich. The big Leafs winger was playing in his first contest since the last time these two teams met (11 games ago) and was greeted with a large ovation from the 16,001 fans in attendance. The Toronto fans seemed to be apologizing to Mahovlich (returning from sick leave) in some small way by cheering his every move and many stood to applaud when he made the play that led to Walton's goal. Mahovlich (who replaced Wayne Carleton on left wing) took two Montreal

defenders away from the play before sliding a pass over to Walton who rapped in a 15-foot drive for his 12th goal of the year. After the game, Mahovlich said he felt great and the Leafs were within two points of first place.

DECEMBER 20, 1967
Montreal 5 Toronto 0 @ The Forum

Dick Duff scored three goals as he negated rumours of his imminent demise with the Canadiens by leading the team to a 5-0 victory over the Maple Leafs. The 31-year-old Duff had not been playing well and stories were circulating that he might return to the Leafs in a trade. Rookie Danny Grant was being groomed to take Duff's spot since the veteran was suffering from assorted ailments, especially a knee problem. However, coach Toe Blake inserted Duff onto a line with Henri Richard (four assists) and Bobby Rousseau (one goal, three assists) and the trio counted for 11 points during the game. Duff scored at 3:24 of the first when he beat goalie Johnny Bower. The hat trick gave Duff seven goals on the season (in 22 games), while goal-tender Gump Worsley recorded his third shutout of the year by stopping 27 Leaf shots on goal. The Leafs had yet to score at the Forum this season and only came close in this game on a hard drive by Frank Mahovlich and when Murray Oliver dinged the crossbar late in the game. Claude Provost got the other Montreal goal.

> *"Tell Punch that I'm sorry I had to spoil his Christmas."*
>
> Dick Duff (*The Toronto Star*, December 21, 1967)

DECEMBER 27, 1967
Toronto 2 Montreal 2 @ Maple Leaf Gardens

The Montreal Canadiens needed two late goals to earn a 2-2 tie with the Maple Leafs in front of

16,091 surprised fans. The Leafs had scored twice in the third period to break a scoreless tie and take a 2-0 lead on goals by Peter Stemkowski and George Armstrong (with his 10th, one more than he scored all of last season). But the Canadiens rookie line of Danny Grant, Jacques Lemaire and Mickey Redmond went to work with Grant getting the goal that made it 2-1 after a good setup by Lemaire. Then, just 91 seconds later, Montreal's John Ferguson stole the puck from Stemkowski just

Montreal goaltender Gump Worsley (#30) tries to make a save against Toronto forward Murray Oliver (#11). Worsley recorded six shutouts in 1967–68 and in 40 games played (19-9-8), he allowed only 73 goals for a 1.98 goals-against average. Along with goaltending partner Rogie Vachon, the two netminders combined to win the Vezina Trophy by allowing 167 goals against in 74 games. Worsley was named as a first-team all-star. After many years with Boston, Oliver was acquired in a deal prior to the start of the 1967–68 season and scored 16 goals and 37 points in 74 games.

VALUE DAYS

the Leafs sent Eddie Shack to the Boston Bruins in exchange for Murray Oliver but the Toronto general manager also got 100,000 US dollars thrown into the deal. Imlach never revealed the actual figure to Shack (who had heard cash was involved) for fear that the former Leaf would ask his new boss, Milt Schmidt of the Bruins, for a big raise if he found out the truth. Imlach did not want to put a fellow management member in any difficulty so he told Shack that the Bruins only paid the regular waiver fee ($30,000 at the time). Later, Imlach boasted that his boss, Stafford Smythe, was absolutely flabbergasted he got that amount of cash for one player.

Mike Walton — a closer look

"I didn't figure to play much this year anyway. I hoped for 15 goals and if I was lucky, maybe 20. I didn't think I'd be getting so much ice time."

Mike Walton (*Toronto Telegram*, January 4, 1968)

Mike Walton (#16) looks to help out goalie Bruce Gamble (#30) in the Leafs' end. Walton scored 30 goals to lead the Maple Leafs and added 29 assists in just his first full season with Toronto. The small but speedy Walton had a good, accurate shot and a feisty nature that made him a crowd favourite (he scored 23 of his goals at Maple Leaf Gardens). Gamble played in 40 games (19-13-3) for the Leafs in 1967–68 and allowed 85 goals for a 2.32 goals-against average with five shutouts. Gamble and goaltending partner Johnny Bower finished second to the Montreal Canadiens in the race for the Vezina Trophy (167 to 176 goals allowed). Gamble was also named as the most valuable player of the 1968 All-Star Game won 4-3 by the Leafs against a team of NHL all-stars.

THE NUMBERS

Mike Walton scored 40 goals for Tulsa in the CPHL and won the Rookie of the Year award in 1964–65. One year later, he had 35 markers for Rochester in the AHL and won the top rookie award in 1965–66. His best year with the Leafs saw Walton score 30 times in 1967–68 (each goal after 20 was worth a $100 bonus), but by 1971 he was dealt to the Boston Bruins.

inside the Leaf blueline and that resulted in Jean Beliveau's game-tying goal at 17:44 of the period when he managed to whack the puck past Johnny Bower into the Leafs net. Both teams played well in this contest that featured great goaltending at either end. Gump Worsley made 29 stops in the Canadiens net.

"There's no way you can get up for every game and play all out like the Leafs did and us did tonight."

Gump Worsley (*The Globe and Mail*, December 28, 1967)

JANUARY 3, 1968
Montreal 1 Toronto 1 @ The Forum

The Maple Leafs finally scored a goal at the Forum and it nearly held up for a win, but the

Canadiens got a third-period marker to even the game at 1-1. The Toronto goal came from the stick of leading scorer Mike Walton who scored his 20th of the year on his 23rd birthday (only Bobby Hull, Stan Mikita and Johnny Bucyk had at least 20 goals in the NHL so far in '67–68). Walton was at the right spot when goalie Gump Worsley dropped Larry Hillman's drive from the point and he pounced on the loose disk to give

Montreal goaltender Rogie Vachon (#30) makes a save against the Maple Leafs with Bob Pulford (#20) in behind looking for a rebound. Vachon got into 39 games (23-13-2) in 1967–68 as he began to establish himself as a full-time goaltender in the NHL. He shared the Vezina Trophy with Gump Worsley by allowing only 92 goals (for a 2.48 goals-against average) and posting four shutouts. Pulford scored 20 goals and added 30 assists in 1967–68 when he played in all 74 games. The consistent Leaf centre was also named the first president of the NHL Players Association in June 1967, under executive director Alan Eagleson.

the Leafs a 1-0 lead at 6:12 of the second period. Gilles Tremblay tied the game in the third when he tipped in a Jean Beliveau drive past goalie Johnny Bower on a Canadiens power-play. Bower stopped all but one of 17 third-period shots taken by the Habs as the Leafs tried to protect a slim lead. Montreal outshot Toronto 30-23 on the night but only the fine work of Worsley kept the Habs in the game.

JANUARY 30, 1968
Montreal 3 Toronto 0 @ The Forum

The Canadiens turned in a workmanlike effort to win their 10th consecutive game with a 3-0 win over the Maple Leafs on home ice. Claude Provost scored the first goal (the 224th of his career) of the game in the opening frame on a shorthanded effort before 15,670 fans. The Habs then got goals from Jean Beliveau (his 19th) and Yvan Cournoyer (his 17th) and Rogie Vachon picked up the shutout by stopping 19 Toronto shots. Desperate to score a goal and down by three, the Leafs pulled goalie Johnny Bower with over a minute to play, much to the displeasure of the partisan fans at the Forum. The Leafs did little with the extra man, as they had done throughout most of the game. The victory kept the Canadiens in first place with 57 points while the Leafs were in a three-way tie for second in the Eastern Division with Boston and Chicago at 54 points. The New York Rangers were in fifth with 52 points. Montreal's Henri Richard was contemplating retirement due to a knee injury that had seen him miss 17 of the first 49 games this season.

FEBRUARY 14, 1968
Montreal 4 Toronto 2 @ Maple Leaf Gardens

The slumping Maple Leafs made a valiant effort to win a game on home ice, but the Canadiens' superiority won the day in a 4-2 Montreal win. The loss was the fifth consecutive defeat for the

Leafs and they had only one win to show for their last ten contests. The Canadiens had won 18 of their past 21 contests, with only one loss during this period. John Ferguson scored the game winner against the Leafs when Claude Provost's shot hit him on the leg at 13:20 of the third and went into the net past a surprised Johnny Bower. The Leafs claimed that Ferguson put the puck in with his hand, but referee John Ashley did not agree. Toronto had come back twice to even the game on goals by Frank Mahovlich (his 19th of the year) and Mike Walton (his 23rd) but could not get the go-ahead goal against a very steady Rogie Vachon. Henri Richard and Terry Harper had given Montreal 1-0 and 2-1 leads respectively, but they needed Ferguson's marker to pull it out. In addition to scoring the winner, Ferguson had a fight with Leaf defenceman Larry Hillman who had a slight advantage in the scrap. Jean Beliveau scored an empty-net goal to seal the win. Toronto used rookie defenceman Mike Pelyk in place of the injured Tim Horton.

"I have worked with Hillman a number of times. I think I broke him in [in 1955] at Detroit [when both were with the Red Wings]. You get so as you instinctively know what your partner is going to do. This helps because you are in position to back his play."

Marcel Pronovost on Larry Hillman
(Maple Leaf program, December 13, 1967)

MARCH 20, 1968
Montreal 3 Toronto 2 @ The Forum

The Canadiens got a good deal of revenge for their loss in the 1967 finals by being the team that officially knocked the defending champions out of the playoffs with a 3-2 win over the

Maple Leafs. Montreal got two goals from Bobby Rousseau and one from Mickey Redmond while the Toronto goals came from Ron Ellis and Tim Horton. Ellis opened the scoring at the 26-second mark of the game but the Habs scored twice on the power-play to take the lead for good. Leafs goalie Johnny Bower was injured in a three-player pile-up and was replaced by Bruce Gamble who got off to a rocky start, giving up two goals in short order. Jacques Lemaire set up Rousseau for the game winner from 20 feet out in front of the Leafs net. The Leafs had not won a game on the road in their last 12 attempts and their overall record away from Maple Leaf Gardens stood at 7-21-6.

Montreal's John Ferguson (#22) crashes into goaltender Johnny Bower (#1) while defenceman Larry Hillman tries to leap over the pile. Ferguson did not have a strong year in 1967–68 with only 15 goals and 18 assists but had, as usual, over 100 minutes in penalties (117) in 61 games played. He added eight points in 13 playoff games. Hillman played in only 55 games for the Leafs in 1967–68 (three goals, 17 assists) after a great season the year before. In contract negotiations, Hillman held out until November 2 for a $500 difference and even though he got what he wanted, Punch Imlach fined him the same amount for reporting late! Bower was still an ageless wonder with 43 games played (14-18-7) and had a goals-against average of 2.25 with four shutouts.

John Ferguson was an intense competitor both on and off the ice. Once while in Toronto, he and teammate Dick Duff went out for dinner, when in walked Eddie Shack of the Leafs. As former colleagues, Shack and Duff exchanged pleasantries while Ferguson started fuming about Duff's talking to the enemy. Ferguson was having none of that and threw down some cash for a meal (a hot, sizzling steak that was just prepared) he would not eat just to avoid being with Shack.

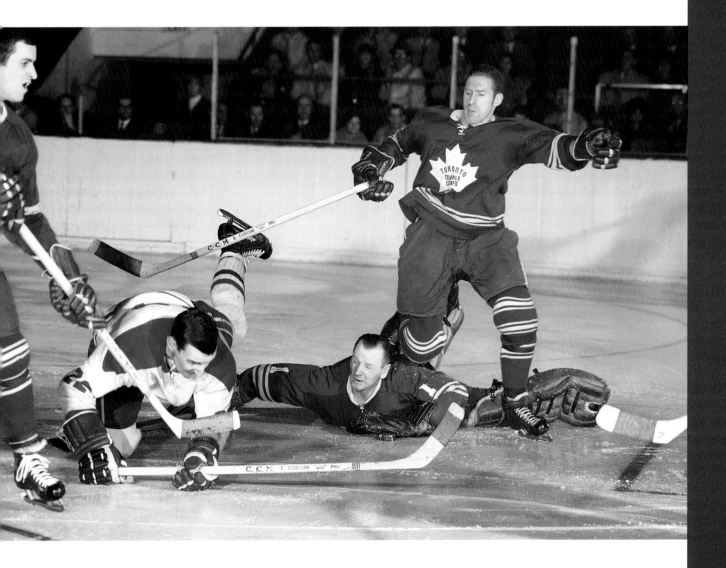

"This is the worst road team I've ever been associated with."

Punch Imlach (*The Globe and Mail*, March 21, 1968)

"I was aware we could put Toronto out tonight. So was the team. But all we thought about was the two points."

Toe Blake (*Toronto Telegram*, March 21, 1968)

"A milestone few people accomplish [1,000 games played]. The most durable sort of player. Really, he was indispensable because you didn't see me trade him in all those years. He is one of the best. I have seen him come along from a fifth defenceman to an all-star."

Punch Imlach on Tim Horton (Maple Leaf program, November 15, 1967)

Montreal forward Bobby Rousseau (#15) takes a shot while Toronto defenceman Tim Horton (#7) moves in to check him. Rousseau did not score 20 goals in 1967–68 (he got 19 for the second year in a row) but he did record 46 assists to give him 65 points (the 14th best mark in the NHL in 1967–68). Horton was one of the few bright spots for the Leafs in 1967–68 when he was named to the first all-star team (for the first time since 1964) with four goals and twenty-seven points in sixty-nine games played. Horton became the first Leaf to play in one thousand career games on November 19, 1967.

Leafs forward Ron Ellis (#6) looks to take a shot at the Montreal net but defenceman Carol Vadnais (#17) is in the way. Ellis had a good year in 1967–68 with 28 goals and 48 points in 74 games played, both career highs to that point in his career. Vadnais played in 31 games for the Habs in '67–68 scoring one goal and adding one assist. He also got into one game in the Stanley Cup finals, which allowed Vadnais to get his name on the coveted trophy for the first time in his career.

MARCH 27, 1968
Toronto 6 Montreal 0 @ Maple Leaf Gardens

Goaltender Johnny Bower recorded his third

shutout of the season and Murray Oliver scored two goals as the Leafs won a meaningless contest 6-0 on home ice in front of 15,887 fans. Oliver's goals both came in the first period and the Leafs coasted from there, with other markers from Mike Walton (his 30th of the year to go along with two assists), Ron Ellis (his 26th), Bob Pulford and rookie Mike Byers. Bower stopped 26 Montreal shots to earn the shutout and the Leafs fired 39 drives at the Canadiens net occupied by Rogie Vachon. The Habs had nothing to play for in this contest, having already clinched first place, but were in a battle for the Vezina Trophy for fewest goals allowed. The Canadiens

For the first time in 10 years (since 1958), the Maple Leafs missed the Stanley Cup playoffs in 1968. The 1967–68 team also matched the record of the 1945–46 Leafs, who also missed the playoffs after winning the Cup the previous season.

No Maple Leaf defenceman has ever won the Norris Trophy since its inception in 1954, but four Toronto rearguards have been the runner-up: Allan Stanley, Tim Horton (twice), Carl Brewer and Borje Salming (twice).

THE NUMBERS

TRIVIA

Montreal forward Jacques Lemaire was one of the top rookies in the NHL during the 1967–68 season when he scored 22 goals and added 20 assists. The determined centre was a strong skater and had a hard, deadly accurate shot that he did not hesitate to use. In the 1968 playoffs, Lemaire showed he was going to be a big game player with 13 points in 13 post-season games, including two overtime winners. He would play for the Canadiens until 1979 and would record 835 points (366 goals, 469 assists) in 853 career games and had an amazing 139 points (61 goals, 78 assists) in 145 playoff games.

were without starting defencemen Terry Harper and Ted Harris and one replacement, Carol Vadnais, had a difficult night being on for four Leaf goals. Duane Rupp, Mike Pelyk and Allan Stanley were all strong along the Leaf blueline.

playoffs

SERIES 1 – MONTREAL VS. BOSTON
SERIES 2 – MONTREAL VS. CHICAGO

Montreal took on third-place Boston in the first round of the playoffs and had no trouble dispensing with the hungry but young Bruins led by Bobby Orr. The Canadiens won the series in four straight by scores of 2-1, 5-3, 5-2 and 3-2. Henri Richard scored his 30th career playoff goal in the first game against Boston while enforcer John Ferguson took apart Bruin tough guy Ted Green in a fight. Jacques Lemaire had a two-goal game in the third contest, while Claude Larose had a pair in the final game of the series for the Canadiens. Gump Worsley played well in goal for the Habs. Chicago knocked out second-place New York in six games and met the Canadiens in the next round. Montreal took the first two games on home ice with convincing 9-2 and 4-1 wins. The Habs took the third game in Chicago 4-2, but lost a chance for another sweep when the Blackhawks snuck out a 2-1 win at the Stadium. The fifth game went into overtime but Lemaire scored the winner at 2:14 of overtime to give the Canadiens a 4-3 win and a berth in the finals.

stanley cup finals

MONTREAL VS. ST. LOUIS

The St. Louis Blues made it to the Stanley Cup finals under the format adopted by the NHL whereby the winner of the Western Division (all the expansion clubs) would gain a berth in hockey's greatest showcase. The Blues played valiantly but they were clearly no match for the

Toronto coach and general manager Punch Imlach cited only five Maple Leafs as untouchables prior to the 1968–69 season: Dave Keon, Norm Ullman, Paul Henderson, Floyd Smith and Ron Ellis.

TRIVIA

Yvan Cournoyer (#12) moves in for a shot against St. Louis Blues goaltender Glenn Hall. Cournoyer led all Montreal scorers in the finals with two goals and two assists in the four games played and had 14 points (the highest total of any Canadien in the post season) in 13 playoff games. Hall was outstanding in the playoffs as the experienced Blues represented the newly created Western Division in the finals. His efforts, which included 19 appearances and a 2.43 goals-against average, were recognized with the awarding of the Conn Smythe Trophy to the veteran goalie.

mighty Canadiens, who were without captain Jean Beliveau. The first two games were played in St. Louis and the Canadiens won both by a goal, 4-3 in overtime (Jacques Lemaire) and 1-0 (on a goal by Serge Savard and a shutout by Gump Worsley). The Blues kept it close at the Forum but Bobby Rousseau got the extra session winner for a 4-3 win in the third game, and then a third-period marker by J.C. Tremblay in the fourth game sealed the Cup for Montreal. The win gave the Habs a 12-1 playoff record in 1968.

St. Louis forward Gordon "Red" Berenson (#7) tries to put the puck past goaltender Gump Worsley in the Montreal net. Berenson scored twice during the third game of the finals versus Montreal, but it was still not enough to beat the Habs who won the contest 4-3 on an overtime goal by Bobby Rousseau. Berenson finished the playoffs with five goals and seven points in eighteen games. Worsley played in 12 playoff contests and allowed only 21 goals for a 1.88 goals-against average with one shutout (in the second game of the finals).

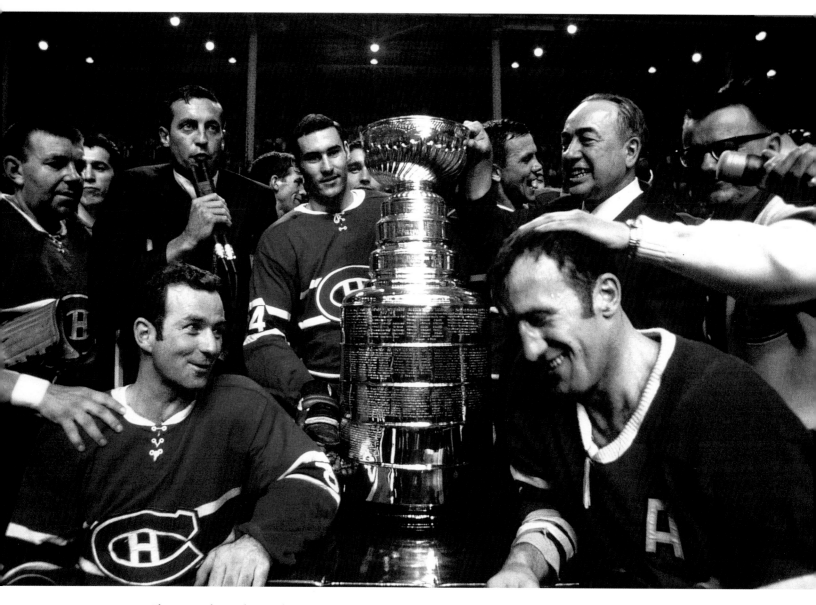

The Montreal Canadiens gather around the 1968 Stanley Cup that they had just won on home ice with a 3-2 win over the St. Louis Blues in the fourth game of the finals. Note that captain Jean Beliveau is in street clothes due to an injury but he came onto the ice to accept the Cup on behalf of the team. Others in the photo include Gump Worsley (#30), Mickey Redmond (#24), coach Toe Blake with Dick Duff (#8) and Claude Provost (#14) kneeling in the foreground.

Both Toe Blake and Jacques Lemaire scored two Stanley Cup–winning goals. Lemaire scored his in 1977 and 1979, while Blake scored his in 1944 and 1946, all for the Canadiens. Both also each coached Cup-winning teams — Blake won eight with Montreal and Lemaire coached the New Jersey Devils to the Cup in 1995.

TRIVIA

"These last few times we have won the Cup have been even more satisfying than when we won it five times in a row from 1956 to 1960. We had a great team in those years … Maurice Richard, Doug Harvey, Jacques Plante, Bernie Geoffrion. But these past few years we didn't have so many stars and we won by working hard."

Jean Beliveau (Pro Hockey Preview magazine, 1968–69 edition)

Montreal captain Jean Béliveau (#4) stands in front of the net while Toronto defenceman Pierre Pilote (#2) keeps a close eye on him. Béliveau led the Canadiens to their second straight Stanley Cup in 1968–69 (and fourth in five years) while Pilote (a three-time Norris Trophy winner) joined Toronto after a deal with Chicago.

The Leafs–Canadiens Rivalry
1968–69

When the last game of the 1968 Stanley Cup finals was played on May 11, Montreal coach Toe Blake packed his bags and walked out of the Forum for the last time as the boss. The fedora-wearing leader decided he had had enough of the big league pressure and after eight championships, there was little left to prove. The stout Claude Ruel, a long-time member of the Canadiens organization, was named as Blake's replacement. He smartly realized that the team was still very strong and did not need much in the way of change. Claude Larose and Danny Grant were dealt to Minnesota while Terry Harper missed all but 21 games during the season with an injury (although he returned for the post season). Gilles Tremblay played in only 44 contests due to injury and missed all of the playoffs. New additions to the club included veteran defenceman Larry Hillman and forward Mickey Redmond, who was now a full-time member of the team. Jude Drouin and Christian Bordeleau also played for the Habs in 1968–69. The other big change in Montreal was a major renovation done to the Forum that re-opened in November.

In Toronto, the heat was turned on coach and general manager Punch Imlach like never before. Controversial moves had many people questioning Imlach, especially those in management. A deal was struck with Imlach whereby he had to be within two points of a playoff spot by December 1 or else he would have to give up the coaching portion of his job. Imlach survived the season and got the team back into the play-offs despite some poor moves like the trading of Jim Pappin to Chicago for an ineffective Pierre Pilote. Gerry Meehan, Larry Mickey, Bill Sutherland, Forbes Kennedy and a returning Brit Selby all made appearances for the Leafs in 1968–69 as forwards. But the biggest change came along the blueline with fresh faces in Rick Ley, Pat Quinn, Jim Dorey, and Mike Pelyk see-ing plenty of action. It was hoped that this group would be the nucleus of a rebuilt team. However, it was the veterans like Tim Horton (a first-team all-star), Dave Keon and Norm Ullman who led the team back to some level of respectability (a 35-26-15 record) with eighty-five points, just six back of third place New York in the Eastern Division. Ron Ellis and Paul Henderson also had good years, while Bob Pulford and Marcel Pronovost faded.

The Canadiens were once again the best team in the NHL with 103 points during the 76-game schedule (46-19-11). Yvan Cournoyer took over as the team's top point producer with 87 and Jean Beliveau was rejuvenated with an 82-point season. Bobby Rousseau had 30 goals, while youngster Jacques Lemaire scored 29, as did tough guy John Ferguson. The other veterans all chipped in and produced good seasons, like blueliner Ted Harris, who gained an all-star berth. But the emerging force was defenceman Serge Savard, who had stardom written all over his play. Just as they breezed through the regu-lar season, the Habs had little trouble in the playoffs, although this year they lost two games (both to Boston) on the way to another Stanley Cup title.

The Leafs faced the Bruins in the playoffs and it was no contest as an emerging powerhouse defeated a crumbling empire. After the Boston four-game sweep, Toronto dismissed Imlach and president Stafford Smythe brought in John McClellan and Jim Gregory. The previous departure of Blake and now Imlach ensured that

the old fire of the Montreal–Toronto rivalry was extinguished. It has been rarely ignited since.

OCTOBER 30, 1968
Montreal 5 Toronto 0 @ Maple Leaf Gardens

The Canadiens jumped out to an early lead and goaltender Rogie Vachon recorded the shutout as the Habs blanked the Leafs 5-0 in the Gardens. A young and jittery Leaf defence gave the Canadiens many opportunities right from the drop of the puck, although they managed to hold Montreal to one goal (by Yvan Cournoyer) in the first period. Jacques Lemaire took a long pass from Serge Savard in behind the Leaf defenders and walked in to beat a beleaguered Johnny Bower in net for the second goal. Gilles Tremblay scored the third goal from a miscue by Leaf rookie rearguard Mike Pelyk, while Bower was at fault on the fourth tally by John Ferguson. Lemaire let go a blast from the blue-line to close out the scoring. Montreal was out to show they were the superior team and they spent most of the night skating circles around the befuddled Maple Leafs. The only Leaf defencemen to look good were 19-year-old Rick Ley and veteran Marcel Pronovost, who likely prevented two more Canadien goals. The win moved Montreal into first place with thirteen points, while the Leafs dropped into fifth spot with nine points.

NOVEMBER 14, 1968
Toronto 5 Montreal 3 @ The Forum

The Maple Leafs scored four second-period goals and goalie Bruce Gamble made 39 saves as Toronto beat Montreal 5-3 in front of 17,953 fans at the newly renovated Forum. The Leafs were eager to make up for the 5-0 shellacking they took from the Canadiens in their last meet-ing and were quite physical the whole night, especially the defence. Tim Horton was named the first star of the game and upset the crowd

Toronto's Norm Ullman (#9) skates away from Montreal's Ted Harris (#10). Ullman had an outstanding season in his first full year as a Maple Leaf with 77 points (35 goals, 42 assists) in 75 games played. He provided Toronto with a great centre to play behind Dave Keon and he stayed with the Leafs until 1975, accumulating 471 points in 535 games. Harris had one of his best offensive years in 1968–69 with 25 points (seven goals, eighteen assists) while recording 102 penalty minutes. His good play was recognized with a selection to the second all-star team in 1968–69.

with his manhandling of Montreal centre Ralph Backstrom late in the first period. The speedy Canadien tried to run Horton into the boards and the Leaf rearguard responded by charging after Backstrom and body-slamming him to the ice with a bear hug. Backstrom had to leave the game for a while with a knee sprain and although he returned in the second period, he was not effective. Mike Walton opened the scoring for Toronto in the first period, but the first of two Yvan Cournoyer goals evened the count. Wayne Carleton gave the Leafs the lead again early in the second, but Cournoyer's 12th of the year tied the game. Norm Ullman scored on a Leafs power-play for the game winner, while Paul Henderson and Murray Oliver also had markers for the visitors in the middle frame. Jacques Lemaire scored for Montreal in the third and Gamble was stellar in keeping the Canadiens from getting any closer. Dave Keon did a masterful job in checking Jean Beliveau of the Canadiens while Jim McKenny replaced the injured Pierre Pilote on the Leaf blueline.

DECEMBER 11, 1968
Toronto 4 Montreal 4 @ Maple Leaf Gardens

John Ferguson scored his 100th career goal (including playoffs) with less than five minutes

to play as the Canadiens came back to tie the Leafs 4-4 before 16,485 fans. The Leafs were up 4-3 going into the third period on goals by George Armstrong, Dave Keon, Ron Ellis and Paul Henderson. Armstrong had returned to the Leafs from another retirement attempt just one week before and he re-directed defenceman Pat Quinn's shot past goaltender Tony Esposito. Keon's goal came on a backhand drive from about 10 feet out and Ellis put in a Keon pass from right in front of the goal. Henderson scored after the Leafs stole the puck from J.C. Tremblay as Norm Ullman and Larry Mickey did most of the work on the play. Montreal also got goals from Mickey Redmond, Jacques

"Sure he got beat by some long shots but he always gave me his best."

Claude Ruel on Tony Esposito (*Hockey Illustrated*, April 1970)

Toronto's Dave Keon (#14) scores on a backhand drive past Tony Esposito of the Canadiens (#1). Keon bounced back from a sub-par season in 1967–68 to score 27 goals and 34 assists in 1968–69, which helped get the Leafs back into the playoffs. He also recorded a career-high 12 penalty minutes in 1968–69. Keon would be named captain of the team in September 1969, and would stay with the Leafs until 1975. He did not leave on the best of terms, but did finish as the Leafs' all-time point leader with 858 (365 goals, 493 assists), a mark not surpassed until Darryl Sittler broke the team record in 1980–81. Esposito played in only one season for the Habs and recorded two shutouts in thirteen games.

Lemaire and Dick Duff. Esposito played in net replacing the injured Gump Worsley and Rogie Vachon, facing 28 Toronto shots. Bruce Gamble had a busier night with 41 Montreal shots on goal, including 17 in the final period. The young netminder was supposedly weak on long shots and had an awkward style, but he came up with key saves to hold the Leafs off the score sheet in the third period.

"Because I don't get many penalties, I think the referees are inclined to think it's an accident when I get into a potential penalty situation. Some even ask me if it was an accident and I always say, 'Oh yeah.'"

Dave Keon (Maple Leaf program, January 28, 1967)

DECEMBER 26, 1968
Montreal 4 Toronto 2 @ The Forum

The city of Montreal was in the midst of a cold snap (15° below zero Fahrenheit, -26° Celsius) but the Canadiens stayed hot and regained first place with a 4-2 win over the Maple Leafs. The game was tied 2-2 late in the second period when Bobby Rousseau scored to give the Canadiens the lead with a backhand drive that hit goalie Bruce Gamble's pad and went in on the short side. John

Toronto's Paul Henderson (#19) knocks down Montreal defenceman J.C. Tremblay (#3). The lightning-fast Henderson played the wrong wing (like one of his boyhood idols, Maurice Richard) but learned how to use his speed to great effectiveness that helped to score many goals. In 1968–69, Henderson scored 27 times and added 32 assists in 74 games played. He stayed with the Leafs until 1974 and scored 162 goals and 318 points as a Leaf in 408 games.

Ferguson scored in the third period to give the Habs an insurance goal, but the Leafs kept fighting until the final siren. Murray Oliver and Norm Ullman scored the two Toronto goals, while Montreal's other goals came from Ralph Backstrom and Henri Richard. The Leafs were injury riddled (Mike Walton, Floyd Smith and, during the contest, Dave Keon) and used Terry Clancy from Tulsa on right wing and defenceman

Pierre Pilote was forced to play left wing in the third period. It was nonetheless an exciting contest, with both teams skating very well. The win moved Montreal into sole possession of first place with 43 points (one ahead of Boston and two ahead of the Leafs) in the Eastern Division.

FEBRUARY 19, 1969
Toronto 5 Montreal 1 @ Maple Leaf Gardens

Goaltender Bruce Gamble was outstanding in net for the Maple Leafs as they handed the Canadiens a 5-1 loss in front of 16,485 fans. Gamble made 40 saves and most agreed he had never played a better game. Montreal lost for the first time in eight games and goaltender Gump Worsley was injured during the contest when he hit his head on the post. The rotund netminder was hurt when three players crashed into the goal area, which was primarily caused by Canadien defenceman Jacques Laperriere cross-checking the Leafs' Bob Pulford into the Montreal net. Norm Ullman, Dave Keon, Ron Ellis, Paul Henderson (his 21st) and Bill Sutherland got the Toronto goals, while Bobby Rousseau (with his 25th) got the only Canadiens marker. Gamble was at his best early in the game (15 saves in the first period alone) as the Habs did everything but score. The Leaf netminder was not the only thing to frustrate the Canadiens, as referee Bob Sloan was not very popular after giving Montreal nine of fourteen penalties. Jean Beliveau and John Ferguson were both given 10-minute misconducts as a result of arguing with Sloan. Ferguson turned down an invitation to a fight extended by Leaf defenceman Pat Quinn. Ullman's goal came on a power-play as he rapped in a rebound and Keon got the winner when his long slapshot eluded Montreal netminder Rogie Vachon.

FEBRUARY 20, 1969
Montreal 2 Toronto 1 @ The Forum

The Canadiens won the second game of the

> *"I've never seen the guy play a better game in this rink. He kept us in the game for the first ten minutes."*
>
> Punch Imlach on Bruce Gamble
> (*The Globe and Mail*, February 20, 1969)

> *"We were robbed. You saw the game. Write what you saw."*
>
> Claude Ruel (*The Globe and Mail*, February 20, 1969)

home-and-home series by squeezing out a 2-1 win over the Leafs at the Forum. Toronto goaltender Bruce Gamble was outstanding once again, but he could not stop two shots from the sticks of Jean Beliveau and Dick Duff. Otherwise, the maskless Gamble had the Canadiens (especially Ralph Backstrom and Yvan Cournoyer) talking to themselves with some great saves. Pat Quinn had an interesting night on the Leaf blueline, as he was responsible for losing the puck on Beliveau's goal and then scoring to tie the game. Quinn kept a puck in the Montreal end and drifted a shot at Rogie Vachon that trickled through the goalie's skates for his second goal of the year. The big defenceman was in the penalty box when Duff scored the winner by putting home a Jacques Lemaire rebound that came off the post.

MARCH 6, 1969
Montreal 5 Toronto 3 @ The Forum

Yvan Cournoyer scored three times as the Canadiens regained first place with a 5-3 win over the Maple Leafs. Montreal clearly outplayed Toronto, and if it were not for the work of Leaf goaltender Bruce Gamble, the score would have been much higher. The Canadiens fired 21 shots on Gamble in the third period alone and 39 on the night as they stormed back to win the game. The Leafs got a big break in the first period when Montreal defenceman Jacques Laperriere was given a five-minute major for cutting Leaf forward Floyd Smith over the right eye with his stick. The Leafs scored twice dur-

---

Leafs defenceman Pat Quinn (#23) gathers in the puck behind the net with Montreal's Jean Beliveau lurking in the background. Quinn was sold to the Leafs by the St. Louis Blues, who had claimed him from the Montreal organization, and the hulking defenceman (six foot three, 215 pounds) finally made his NHL debut with Toronto in 1968–69. He was a stay-at-home defender who managed to score two goals and seven assists in 40 games with 95 penalty minutes. He became much more known during the 1969 playoffs when he levelled Boston superstar Bobby Orr with a ferocious hit.

ing the major on goals by Tim Horton and Ron Ellis but Cournoyer also scored a pair to negate any Leaf advantage. Ted Harris gave the Habs the lead in the second period, but Paul Henderson tied it up for Toronto. Goals by Cournoyer (his 39th of the season) and Duff gave the Canadiens their margin of victory although the Leafs pulled Gamble with over two minutes to play in a futile effort to even the score. The Habs were now one point up on Boston in the Eastern Division standings.

MARCH 26, 1969
Toronto 6 Montreal 4 @ Maple Leaf Gardens

In one of their greatest games of the past two years, the Maple Leafs overcame a 3-0 Montreal lead to defeat the Canadiens 6-4 before 16,485

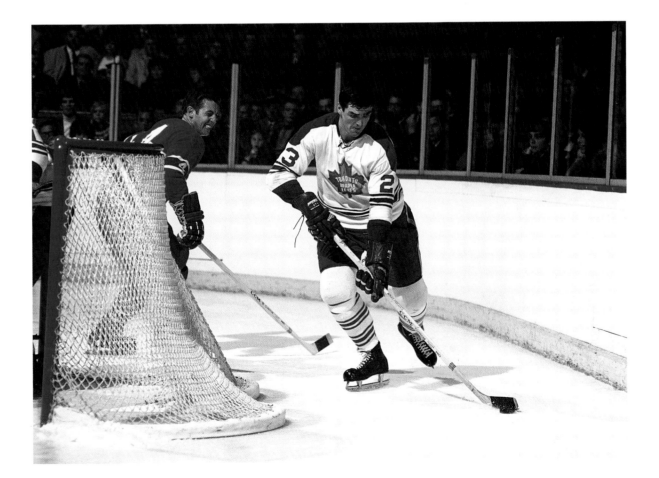

Canadiens captain Jean Beliveau is closely watched by Tim Horton (#2) of Toronto with Bruce Gamble in the net (#30). Beliveau kept on getting better with age, as his statistics for the 1968–69 season indicate. He scored 33 times (his best total since 1959–60 when he had 34) and added 49 assists in 69 games played. He was just as sharp in the playoffs with 15 points in 14 games. Beliveau was selected to the second all-star team. Horton had another top season in '68–69 with 11 goals and 40 points in 74 games, which gained him a berth on the first all-star team alongside Bobby Orr of Boston. Gamble was now the Leafs' number-one goaltender playing in 61 games (28-20-11), posting three shutouts to go along with a 2.80 goals-against average.

happy fans. Henri Richard, Ralph Backstrom and John Ferguson (his 20th) scored in a six-minute span in the first period to give Montreal the early lead. Ron Ellis got one back for Toronto before the first period ended on a laser beam from outside the blueline that beat Rogie Vachon in the Canadiens net. Jacques Lemaire got the only Montreal goal of the middle stanza but Norm Ullman (his 35th), Dave Keon (his 27th) and Jim Dorey (on a shot from the point at 19:44) scored in the second to pull the Leafs into a 4-4 tie. Third-period goals by Floyd Smith and Mike Walton (with his 23rd) put the game away for the Leafs. The win was very important to the

"Any parent could use Jean Beliveau as a pattern or model. He provides hockey with a magnificent image. I couldn't speak more highly of anyone who has ever been connected with our game than I do of Jean."

NHL president Clarence Campbell (*Hockey Illustrated*, November 1968)

Toronto goaltender Johnny Bower appears exasperated after Boston's Phil Esposito (#7) has crashed into his net during the playoffs. Bower appears to be asking for help from defenceman Jim Dorey (#8). Bower was now using a mask but only got into 20 games (5-4-3) in 1968–69, although he did manage two shutouts. He was aged 45 when he played against Boston in the '69 post season and would only play one more game for the Leafs, a 6-3 loss to Montreal on December10, 1969.

Leafs, who were trying to clinch a playoff spot. The loss was the Canadiens' fourth in their last 27 games.

playoffs

TORONTO VS. BOSTON

Although the Maple Leafs played well in the last portion of the season to make the playoffs ahead of Detroit, they were no match for the powerful Boston Bruins in the first round of the post season. The first two games were the most embarrassing in Leaf history as they were destroyed 10-0 and 7-0. These contests were more notable for the fighting and brawling that took place in Boston Garden than anything else that happened on the ice. Pat Quinn knocked out Bruins star Bobby Orr with a tremendous bodycheck (and some say part elbow) for which he was assessed a five-minute major. The Boston fans tried to get at Quinn in the penalty box, pouring beer on him and punching him in the back of the head, and the big Leaf had to make a hasty exit from the sin bin. Forbes Kennedy went wild later in the same game and punched a linesman who was trying to restrain him in a fight. None of this activity helped the Leafs, not even when they returned home and dropped the next two games by more respectable scores of 4-3 and 3-2. Shortly after the final game was over, the Punch Imlach era in Toronto was brought to an end with his prompt dismissal by Leaf president Stafford Smythe.

SERIES 1 – MONTREAL VS. NEW YORK
SERIES 2 – MONTREAL VS. BOSTON

The first-place Canadiens had no trouble knocking off the New York Rangers in the first round of the playoffs. They did it with remarkable ease as they took the series in four straight games by scores of 3-1, 5-2, 4-1 and 4-3. The next series against the surging Boston Bruins was much tougher and the Canadiens were forced to win three of the games in overtime. The Habs were

Montreal defenceman Serge Savard (#18) was outstanding during the entire 1969 playoffs and was rewarded with the Conn Smythe Trophy. In just his second season, Savard was showing signs of becoming a superstar with 8 goals and 23 assists in 74 games. In the playoffs, he scored four goals and added six assists in fourteen games with a commanding presence along the Montreal blueline that would last for many years. In 840 career games, Savard scored 96 goals and 395 points. His post-season record shows 19 goals and 49 assists in 120 games.

Jean Beliveau

"At my age [37], these things [individual records] are not too important anymore. To know that I have done my best, that is important. That is very important. I have always said I do not play for records, when they happen, they are nice but hockey is something I want to do."

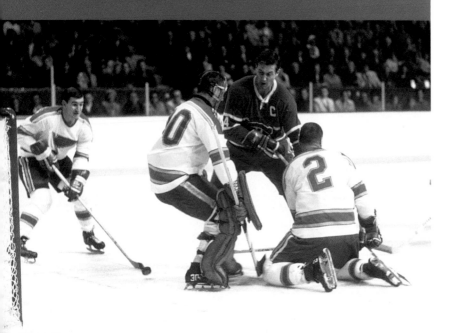

Montreal captain Jean Beliveau tries to sweep a puck past St. Louis goaltender Jacques Plante (#30) with Doug Harvey (#2) down on the ice. The 1969 Stanley Cup was the second-last championship won by Beliveau in his illustrious career and it is ironic that he would win it against former teammates Plante and Harvey who had helped him win so many other Cups previously. His 10 assists in the '69 post season tied him for the lead with Phil Esposito among all playoff scorers.

actually fortunate to win the first two at the Forum, since they had to tie the game late in the contest on both occasions and then score the winner in overtime. Ralph Backstrom scored in extra time in the first game to give Montreal a 3-2 win and Mickey Redmond got the winner in the second contest to give the Habs a 4-3 overtime victory. Boston roared back on home ice to win the next two 5-0 and 3-2, but Montreal won 4-2 on home ice to regain the series lead. The sixth game was a playoff classic that ended when Jean Beliveau scored the only overtime goal of his career to give Montreal a very hard-fought 2-1 win and another trip to the finals. On the winning goal, Beliveau won the face-off from Phil Esposito and he went to the net as defenceman Jacques Laperriere drilled a shot on goal. Serge Savard took a swipe at the puck and then Beliveau drove home the rebound over goaltender Gerry Cheevers.

stanley cup finals

MONTREAL VS. ST. LOUIS

The same two teams met for the second straight year and the results were predictable. Another Montreal sweep was executed with great efficiency as the Habs gave the Blues just three goals in the entire four-game series. Montreal opened with a pair of 3-1 victories at the Forum and followed that up with a 4-0 win in St. Louis. The final game was tight, but John Ferguson got the winner in a 2-1 Montreal victory that clinched another Stanley Cup for the Habs. Dick Duff had a great series against St. Louis with four goals and two assists and Jean Beliveau was back in the finals with five assists. Defenceman Serge Savard was awarded the Conn Smythe Trophy for his outstanding play during the entire playoffs. The Montreal win brought an end to the 1960s, a great decade of hockey dominated by the Canadiens and Maple Leafs.

Montreal coach Claude Ruel comes off the ice during the finals between his Canadiens and the Blues. Ruel was only 30 years old (the youngest coach ever in NHL history) when the Canadiens won the Stanley Cup during his first year behind the bench. It was not easy to replace a legend like Toe Blake but Ruel managed to do it for one year at least. The Habs missed the playoffs the next season and Ruel did not make it through the entire 1970–71 season. The nervous coach returned behind the bench in 1979 and coached for a couple of seasons to bring his total to 172 wins, 83 losses and 51 ties for a winning percentage of .648. His ability to develop players was perhaps his greatest contribution to the Canadiens organization over many years.

"We've planned and recruited and when older people have left us, our development program has been good enough to provide us with replacements as soon as we needed them … Our young players always have looked ahead to the day when they could play with the big team. They worshipped the men on the team. A kid plays for the Canadiens — he's somebody special. He's with champions. He's on a team with a history of winning."

Montreal general manager Sam Pollock (*Hockey Illustrated*, April–May 1967)

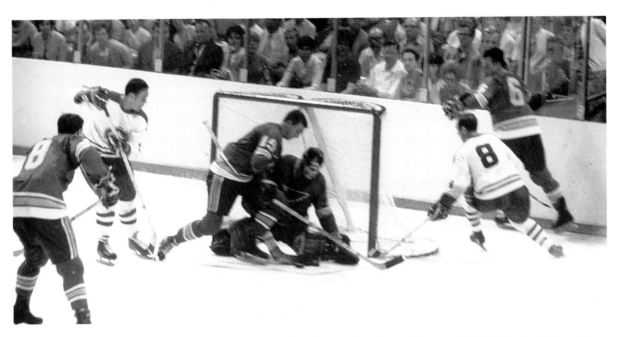

Montreal's Dick Duff (#8) tries to score on St. Louis netminder Glenn Hall in the fourth game of the 1969 finals. Duff was the top Canadien scorer (six points in total, including four goals) during the final series and got one goal in the final game.

"It took Toe Blake a long time to build this team and I don't feel I should start tampering with it."

Claude Ruel (*Pro Hockey preview magazine, 1968–69*)

*The Canadiens congratulate the Maple Leafs on winning the 1967 Stanley Cup. Pictured here are
(left to right) Gump Worsley, Bobby Rousseau, Dave Keon, Henri Richard and the Big M.*

The Leafs–Canadiens Rivalry
Afterword

The year 1967 was very special for Canada. It marked the Centennial for a young nation and many celebrations were held as Canadians looked to the future and commemorated the past. A special logo was designed and a happy tune by composer Bobby Gimby rang out as a cheery "Ca-na-da." As a proud nation beat its chest for one great year, it was only fitting that Montreal and Toronto would meet for the Stanley Cup. The Canadiens wanted to win the Cup so that it could be put on display at Expo '67, while the Leafs were just as determined to prove that their over-the-hill gang had one more championship in them.

The 1967 finals started in predictable fashion. Montreal beat Toronto 6-2 as the weary Maple Leafs showed their age. The Leafs had just come off a gruelling six-game upset of first-place Chicago, while the Habs had wiped out the New York Rangers in four straight. But the Leafs were a resilient group and came back to win the next two games 3-0 and 3-2. However, the Canadiens again whipped Toronto 6-2 to even the series. But the Leafs won the crucial fifth game 4-1 at the Forum behind the stellar work of goaltender Terry Sawchuk. That victory set up a potential clinching game at Maple Leaf Gardens for May 2, 1967. Realistically, the Leafs knew they had to win the sixth game if they were to win the Cup. It had been a magical spring for the Leafs to this point but going back to the Forum for a seventh game was simply not in their game plan.

However, the Canadiens would not give up the Cup without a great fight. As soon as the puck was dropped to start the sixth game, Montreal defenceman Terry Harper made a statement by hitting Toronto's Bob Pulford with a bodycheck. The Habs got the first good scoring chance when Sawchuk had to stop Jean Beliveau on a two-on-one break. The Leafs were then penalized when referee John Ashley whistled off Brian Conacher. But Sawchuk made a good stop on Yvan Cournoyer, who later was belted hard by Leaf defenceman Tim Horton. There were more physical confrontations in the first period as Frank Mahovlich and Leon Rochefort clashed, and Leaf blueliner Allan Stanley had confrontations with Henri Richard and Beliveau. Horton was nearly decked by Beliveau (in a nasty mood all night long) behind the Leaf goal and the Montreal captain was called for cross-checking.

The Habs kept coming at the Leafs and fired 17 shots at Sawchuk in the first but could not score. Toronto had 11 drives on Gump Worsley in the Montreal net but could not get a goal either. The energy level on the ice and in the stands was electric and everyone seemed to sense they were all a part of history; after all, this was the last game of the "Original Six."

The Leafs finally opened the scoring early in the second when Ron Ellis put in a rebound of a Red Kelly drive over a falling Worsley at 6:25. Sawchuk was still the busiest player on the ice, making saves on Dick Duff, John Ferguson, Bobby Rousseau and Jean Beliveau. He also got help from one of his goalposts. The Leafs caught a large break when Jim Pappin floated a shot toward the Montreal net hoping to hit teammate Peter Stemkowski with the drive. Instead, the puck hit Harper on the skate and went past a startled Worsley at 19:24 of the middle period. The lucky bounce for the Leafs was a back-breaker for the Canadiens.

During the second intermission, Montreal team president David Molson told a national television audience that with the upcoming expansion this "could be the last time we see two Canadian teams in the finals." It turned out to be

a prophetic statement since it took until 1986 before Montreal and Calgary met for the Cup.

But that would be for the future. There was still one great period of hockey to be played and Duff made it memorable with a great individual effort that ended when he beat Sawchuk with an over-the-shoulder shot. Duff's well-placed drive finally shattered Sawchuk's armour at 5:28, leaving the Habs with plenty of time to tie or even win the game. But the Leafs were very determined to protect the lead and Sawchuk was not rattled by the goal he allowed.

Montreal defenceman J.C. Tremblay was robbed by Sawchuk, but Worsley kept the Canadiens within one by making saves on Kelly and Conacher. For the most part, the Leafs were absorbing the Montreal onslaught and counter-attacking whenever possible. The Leafs had to kill off a penalty to Pappin at 11:46, but Montreal nearly got a lucky goal when Richard bounced a long shot on goal that Sawchuk misplayed. The crowd let out a groan but the puck stayed out. Sensing that the home team needed a boost, the crowd took up a "Go Leafs Go" chant. The Leafs seemed to get re-energized; they threw a defensive wall up at their own blueline and would not let the Canadiens get too close.

However, with 55 seconds to play, Leaf defenceman Larry Hillman iced the puck. With the face-off in the Toronto end, Montreal coach Toe Blake paced behind his bench hesitating for a moment but then finally waving Worsley over for the extra attacker. Blake made a late change and put Jim Roberts out on the ice, while Beliveau conferred with Ferguson about where to line up. On his radio broadcast that night, the legendary Foster Hewitt set the scene this way:

The crowd can hardly contain themselves during this dramatic struggle. It has been a terrific game all the way. The home crowd is anticipating a Stanley Cup victory while the Canadiens are using every strategy to get the tying goal and push the result into overtime.

Toronto coach Punch Imlach sent out his

veterans—Horton, Kelly, Pulford, Stanley and team captain George Armstrong—to defend in front of Sawchuk. Stanley, who had been taking face-offs in his own end all night long (as did all Leaf defencemen during the Imlach era), moved into the circle to face Beliveau. Hewitt described the action:

The puck is dropped, Stanley gets possession; he snaps the puck to Kelly; Kelly kicks over to Pulford; Pulford passes over to Armstrong: Armstrong is driving hard; Armstrong shoots toward the empty net. It's on target. It's in. He scores! Armstrong has scored the insurance goal.

The goal came with 47 seconds to play and all the Leafs had to do was run out the clock with a secure lead. Hewitt's description of the last few seconds went as follows:

Seven seconds, six, five, four, three, two, one. The game is over! Leafs have won the Stanley Cup. The Toronto players are mobbing each other. The crowd is wild. There's no use trying to talk against that uproar. The final score is Leafs three and Canadiens one.

When the game was over, Blake came out on the ice to congratulate Imlach who was shaking hands with his own players. The two teams then lined up for the traditional handshake and Armstrong, along with his son Brian, accepted the Cup on behalf of the Leafs from NHL president Clarence Campbell.

Later, in the dressing room area, Ward Cornell and Frank Selke, Jr., interviewed most of the victorious players. It was a tired and relieved group of Maple Leafs that came before the cameras.

"Johnny [Bower] played two great games, Terry [Sawchuk] played two great games," said Dave Keon of the Leaf goaltending during the finals.

"I wasn't the slowest on the ice," said the ancient Stanley.

"[It's] the greatest thrill of my life," chimed in Sawchuk, who added he would retire (he did

not). Mahovlich simply stated, "I'm just glad to be associated with this club."

But Horton summed it up best when he said, "This is what you live for."

The same could be said for hockey fans all across Canada. What could ever be better than a Leafs–Canadiens Stanley Cup final? Both teams battled hard for the affection of hockey fans all over the country, which made their rivalry a lasting legacy from the days of the six-team league.

Much has changed since the 1967 finals and the rivalry has never been the same, mostly because the Canadiens kept winning while the Leafs did not. But there are other reasons. Every player who dressed for the last game of the '67 finals was born and trained in Canada. Today with 30 teams and players from all over the world on the clubs, it is not realistic to expect them to understand the rivalry the way those who experienced it do. Talk to any Toronto player on the '67 Leafs team and they'll tell you they relish the Cup win over Montreal the most. Ask any Canadiens player involved in the '67 final and they'll say it still disturbs them that they were denied five Cups in a row.

Now that the two teams are in the same conference it is quite likely that they will meet in the playoffs, although not in the finals—remember the excitement when the two teams nearly met for the Cup in 1993? When there is something on the line, the excitement of a Toronto–Montreal contest still captures the imagination. During the 1999–2000 season, a March 4 game (a 4-3 Toronto win at the Air Canada Centre) drew a national television audience of over 1.5 million people. It is obvious that a Leafs–Canadiens contest rises above the usual fare offered by the NHL today and the intensity level goes up among players and fans alike.

But when they meet in the Stanley Cup playoffs the passion for the age-old rivalry will be rekindled. Until that time, we have the work of Harold Barkley to look back on and remember the rivalry that once was and what all fans in Canada hope might be again some day. Barkley's superb photography captured Canada's great rivalry at its best and helps to recall a time when a Toronto–Montreal game represented hockey at its finest.